Edinburgh Law Essentials

SCOTTISH MEDICAL LAW ESSENTIALS

EDINBURGH LAW ESSENTIALS

Series Editor: Nicholas Grier, Abertay University, Dundee

Delict Essentials
Francis McManus

Scottish Evidence Law Essentials
James Chalmers

Scottish Commercial Law Essentials
Malcolm M Combe and Alisdair D J
MacPherson

Scottish Legal System Essentials
Gerard Keegan

*Scottish Environmental Law
Essentials*
Francis McManus

Roman Law Essentials
Craig Anderson

Scottish Criminal Law Essentials
Claire McDiarmid

*Legal Method Essentials for Scots
Law*
Dale McFadzean and Lynn Allardyce
Irvine

Public Law Essentials
Jean McFadden and Dale McFadzean

Scottish Contract Law Essentials
Tikus Little

Scottish Family Law Essentials
Kenneth McK. Norrie

Private International Law Essentials
David Hill

Revenue Law Essentials
William Craig

Succession Law Essentials
Frankie McCarthy and Duncan Adam

Contract Law Essential Cases
Tikus Little

Trusts Law Essentials
John Finlay

Company Law Essentials
Josephine Bisacre and Claire
McFadzean

Jurisprudence Essentials
Duncan Spiers

Human Rights Law Essentials
Valerie Finch and John McGroarty

Planning Law Essentials
Anne-Michelle Slater

Employment Law Essentials
Jenifer Ross

International Law Essentials
John Grant

Media Law Essentials
Douglas Maule and Zhongdong Niu

Intellectual Property Law Essentials
Duncan Spiers

European Law Essentials
Stephanie Switzer

www.edinburghuniversitypress.com/series/ele

Edinburgh Law Essentials

SCOTTISH MEDICAL LAW ESSENTIALS

Second edition

Murray Earle

EDINBURGH
University Press

Edinburgh University Press is one of the leading university presses in the UK. We publish academic books and journals in our selected subject areas across the humanities and social sciences, combining cutting-edge scholarship with high editorial and production values to produce academic works of lasting importance. For more information visit our website: edinburghuniversitypress.com

Previous edition published in 2007 by Dundee University Press

Edinburgh University Press Ltd
13 Infirmary Street
Edinburgh EH1 1LT

Typeset in 10/13 Bembo
Deanta Global Publishing Services, Chennai, India

A CIP record for this book is available from the British Library

ISBN 978 1 3995 1778 2 (hardback)
ISBN 978 1 3995 1779 9 (paperback)
ISBN 978 1 3995 1780 5 (webready PDF)
ISBN 978 1 3995 1781 2 (epub)

CONTENTS

TABLE OF CASES

TABLE OF STATUTES

1 INTRODUCTION

1.1 SCOPE

Medical law has been acknowledged as a legal specialism since the 1970s, with the Law Society recognising accredited specialists in the subject. The scope of the specialism is fluid, and expanding, insofar as several branches of law fall within its remit. In essence, the subject is concerned with the legal interaction between medical practitioner and patient.

1.2 INCLUSIONS

Actions were at one time limited to allegations of medical negligence, which remains the backbone of the discipline. Yet the field encompasses more than actions in negligence or litigation at all. Where the matter is a legally regulated one involving the human body and medical or biological science, it falls within medical law. If, for example, one considers the beginning of life, subjects within the medical law field will include abortion, sterilisation and control of fertility, wrongful life and wrongful birth. Issues at the end of life may include ownership of body parts, organ donation, euthanasia and assisted suicide.

1.3 EXCLUSIONS

Having defined the area in this way, it may seem that it is a very large field. But it can be distinguished from other branches of law. It does not usually cover matters relating to medicines, except insofar as the administration of medicines may lead to harm, which may lead to an action in negligence. Even so, product liability will be considered in this book, principally on the basis of the harm criterion. Neither does it cover health care law or health services law, other than in similar circumstances. The structure of the National Health Service, resource allocation and the delivery of health care are subjects worthy of a separate book.

1.4 MEDICAL LAW IN CONTEXT

The principles on which medical law operates did not, as the discipline did, emerge in the 1970s. For example, medical negligence draws on professional negligence, which itself draws on the law of negligence in general, all of which have a long history. Another example is abortion, which forms part of the criminal law. Existing principles have been gathered together under a single banner.

Arguably, ethics is what links those legal categories involving the disciplines of both law and medicine. Ethical codes may be iterated in the courts, laid down by professional bodies such as the General Medical Council or set out in statute by the UK legislatures. These ethical codes may either drive or be driven by legal developments. Professional ethics and law are not always in accord with one another. The General Medical Council recognises this in *Good Medical Practice*. Professional ethics and law may be in agreement (e.g. duty of care in negligence) or in conflict (e.g. therapeutic privilege and conscientious objection). Ethics may pre-empt law (e.g. artificial procreation and information disclosure requirements) or vice versa (e.g. surrogacy).

1.5   PRIVATE LAW

Medical law combines aspects of private law under its banner. It is also inherently comparative. For example, the case law on consent has drawn heavily on the law in the United States of America, Canada, Australia and South Africa, to agree with those regimes. For the most part, Scots medical law draws on or has developed alongside English medical law. While the legal positions north and south of the Border are broadly similar, some crucial differences have emerged over the years, primarily because both civil and criminal law have been allowed to develop separately under the Act of Union of 1707. It has also been recognised, both implicitly and explicitly, that cross-border differences that may lead to 'bio-tourism' should be discouraged. This was one of the principles on which the devolution settlement was built: that it would be inappropriate that people should move from England to Scotland or from Scotland to England in order to take advantage of a different regime. This is particularly true of issues such as abortion, *in vitro* fertilisation and medically assisted suicide, although the first of those has become devolved to the Scottish Parliament since the last edition of this book.

While English cases are recognised as important in Scottish courts, they can never be more than persuasive. English jurisprudence from the House of Lords or United Kingdom Supreme Court is not binding on Scots law. Nevertheless, where there is a similarity of basic doctrinal ideas, Scottish judges may be persuaded to follow those cases. This may be done on the basis of logic or policy, or may even be considered as binding where the circumstances are sufficiently similar. This was the case in *McCallum v Morrison* (2023), where the House of Lords decision in *Rothwell v Chemical Insulation*

Co Ltd & Another (2008) on psychiatric harm, proximity and the duty of care was considered binding on the Sheriff Court. That was because the appellant in *McCallum* was in the same position as the plaintiff in *Rothwell*. A not dissimilar argument allows for the selective inclusion of English jurisprudence in this book.

Possibly the best example of a cross-border exchange is the law of negligence. The law has been similar in the two jurisdictions since the 1950s, when the test of the standard of care was laid down by the Court of Session in *Hunter v Hanley* (1955). The test was adopted in a modified form by English courts a few years later, in *Bolam v Friern Hospital Management Committee* (1957), and modified again by Scottish courts in *Moyes v Lothian Health Board* (1990).

Differences that have emerged are small, yet arguably important. For example, the law on legal capacity and guardianship is different as regards capacity and consent, and breach of confidence is an equitable wrong in England but a delict in Scotland. In Scots law, an action for wounded feelings may be considered a personality right, while there is no recourse to the *actio iniuriarum* in England. Property law is another aspect of private law that falls within medical law. Principles of property law may be brought to bear on cases in which ownership and possession of body parts are concerned, indicating a further divergence with the law in England and Wales. Where possible these differences and similarities will be teased out throughout this book.

1.5.1 Human rights law

Some commentators have considered with approval that medical law is a sub-set of human rights law. This means that the notion of rights is embedded within medical law because of the latter's dependence on ethics for its development. That said, the European Convention on Human Rights and the Human Rights Act 1998 have had a horizontal effect on medical law, not least because it is unlawful for a public authority to act in a way that is incompatible with a Convention right under the Human Rights Act 1998, s 6. It is clear, for example, that the 1998 Act has a direct effect on confidentiality and public disclosure of private information. Since the reception of Ulpian's rights of personality under the *action iniuriarum* such rights have coexisted with nominate delicts, which are distinguished from the English law of torts and equitable wrongs.

1.5.2 Medical law: reserved or devolved?

Section 30 of the Scotland Act 1998 deals with the legislative competence of the Scottish Parliament. It refers to Pt II of Sch 5, which lists 'specific reservations', so defining those powers reserved to Westminster. The general rule is that matters are devolved unless they are reserved by the Scotland Act. Under Sch 5, the law on human fertilisation; regulation of the medical professions; xenotransplantation; embryology; surrogacy and genetics; and medicines and poisons are reserved to Westminster and cannot be changed by the Scottish Parliament. Similarly, data protection is reserved. This affects access to medical records. Intellectual property is similarly reserved, affecting cloning and ownership of cell lines. Consumer protection is the branch of law dealing with (medical and other) products liability. This area is also reserved to Westminster. On the other hand, abortion was reserved to Westminster until the passage of the Scotland Act 2016, indicating that these competencies are shifting. These constitutional differences will be noted in relevant parts of this book.

1.6   THE NATIONAL HEALTH SERVICE IN SCOTLAND

The statutory basis of the National Health Service in Scotland (NHSiS) is set out in the National Health Service (Scotland) Act 1978. It requires the Scottish Ministers to promote a comprehensive integrated health service geared towards the improvement of the physical and mental health of the people of Scotland. Services are to be free except where expressly provided for under the National Health Service (Scotland) Act 1978, s 1(2), as amended.

Under the same Act, Ministers are under a duty to promote good health. This falls outwith the scope of this book except insofar as the professions working within the NHSiS are covered in Chapter 2, and it is the health service that will be vicariously liable for the actions of medical practitioners in its employ (e.g. negligence), will perform the services allowed under certain enactments (e.g. *in vitro* fertilisation and surrogacy) and will perform the functions allowed under the common law (e.g. acting in the interests of the *incapax*).

2 MEDICAL AND ALLIED PROFESSIONS

2.1 STATUTORY CONTROL

Regulation of the health care professions is affected by a large body of statute, which is itself an area reserved to Westminster, with some minor exceptions on suitable experience and vocational training (Scotland Act 1998, s 6(1) and Sch 5, s G2). The broad aim is public protection. The relevant professions which are regulated include doctors, dentists, nurses, pharmaceutical chemists, opticians and certain professions allied to medicine. These are each discussed separately.

While there is no bar on providing healing services, the legislation seeks to ensure that those holding themselves out as having a particular skill should be subject to a system of licensing and testing of their competence. Degrees of professional control differ. At the extreme end, it is an offence to practise as a registered dentist or medical practitioner when one is not. At the other end of the scale, professional censure may be imposed for unethical behaviour.

Under s 60 of the Health Act 1999, as amended, primary legislation is not necessary to bring new professions within the ambit of the Acts governing the health care professions. This may be done by His Majesty by Order in Council and includes, for example, modifying the regulation of the health care professions. That includes professions regulated by the Professions Supplementary to Medicine Act 1960 and modifying the functions, powers or duties of the Professional Standards Authority for Health and Social Care, the list of regulatory bodies and the range of functions of those bodies. Such Orders in Council can repeal or revoke any enactment, amend it or replace it, in effect deregulating a profession previously regulated by enactment. For example, the Hearing Aid Council Act 1968 was abolished by the Health and Social Care Act 2008. Some matters remain outside the scope of Orders, such as abolition of an existing regulatory body.

2.2 PROFESSIONAL STANDARDS AUTHORITY FOR HEALTH AND SOCIAL CARE

On the recommendation of the Report of the Bristol Royal Infirmary Inquiry (*Learning from Bristol* (Cm 5363, 2002)), the National Health Service Reform and Health Care Professions Act 2002 created a body corporate known as the Council for the Regulation of Health Care Professionals (CRHCP). Its function was to oversee the activities of those bodies charged with regulation of health care professions. Part 1 of the Act extends to England and Wales only but Parts 2 and 3 extend to the whole of the United Kingdom. Structural reforms of the National Health Service in Scotland were made by the National Health Service Reform (Scotland) Act 2004. Following several reviews, the Council was renamed the Professional Standards Authority (PSA) for Health and Social Care under the Health and Social Care Act in 2012.

The Authority has several functions under s 25 and powers under s 26. It must promote the interests of users of health and social care, and the public in relation to specified regulatory bodies, promote best practice in the performance of those functions, promote co-operation among regulatory bodies and formulate and encourage adherence to principles relating to good professional self-regulation.

2.3 REGULATORY BODIES

The following regulatory bodies are required, in the exercise of their functions, to co-operate with the Authority:

- General Medical Council;
- General Dental Council;
- General Optical Council;
- General Osteopathic Council;
- General Chiropractic Council;
- General Pharmaceutical Council;
- Nursing and Midwifery Council;
- Health and Care Professions Council;
- Social Work England and
- any other regulatory body established by an Order in Council under s 60 of the Health Act 1999.

2.4 DUTIES AND POWERS OF THE AUTHORITY

Under s 26 of the National Health Service Reform and Health Care Professions Act 2002, the Authority has wide discretion in the performance of its functions. An exception exists in relation to an individual whose case is before a committee of a regulatory body, or where an allegation has been made to that committee, for example the Disciplinary Committee of the General Medical Council. In this circumstance, the Council may not do anything in relation to that individual.

Otherwise, the Authority may, for example, investigate and report on the performance by each regulatory body and on how the performance of such functions compares. It may also recommend changes to the practices of regulatory bodies.

Scottish Ministers and the Secretary of State may ask the Authority for advice, which the Authority must provide. They may also require the Authority to investigate and report on a matter within its remit, and to publish the results of that investigation, as well as to seek the views of members of the general public as users of health care.

The Authority may, on the basis of public protection, give directions requiring a regulatory body to make certain rules. These are sent to the Secretary of State and laid before both Houses of Parliament. Under s 28 of the 2002 Act, the regulatory body must comply with the directions, which may include provision for the investigation by the Authority of complaints made to it about how a regulatory body has exercised its functions.

If the Authority considers that a decision made by a Disciplinary Committee of one of the regulated bodies has been unduly lenient or should not have been made (in the interests of public protection), the Authority may refer the case to the relevant court under s 29 of the 2002 Act. In Scotland that means the Court of Session. Referral must be made within 40 days of the last date on which the practitioner had the right to appeal against the decision, or 56 days if no appeal was possible. The court will treat the case as an appeal by the Authority against the decision in question. It may dismiss the appeal; allow it and quash the relevant decision; make a substitute decision; or remit the case to the committee or other person or to the Medical Practitioners Tribunal Service, for disposal. In these circumstances the Authority must also notify the General Medical Council of the reference.

2.5 MEDICAL PRACTITIONERS

The medical profession is self-regulating, under the auspices of the General Medical Council (GMC), which is itself regulated by the Medical Act 1983. Under the General Medical Council (Constitution) Order 2008, the GMC continues to set standards and remain responsible for investigating allegations of professional misconduct, but adjudication of such allegations falls to an independent tribunal.

2.5.1 Registration and qualification

2.5.1.1 The General Medical Council

The GMC is a body corporate. It was established in 1858 to oversee training in and practice of medicine. It is regulated under the Medical Act 1983. Its constitution is set out in the General Medical Council (Constitution) Order 2008. The Council comprises six lay and six registered registrant members, elected from constituencies in the United Kingdom (such as Scotland). The Privy Council must ensure that at least one member lives in each of the constituencies of the United Kingdom. Members serve a term of office of up to 8 years within any 20-year period.

2.5.1.2 Registration and liability of unregistered practitioners

Any person may practise medicine or surgery – but not anatomy (under the Anatomy Act 1984) – regardless of qualification. What is unlawful is wilfully and falsely holding oneself out to be a registered medical practitioner (physician, medical doctor, licentiate in medicine and surgery, Bachelor of Medicine, surgeon, general practitioner, etc.). Unregistered practitioners may not fall foul of the law, if they do not hold themselves out as registered medical practitioners and do not contravene provisions on medicinal products or controlled drugs. Further, according to the Cancer Act 1939, an unqualified practitioner may not advertise a treatment for cancer.

What amounts to holding oneself out under the Medical Acts has been discussed by the courts. In *Younghusband* v *Luftig* (1949), the court found that the accused had not in fact claimed one of the qualifications mentioned in the legislation, by using the designation 'MD Berlin' to denote his degree from that university. In *Wilson* v *Inyang* (1951) the court found that it would be a defence that the accused held a genuine belief of entitlement to hold himself out as a doctor. Although unregistered practitioners may not hold appointments at hospitals, an exception exists for non-Commonwealth citizens who are medically qualified in their home countries.

Different provisions exist for dentists and opticians. The 'holding out' provisions in the Dentists Act 1984 and the Opticians Act 1958 do not use the terms 'wilfully and falsely' and so do not require *mens rea*.

Where the conduct of an unregistered practitioner leads to the harm of a patient, that practitioner may be liable to criminal or civil redress. Death may amount to murder in cases of wicked recklessness (e.g. administering a substance of unknown chemical properties); it may also amount to culpable homicide. Negligently causing harm would be judged by the standard of a medical practitioner where the defender held themselves out as such. Lack of skill amounts to fault in the law of delict. Much will depend on whether the patient knew of the practitioner's lack of registration. Indeed, in *Dickson* v *Hygienic Institute* (1910), it was said *obiter* that an unregistered practitioner, who the patient did not know was unregistered, must attain the standard expected of a registered practitioner.

The GMC Registrar is to maintain and publish an up-to-date register of all registered medical practitioners. The main register is divided into different lists, such as the principal list, the emergency powers doctors list, and the visiting overseas doctors list. Provisional registration is available to European Economic Area (EEA) nationals with certain overseas qualifications, as long as their application was made before the Brexit implementation period (IP) completion day. They may work in recognised hospitals as if fully registered, but may not undertake certain work.

Practitioners pay an annual fee for inclusion on the list and are entitled to a certificate of registration. Retired practitioners may remain on the register even after retirement.

Entries in the register which, in the view of the GMC, were fraudulently or incorrectly made may be erased at the direction of the GMC. The person whose name was erased must be notified and has a right of appeal.

2.5.1.3 Training, qualifications and experience

The supervision and granting of medical qualifications were undertaken by the Education Committee of the GMC, until it ceased to exist following the Medical Profession (Miscellaneous Amendments) Order 2008. The GMC itself now determines the veracity of qualifying examinations and the appropriate level of proficiency. It also ensures that doctors with provisional registrations have access to programmes that will lead to full registration as a medical practitioner. Similarly, it also ensures that the required post-graduation training is adequate (pre-registration experience or graduate clinical training). The Committee may appoint visitors to the medical schools charged with gathering course, teaching and examination details. Institutions offering pre-registration experience may also be inspected.

Medical practitioners should have both a primary qualification (e.g. degree of Bachelor of Medicine or of Bachelor of Surgery or membership of the Royal College of Surgeons) and a qualification of experience (clinical experience in an approved hospital or institution). Primary qualifications are gained by passing the examinations of one of the bodies on the approved list, set out in statute. The Scottish universities included are those of Aberdeen, Dundee, Edinburgh, Glasgow and St Andrews. A primary qualification may be acceptable if obtained from a university in a relevant European state, provided that the GMC Registrar is satisfied as to equivalence, and their application was made before the Brexit implementation period (IP) completion date. Alternatively, the Registrar may be satisfied by evidence of the quali-fication being accompanied by a certificate, of having lawfully engaged in the practice of medicine, from the medical authorities of the Member State, or on evidence of having carried out a professional traineeship in a third country, which the GMC must take into account. Practitioners disqualified in their home state are not entitled to registration in the United Kingdom. Disqualification will be on the grounds of the commission of a criminal offence or professional misconduct. Appeals against disqualification may be made to the GMC.

The GMC and the specialist training authority of the Royal Colleges are designated for the United Kingdom in relation to specialist medical quali-fications. These two authorities award certificates to those who have com-pleted approved specialist training. The GMC publishes a register of such specialists. This is required for employment as a consultant in the National Health Service. Appeals may be made to a panel of independent persons, which must give reasons for its decision.

Following the abolition of the Postgraduate Medical Education and Training Board, by the General and Specialist Medical Practice (Education, Training and Qualifications) Order 2010, the GMC assumed responsibil-ity for the establishment and maintenance of postgraduate training in the United Kingdom. It sets the standards and requirements for a doctor to be awarded a certificate of completion of training as a general practitioner or as a specialist. The GMC may also appoint visiting panels to visit persons or institutions involved in postgraduate medical education and training. Appeals against decisions of the Council may be made to an appeal panel; appeals from a decision of the panel can be made to a sheriff.

2.5.1.4 The medical registers

The GMC must maintain and publish a general practitioner and a special-ist register, and make regulations for those applying for inclusion. It must also establish and maintain education and training standards and develop postgraduate training, including the approval of courses and training posts. Copies and information in the registers must be provided to those making enquiries as to whether a person's name is included in the registers. A name may be removed in prescribed circumstances, such as when a person ceases to be a registered medical practitioner. Inclusion in one of these registers is required in order to practise as a general practitioner or consultant in the National Health Service in the United Kingdom. A decision by the Council not to include a person's name is subject to a right of appeal under the Medical Act 1983.

Overseas practitioners, such as those who are EEA medical practitioners, are entitled to full registration, subject to certain criteria, such as application before the Brexit IP. The same provision applies to those who would have been entitled to such registration by virtue of an enforceable Community right, subject to the IP completion date provision. The Registrar must also be satisfied that they hold equivalent qualifications and are of good character. In the case of qualifications gained outside the EEA, the Registrar must be satisfied that they have gained the qualifications necessary for overseas certificates and undertaken training and gained clinical experience sufficient for registration as a medical practitioner. In addition the GMC must have regard to whether the qualification has been accepted by European state.

Registration may be full, or provisional in the case of practitioners undertaking employment intended to qualify for full registration. Demonstrating proficiency in English is no longer required, but the application is still required to have been made before the IP completion date.

Temporary registration is available on notice of the Secretary of State in the case of emergencies involving loss of human life or human illness.

Limited registration is available on the basis of demonstration of knowledge, skill and experience, depending on the post for which registration is sought. This may be converted to full registration on demonstration of good character and being deemed to have the necessary knowledge, skill and experience. In determining whether to grant full registration to a doctor with acceptable overseas qualifications, the GMC need not make a comparison with a hypothetical European Union equivalent applicant: *R* v *General Medical Council, ex p Virik* (1996).

A medical practitioner may apply to have his name removed from the register, but restoration requires the approval of the Council.

2.5.2   Licence to practise

A medical practitioner may be granted a licence to practise when first registered. The GMC may make regulations as to granting or refusing such certificates, and for revalidation of practitioner certificates, and the restoration of licences to those from whom they may have been withdrawn. Where a practitioner is being revalidated, the licencing authority has a public interest duty to disclose information that arises in that process to the Scottish ministers and the practitioner's employer. The GMC may also publish guidance on the issue of certificates, and the requisite documentation for licences to practise. If the Council is satisfied that an entry has been incorrectly made or fraudulently procured, it may direct that it be erased. The Registrar must notify the person of that erasure, and of their right to appeal. That and other appeals may be made to a Registration Appeals Panel.

2.5.3 Conduct of practitioners

2.5.3.1 Committees and proceedings of the General Medical Council

The GMC has the power to provide advice to members of the medical profession, on standards of performance, conduct and medical ethics. It also makes procedural rules for the three bodies dealing with the conduct of practitioners. These are the Investigation Committee, Medical Practitioners Tribunals Service (MPTS) and Interim Orders Tribunals. The role of the GMC is set out in Sch 4 to the Medical Act 1983, as substituted by the General Medical Council (Fitness to Practise and Over-Arching Objective) and the Professional Standards Authority for Health and Social Care (References to Court) Order 2015.

The Council must make rules for reference of cases to the MPTS, and for the arrangements by the MPTS for either a Medical Practitioners Tribunal or an Interim Orders Tribunal to consider matters. Those rules are to be made with regard to dealing fairly and justly with cases. The Committee or Tribunals may administer oaths, which will have the same power as an action in the Court of Session. That means the power to grant warrants for the citation of witnesses to give evidence, the recovery of documents and granting commissions to persons to take evidence from witnesses.

The Council may make rules that authorise the Investigation Committee, a Medical Practitioners Tribunal or other specified persons, requiring an assessment to be carried out of the standard of a practitioner's professional performance, and their physical and mental health. The same applies whether a person is applying for their name to be restored to the register, or whether the case involves the person's name being erased from the register. The Registrar gives directions as to whether the assessment is to be carried out by an Assessment Team or by an individual assessor.

A sheriff may issue a warrant if on the evidence of that team or individual there are grounds for believing that this will be needed for them to carry out their investigations. The MPTS must appoint an assessor to a Medical Practitioners Tribunal or Interim Orders Tribunal to advise the Investigations Committee on questions of law that may arise from the proceedings. Although it is an English case, there is persuasive authority in *R (Kuzmin)* v *General Medical Council* (2019) that tribunals may draw adverse inferences were the person charged with breaches to remain silent.

2.5.3.2 Responsible officers

In 2010 Regulations were made that require the appointment of 'responsible officers' by specified designated bodies, including NHS Trusts and Local Health Boards, i.e. those bodies that arrange for the provision of health care and employ medical practitioners. A responsible officer must be a fully registered senior medical practitioner. They have responsibility to ensure regular appraisal of medical practitioners and to establish procedures for investigation should patients raise concerns around a practitioner's fitness to practise. Where appropriate that responsible officer may refer a case to the GMC, and make recommendations to the Council, and must co-operate with the GMC in respect of its fitness to practise evaluations. As well as monitoring any conditions to which a medical practitioner may be subject following an investigation, a responsible officer must also maintain records of practitioners' fitness practise evaluations. The Secretary of State may create offences for non-compliance with Medical Profession (Responsible Officers) Regulations 2010, SI 2010/2841.

2.5.3.3 Fitness to practise and medical ethics

Among the powers of the GMC is the provision of advice on standards of professional conduct, performance and ethics of members of the medical profession. If an allegation of impaired performance of a registered medical practitioner is made, this must be investigated by the Investigation Committee, which will determine whether it should be referred to the Medical Practitioners Tribunal Service, which must arrange for the allegation to be considered by a Medical Practitioners Tribunal. The grounds for a finding of 'impaired' fitness to practise include conviction or caution for a criminal offence, adverse physical or mental health, deficient professional performance or misconduct. Where the Fitness to Practise (FTP) tribunal finds practise to have been impaired the adjudicator may make one of the following appealable directions:

- erasure from the register (except in a health case);
- suspension of registration;
- registration made conditional upon compliance with requirements specified by the panel.

Appeals must be made to the Court of Session within 28 days, or to a sheriff in the case of a decision for erasure made by the GMC. The Council may appear as the respondent. On appeal, the court may dismiss the appeal; allow the appeal and quash the direction; make a substitute direction or variation or remit the case to the Registrar, who will refer the case to the Council for disposal according to the court's directions.

Following an appeal from a Council decision, the sheriff may dismiss the appeal; allow it and quash the direction; or remit the case to the Council for disposal.

Both courts may make any costs order they think fit.

2.5.3.4 Impaired fitness to practise

The grounds on which fitness to practise may be regarded as impaired are as follows:

2.5.3.4.1 Misconduct

What remains important is that patient care, treatment and safety are paramount. The same principle applies to medical practitioners and to chief executives of NHS Trusts. In *Daly* v *General Medical Council* (1952) the Chief Executive, who was also a practitioner, had a duty in both capacities, and in *Roylance* v *General Medical Council (No 2)* (2000) a Chief Executive was found guilty of serious professional misconduct for failing to act over high infant mortality rates and on those grounds to prevent the surgery of a child who later died.

A high standard of proof is required in such cases. According to *Lanford* v *General Medical Council* (1990), both the onus and the standard are those of the criminal law. Evidence of the use of indecent language and behaviour towards one female patient corroborated the same conduct against another female patient. This is an example of the use of the *Moorov* doctrine in the law of criminal evidence (*Moorov* v *HM Advocate* (1930)). Evidence of previous misconduct may also be considered, as set out in *Daly* v *General Medical Council* (1952).

2.5.3.4.2 Unethical behaviour

This is defined by codes of medical ethics, which have no formal legal status. Such behaviour may be on the basis of the Hippocratic Oath, or based on published guidelines of the GMC, for example the importance of patient confidentiality, discussed in Chapter 6. Breach of confidence may lead to civil proceedings; it may also lead to an allegation of serious professional misconduct.

Under s 35C of the 1983 Act, the question of impairment to fitness to practise is not limited to the medical practitioner acting in a specific capacity. While the conduct in question must maintain a link to the medical profession, the key question is whether that conduct brought the profession into disrepute. It does not matter whether the medical practitioner was acting in that capacity. This was the case in *Ogunsanya v General Medical Council* (2021), in which a dual qualified medical practitioner was acting in their capacity as a solicitor.

2.5.3.4.3 Sexual involvement with a patient

This would amount to serious professional misconduct, as discussed above. In *De Gregory v General Medical Council* (1961), Lord Denning held that if a practitioner has used a professional position to gain access to family confidences, the same standard must be maintained if the practitioner befriends the family. In the *De Gregory* case, this applied to a practitioner who had an affair with the wife of a patient, even although it took place after she ceased to be his patient. It was still found to be serious professional misconduct. Neither would it make a difference if both parties were unmarried. That said, the opposite conclusion was reached in *Nwabueze v General Medical Council* (2000).

In *Bhattacharya v General Medical Council* (1967), the court held that whether the conduct brings the profession into disrepute will differ from case to case. In that case the appellant argued that the intimate relationship had taken place before the woman had become his patient. Lord Hodson said that a pre-existing relationship may be considered less serious.

Although the penalty will itself depend on the seriousness of the conduct, erasure from the register will be the most likely outcome.

2.5.3.4.4 Neglect of duty

Negligence will be discussed in Chapter 4. Neglect of duty will usually be actionable in civil law, but behaviour amounting to culpable carelessness or indifference to consequences may be 'gross neglect' and may lead to erasure from the register. This will constitute serious professional misconduct and may *also* amount to negligence. One example is failure to visit a patient, although this is difficult for the practitioner as he must distinguish frivolous requests. The issue of what in English jurisprudence is called 'gross negligence manslaughter' (discussed in Chapter 5) was raised in *R v Bawa-Garba* (2016) and led to an FTP tribunal inquiry, that in turn led to the sanction of erasure from the register, in *General Medical Council v Bawa-Garba* (2018), that was reversed in *Bawa-Garba v General Medical Council* (2018). Another example is the failure to supervise medical students properly (*R v Secretary of State for Health, ex p Spencer* (1989)).

2.5.3.4.5 Advertising and dishonesty

Advertising may be penalised with erasure, but only if the intention was to attract patients or gain financial advantage. The definition of advertising is straightforward in cases of blatant marketing, but more problematic in a publication in which there is reference to the practitioner's skills or reputation. This may depend on the medium, such that use of the mainstream press to showcase the practitioner's expertise may be seen as advertising. The GMC publishes guidelines which allow practitioners to publish factual information about their practices at local information centres, although the same information cannot be used in the mainstream press (*R* v *General Medical Council, ex p Colman* (1990)).

Dishonesty may lie in claiming payment to which the practitioner is not entitled. Similarly, improper prescribing of drugs for financial incentive may also amount to serious professional misconduct.

2.6 DENTAL PRACTITIONERS

The dental profession – including dentists and dental care professionals – is principally regulated by the Dentists Act 1984 which consolidated more than a hundred years of legislation. The General Dental Council (GDC) is a United Kingdom body. Regulation of the profession is also national. Like the GMC, the main objective of the GDC in exercising its powers is the protection of the public, insofar as it must have regard to the interests of persons using the services of registered dental practitioners. The GDC is also charged with the promotion of high standards of education and professional conduct among dentists. It has a duty to co-operate with certain public authorities, bodies and persons, such as those concerned with the employment of dental practitioners or those regulating services in which such practitioners are engaged. It must publish annual reports, statistical reports, accounts and strategic plans on an annual basis, and submit those to the Privy Council, along with a register of members' private interests.

As of October 2013, the GDC agreed that the Council should comprise six registrant and six lay members, and a chair elected from that membership. All members will be appointed by the Privy Council, and at any time at least one member must live or work in each of the four nations of the United Kingdom.

According to s 37 of the Dentists Act 1984 as amended, the 'practice of dentistry' includes the performance of any such operation and the giving of any such treatment, advice or attendance as is usually performed or given by dentists. It includes operations, treatment and advice on dentures, artificial teeth and appliances and excludes medical tasks carried out by qualified medical professionals.

Dentistry may be lawfully practised *only* by a registered dentist. An unregistered dentist treating a patient may be negligent, but that will not amount to a criminal assault (see *R* v *Richardson* (1998)).

Certain exceptions exist, however. Dental care professionals undertaking dental work is permissible in the circumstances discussed below. Dental work carried out by dental and medical students undertaken in the course of studies and under direct supervision is no longer, strictly speaking, treated as the practice of dentistry.

It is an offence to practise dentistry unlawfully or falsely to hold oneself out as a practising dentist or to be listed as such. It is also an offence to use the title 'dentist', 'dental surgeon' or 'dental practitioner', or to describe oneself as such, if unregistered.

Dentistry is run as a business in the United Kingdom, with patients drawn from the private sector and covered by the National Health Service. As a business, it is controlled by the 1984 Act, which sets out those persons considered to be carrying on the business of dentistry – that is, a partnership of which each member receives payment for dental services performed by that member, by a partner or by an employee.

The rules set out in the 1984 Act are aimed at preventing persons from employing dentists as a commercial proposition. Corporate bodies may carry on the business of dentistry only if the majority of directors are registered dental practitioners. The maximum penalty on summary conviction is a fine of up to level 5 on the standard scale, although the Professional Conduct Committee may also impose financial penalties of up to £1,000 in the case of an individual and £5,000 in the case of a body corporate.

2.6.1 Training and registration

Medical authorities permitted to grant degrees in surgery are also allowed to grant licences in dentistry. The GDC appoints boards of examiners to examine candidates for the degree or licence. These are available to those aged over 21 years. Any medical authority entitled to grant surgery degrees may grant licences in dentistry, as can the colleges of Surgeons of Edinburgh and Physicians and Surgeons of Glasgow. The GDC maintains a dentists register of two lists: the principal list and the list of temporary registrants.

Those with recognised overseas diplomas in dentistry are entitled to registration if the qualification is recognised by the GDC as demonstrating possession of the requisite knowledge and skill. The holder must also satisfy the Registrar of their identity, good character, knowledge of English and good physical and mental health. The council is required to publish guidance on the evidence and documents required to satisfy the Registrar that the applicant has the necessary knowledge of English. Where the qualification is not a recognised one, the GDC may arrange for examinations to be sat. It may also grant temporary registration or registration permitting practice only in particular posts. Registration decisions are subject to appeal to the sheriff court.

Dental authorities must, on request, submit to the GDC information on course content. Visitors may be appointed to visit dental schools to assess instruction given. The Privy Council may be informed by the GDC of shortcomings in educational standards and may direct that the qualifications will not, after a certain date, entitle the holders to registration. This may be revoked if the dental authority takes remedial action. Neither may a dental authority make the adoption of a particular theory of dentistry a require-ment of qualification. In these circumstances the authority runs the risk of being reported to the Privy Council, which may withdraw the power to grant certificates.

Dentists must undertake continuing professional training and develop-ment during their careers. The GDC may make rules prescribing the train-ing of registered dentists and of anyone seeking restoration to the register.

The Registrar appointed by the GDC keeps the dental register contain-ing the lists of principal and temporary registrants. The registration proce-dure is set out in the Dentists Act 1984, as are the required qualifications. These may be a degree or licentiate in dentistry of a dental authority, or a national of an overseas state holding an appropriate diploma. Holders of such qualifications must satisfy the GDC of their identity, good character and good physical and mental health.

The Registration Appeals Committee makes provision for decisions not to register a person, as well as decisions to remove a name from the register and failure to restore a name.

Decisions of the Registration Appeals Committee may be appealed to the sheriff court, although such decisions made on the basis of non-payment of the prescribed fee are not appealable (s 37). The Registrar is to notify a person whose registration is appealable that the decision against registration is appealable, and must give reasons for the decision. Provision is made as to procedure and applicable time limits and extensions of time limits (Dentists Act 1984, Sch 2A).

Further matters affect both registration and sanction, such as the require-ment to have adequate insurance and proceedings following conviction of a criminal offence.

2.6.1.1 Insurance

Registered dentists are required under the Dentists Act s 26A to have 'appro-priate' indemnity cover to practise as such, and in order for their name to be entered and retained on the register. This means a contract of insurance covering possible liabilities in the work of a dentist. Rules are in place in respect of the information that is to be provided to the Registrar in this connection. Breach of either requirement may be a ground for erasure from the register.

2.6.1.2 Criminal offences

A dentist who commits a criminal offence before or after registration may face disciplinary proceedings before the Professional Conduct Committee. This applies whether or not the offence was committed outwith the United Kingdom. The Investigating Committee may refer further matters to the Professional Conduct Committee (SI 2005/2011, art 18), including that the person has:

(1) accepted a conditional fixed offer under the Criminal Procedure (Scotland) Act 1995; or

(2) agreed to pay a penalty as alternative to prosecution under the Social Security Administration Act 1992 or

(3) received an absolute discharge under the Criminal Procedure (Scotland) Act 1995.

Although petty offences are excluded, they may attract professional penalties if part of a string of similar offences which also speak to professional or ethical practice, or which lead to a concern for patient safety.

In *Dad* v *General Dental Council* (2000) the dentist appealed against his temporary removal from the register on the ground of convictions for road traffic offences. The Privy Council set the suspension aside, finding that it was not a question of the gravity of the offences themselves; it was a question of whether the appellant was fit to practise as a dentist. It is necessary and important to balance the gravity of the offence against fitness to practise. There is also a duty on the Committee, where practicable, to suspend its determination where police investigations are ongoing: see *R (on the application of Zietsman)* v *Dental Practice Board* (2002), where police investigations were ongoing into suspected fraud by the appellants.

2.6.2 Professional conduct and fitness to practise

The GDC comprises six statutory committees:

(1) Professional Conduct Committee;

(2) Health Committee;

(3) Investigating Committee;

(4) Professional Performance Committee;

(5) Interim Orders Committee and

(6) Registration Appeals Committee.

The GDC is required, after consultation, to issue guidance as to the standards of conduct, performance and practice expected of registered dentists, which it must keep under review.

2.6.2.1 The Investigating Committee and the Practice Committees

The Investigating Committee considers allegations made against a registered dental practitioner that their fitness to practise as a dentist is impaired. One of the Practice Committees must investigate allegations of professional misconduct referred to it by the Investigating Committee. Before referral to the appropriate Practice Committee the Investigating Committee may first agree with the subject of the allegation that they will comply with such undertakings as the Investigating Committee considers appropriate. If the Investigating Committee finds the allegation ought not to be considered by a Practice Committee, it may issue a warning or advice, if the Committee has had regard to the over-arching objective. Such warnings are subject to review by the Investigating Committee with a view to its revocation or removal from the register entry.

Allegations may also be referred by the Investigating Committee to the Interim Orders Committee. In that instance, or if the Investigating Committee refers a case to the Practice Committee or the Registrar, the Interim Orders Committee may impose an interim order. The Registrar may refer an allegation to the Interim Orders Committee at any time before the Investigating Committee has begun its consideration of that allegation. The Registration Appeals Committee will deal with appeals against decisions affecting that person's registration.

The grounds on which fitness to practise is considered 'impaired' include misconduct, deficient professional performance, adverse physical or mental health and conviction of a criminal offence (Dentists Act 1984, s 27). Matters may be referred regardless of whether they allegedly took place outwith the United Kingdom or when the person was not a registered dental practitioner.

The Investigating Committee investigates the allegation and determines whether it should be considered by one of the Practice Committees (the Professional Conduct Committee, the Health Committee and the Professional Performance Committee). It is then referred to a Practice Committee or, if deemed appropriate, to the Interim Orders Committee. If it does not refer the matter, the Investigating Committee may issue a warning or advice to the person who is the subject of the allegation. The Practice Committees are required to investigate allegations referred from the Investigating Committee and to determine whether fitness to practise is impaired, taking account of adherence to any published guidance. An example of a 2016 case in which practise was found by the then Professional Conduct Committee of the General Dental Council to have been impaired involved the same set of facts that led to the Sheriff Court case of *McCallum* v *Morrison* (2023), considered in Chapter 5. The respondent was removed from the Dentists Register due to failure to comply with dental infection control procedures, that led to the patient's distress and psychiatric injury, at the possibility of having contracted a blood-borne virus.

Where the investigating committee or a practise committee is considering an allegation of impaired practise it may direct the subject of that allegation to undergo an examination or other assessment, in respect of their knowledge of English. The same is true where a person whose name has been removed from register applies to have it restored. This is subject to particular rules of procedure.

The GDC must appoint legal advisers to give advice on questions of law arising in connection with the functions of the committees and the Registrar and may also appoint medical advisers and professional advisers (dentists). It may require the production of details useful to the investigation. This requirement has its basis in the civil law of disclosure. The GDC may seek a court order if the practitioner fails to disclose the required information.

Once an allegation is referred to the Investigating Committee, the GDC must notify the Scottish Ministers and in some instances the person's employer. It may also inform any person, if that is deemed to be in the public interest.

If it is determined that fitness was *not* impaired, the GDC must, at the request of the practitioner, publish a statement to that effect, and may do so with consent of the practitioner. If fitness to practise is found to have been impaired, the Committee may recommend a change to the register, or impose further sanctions on the practitioner.

2.6.2.2 Changes to the register

In certain circumstances a person's name may be erased from the register. These include where the entry was incorrectly made or was fraudulently procured, as determined on reference to the Professional Conduct Committee. The person may apply to the GDC for restoration, which may be done through referral to the Professional Conduct Committee which decides the matter.

A Practice Committee may direct that a person's registration be suspended. For practical purposes, this is treated as not being registered. The committee may also end, extend or attach conditions to that suspension. It may also determine that a person's registration should be conditional or that conditions should cease, continue for a longer period or be supplemented with further conditions. It may also direct that registration be suspended. These provisions apply to resumed hearings. They allow a Practice Committee to vary determinations previously made, although the person concerned must be notified.

A person may apply to the Registrar to have their name restored, but only after five years of erasure and after 12 months of a previous application for restoration. The Professional Conduct Committee considers the application. It may require evidence as to fitness to practise and must be furnished with evidence that the applicant meets the requirements for fitness to practise as regards education, training, good character, etc.

Restoration may be conditional, for example on the existence of adequate insurance or other conditions the Professional Conduct Committee thinks fit for public protection or in the interests of the applicant. Following two or more refused applications for restoration, the Professional Conduct Committee may order that the right to make further applications be suspended indefinitely.

Certain decisions of the Professional Conduct Committee are appealable, for example directions for erasure from the register. Similarly, decisions of the Practice Committees for erasure, suspension, conditional registration or variance of conditions are also appealable.

Appealable decisions may also be appealed to the Court of Session, which may quash the decision, substitute another decision or remit the matter back to the relevant committee of the GDC.

2.6.2.3 General Dental Council sanctions

Following a criminal conviction or a finding of serious professional misconduct, the Professional Conduct Committee may order erasure from the register or the suspension of the dentist's registration. This amounts to disciplinary proceedings on the ground of serious professional misconduct. The standard is that of the ordinarily competent dental practitioner and not the adoption or failure to adopt a particular theory of dentistry. As this is a new provision, any analysis illustrative of serious professional misconduct must be done on the basis of convictions of the Disciplinary Committee (as it then was).

For example, in *Felix* v *General Dental Council* (1960), the appellant, a registered dentist, had been convicted by the Disciplinary Committee of infamous and disgraceful conduct in a professional respect, for wrongfully claiming fees for fillings he had not made and of doing more fillings than were necessary. His defence was carelessness as regards the fees and honestly held professional opinion as regards the need for fillings. As regards the fees, the Privy Council held that it was necessary to prove moral turpitude, fraud or dishonesty, or persistent recklessness as to amount to dishonesty. As regards the fillings, it was held that it was possible that the Committee might have accepted that there had been an honest belief in the necessity of the treatment.

Conversely, in *Carmichael* v *General Dental Council* (1990), it was held that the administration of general anaesthetic contrary to proper practice amounted to serious professional misconduct. The standard applied to serious professional misconduct was similar to that applied in medical negligence.

If fitness to practise is impaired, the Practice Committee may direct:

1. erasure from the register (but not if the sole ground is impaired physical or mental health);

2. suspension for up to 12 months;

3. conditional registration for up to 3 years or

4. that a reprimand be issued.

The Practice Committee is to notify the person of its determination and of the right of appeal, while at the same time revoking any interim order made. In the interest of public protection, a Practice Committee may also make an interim order, or orders for immediate suspension or immediate conditional registration.

Such disciplinary orders will have financial and career consequences for the practitioner, which should be weighed against the conduct of the practitioner when the matter is considered (see *Dad* v *General Dental Council* (2000)).

2.7 DENTAL CARE PROFESSIONALS

Dental hygienists and dental therapists are known as 'dental care professionals' (formerly known as 'dental auxiliaries'), as are dental nurses, dental technicians, clinical dental technicians and orthodontic therapists. They are members of professions complementary to dentistry. In order to fall within the definition, the majority of members of the profession must work in connection with dental care and the profession must also be one regulated by the Professional Standards Authority for Health and Social Care.

2.7.1   Training and registration

The GDC supervises the training of dental care professionals. It has power to appoint visitors to determine the adequacy of instruction and examination. It also has the power to withdraw approval of a qualification if its contents and/or standards are considered to no longer provide the necessary knowledge and skills for a person to acquire the requisite standard of proficiency. Those in possession of a recognised qualification may be entered on the register, as long as they are of good character. The use of the title of 'dental hygienist' or 'dental therapist' by one not enrolled as such is an offence that carries a penalty on summary conviction of a fine of up to level 3 on the standard scale (£1,000). The same penalty follows conviction of the offence of using such a title to suggest qualifications in dentistry.

For each of the following classes, the GDC is to determine the appropriate standard of proficiency required and specify the content and standard of education and training (including practical experience): dental hygienists, dental therapists, dental nurses, dental technicians, clinical dental technicians and orthodontic therapists.

The Council may also approve particular qualifications from particular institutions and may withdraw institutions from the approved list in certain circumstances, which may be based on the sufficiency and adequacy of the courses on offer. It may also withdraw approval of a qualification where it considers the standard of content to no longer provide the necessary level of knowledge and skill required.

Rules must be made requiring registered dental care professionals to undertake professional training and development. Failure to do so may lead to removal of the person's name from the register. It may be restored on application, as long as adequate insurance is in place and training and development requirements have been fulfilled.

The same provisions that apply to dentists' insurance will apply to dental care professionals (Dentists Act 1984 s 36L, added by the Dentists Act 1984 (Amendment) Order 2005, art 31).

Persons registered on the dental care professionals register may be registered only under the titles set out in these regulations. They must satisfy the Registrar as to their identity, good character and good physical and mental health. In addition, dental hygienists and dental therapists must satisfy the Registrar:

1. that they hold the requisite qualifications, or that they hold qualifications from an institution outwith the United Kingdom and have satisfied the Council that they hold the requisite knowledge and skill to practise, and

2. that they have the necessary knowledge of English, that they are of good character, and that they are in good physical and mental health.

The registration procedure is set out in rules drawn up by the Council, specifying the form and manner of registration and what will constitute adequate qualifications. The Council may charge a fee for registration, alteration and restoration of a name to the register. Restoration will be possible only if the applicant satisfies the Registrar that the fee has been paid, insurance is in place, the person is of good character and in good physical and mental health and that they have complied with any requirements as to training and development.

The Registrar has certain duties *vis-à-vis* the register. For example, they must make parts of it publicly available and erase the names of those who are deceased. If the Registrar has referred a person to the Professional Conduct Committee and that committee has recommended erasure, the Registrar is to erase that person's name from the register. This may also occur if the entry in the register was fraudulently procured. Detailed provision is made as to appeals (Dentists Act 1984, s 36J and Sch 4A, prospectively added by SI 2005/2011, art 30(2) and Sch 3 and SI 2006/1668).

2.7.2   Indemnity arrangements

Since the passage of the Health Care and Associated Professions (Indemnity Arrangements) Order 2014, dental professionals must have appropriate indemnity in force in relation to the title under which they practise. Rules may be made in respect of the information that is required to be given to the Registrar. Failure to comply with those rules may be dealt with as a fitness to practise issue, and the person's name subject to erasure from the register. Their name may be restored if they satisfy the Registrar that the appropriate indemnity is in place and that they are of good character and in good physical and mental health, as well as having complied with any conditions, training or development as laid down when their name was removed from the register.

2.7.3   Professional conduct and fitness to practise

Following consultation with appropriate bodies and persons, the GDC is required to publish guidance on the expected conduct and performance of dental care professionals. This must be kept under review. It may differ for different classes of dental care professional. Allegations of impaired fitness to practise may be made on specified grounds similar to those applicable to dentists, that is, misconduct, deficient professional performance, adverse physical or mental health and conviction of a criminal offence.

As is the case with dentists, the Registrar must refer the matter to the Investigating Committee and may refer it to the Interim Orders Committee. The Investigating Committee must investigate and determine whether the matter should be referred to a Practice Committee for further investigation. The Practice Committee is required to make a separate determination in relation to each title under which the person is registered. Where the Investigating or a Practice Committee are considering a misconduct allegation of impaired fitness to practise, it may direct that the person undergoes an assessment to determine whether they have the necessary knowledge of English. This will happen subject to rules that must determine the procedures to be followed.

The Practice Committee of the GDC has the same powers in respect of dental care professionals as it has in respect of dentists and the same provision is made for resumed hearings, restoration of names to the register, immediate suspension orders, conditional registration, interim orders, recording, the Council's power to require disclosure of information and notification and disclosure by the Council. These provisions were discussed above, in respect of dentists.

2.8   NURSES, MIDWIVES AND HEALTH VISITORS

2.8.1   The Nursing and Midwifery Council

The Nursing and Midwifery Council was established by the Nursing and Midwifery Order 2001. It sets standards of education, training, conduct and performance, and its over-arching objective in exercising its functions is the protection of the public. Its current composition is specified by the Nursing and Midwifery Council (Constitution) Order 2008 (SI 2008/245). Its members are appointed by the Privy Council and serve for four years. The Council comprises six registrant and six lay members, where at least one wholly or mainly lives in each of the regions of the United Kingdom, that is, England, Scotland, Wales and Northern Ireland. A president is elected from among the members. The Council's two 'practice committees' are the Investigating Committee and the Fitness to Practise Committee.

2.8.2   Education and registration

The Council maintains and makes rules for the register of nurses and midwives and for the collection of prescribed fees. Registration is open to those with adequate qualifications as reflected in different parts of the register. Applicants must also have appropriate indemnity cover and evidence of the necessary knowledge of English. Further rules apply to further evidence which the Registrar may request in support of the application, or to any examination or other assessment that may be required. Renewal is open to those who complete the required continuous professional development and additional educational training and experience. In emergency circumstances the Council may make temporary annotations to the register in circumstances of loss of life or major illness.

Following Brexit, the same provisions apply to those with European Economic Area qualifications as apply to those with qualifications from any other country outside the United Kingdom. If an applicant has been trained other than in the United Kingdom, they are regarded as holding an approved qualification, if the council is satisfied the qualification is equivalent to those awarded by approved UK institutions. They still need to prove their proficiency in English.

In order to train as a health visitor, a person must be a registered first-level nurse or hold a midwifery qualification and satisfy other specified educational qualifications. Training takes 51 weeks at a prescribed institution. Eligibility depends on completing a training course and passing an examination.

2.8.3   Fitness to practise and restrictions on practice

Standards of conduct and ethics are made and reviewed by the Council. It may issue guidance and take action if the fitness to practise of a nurse or midwife is impaired through misconduct, incompetence or ill health. The Council may make rules that allow the Registrar or other council officer to exercise functions of the Investigating Committee or the Council, and give the Council the power to review a decision of the Investigating Committee.

If there appears to be a case to answer, the Fitness to Practise Committee is then required to consider the allegation referred to it by the Council.

The Practise Committee may order that the person be struck off the register, be suspended for up to a year or be subjected to a 'conditions of practice order' or a 'caution order'. In *Professional Standards Authority for Health and Social Care* v *Nursing and Midwifery Council* (2017) the Inner House of the Court of Session found that a perceived need for a penalty did not mean that a finding of current impairment had to be made. Such a finding would depend on the merits of the case and the discretion of the Committee. Any person who has been struck off the register may apply for the restoration of their name.

Falsely representing oneself as registered is an offence, as is use of the title 'nurse' or 'midwife' or claiming to have qualifications for those professions. It is also an offence to permit another person to do so, knowing the representation to be false. Other offences include trying to change the register, failure to comply with requirements imposed by one of the committees and for anyone other than a midwife to attend a woman in childbirth, except in an emergency. The penalty is a fine of up to level 5 on the standard scale (£5,000).

2.9 OTHER HEALTH CARE PROFESSIONALS

2.9.1 Pharmaceutical chemists

2.9.1.1 Organisation and registration

The General Pharmaceutical Council is a corporate body constituted by an order of the Privy Council under the Pharmacy Order 2010, SI 2010/231. The council's two 'practice committees' are the Investigating Committee and the Fitness to Practise Committee; it also has a separate Appeals Committee. The council's functions are to:

1. establish and maintain a register of pharmacists, pharmacy technicians and retail pharmacy premises;

2. set and promote standards for the safe and effective practice of pharmacy;

3. set requirements of fitness to practise;

4. promote the safe and effective practice of pharmacy;

5. set standards and requirements for education, training, acquisition of experience and continuing professional development to be entered into the register and

6. ensure the continued fitness to practise of registrants.

The Registrar – appointed by the council as a fit and proper person to hold the post – maintains separate registers of pharmacists, pharmacy technicians and premises. Appropriately qualified persons are entitled to be entered into the applicable part of the register for one year, provided they conform to the rules established by the council, pay the annual fee and hold the appropriate indemnity cover. The Registrar's role includes restoring a person's name to the register as appropriate.

Some decisions of the Registrar may be appealed to the appeals committee, by giving notice to the committee within 28 days of the making of the decision that is being appealed. Such decisions relate mainly to the refusal to grant registration. The Appeals Committee may dismiss the appeal, allow the appeal and quash the decision being appealed or refer the case to the Registrar for disposal in accordance with its directions. In the latter two instances a person may appeal against the decision to the sheriff in the sheriffdom of their domicile or of the location of their premises.

As part of its general function to set standards of education and training, the General Pharmaceutical Council must:

1. set the standards of proficiency for the safe and effective practice of pharmacy by pharmacists and pharmacy technicians that are adequate for entry to the register and

2. set standards of education, training and experience that education providers must meet in order to enable such a person to achieve those standards.

Both standards must be published by the council, which may approve the courses of training, qualifications granted, tests of competency and knowledge of English and the institutions of postgraduate education providing training. Similar provisions apply to continuous professional development (CPD) standards, a framework for which must be adopted and maintained by the council. The council must require registrants to comply with CPD conditions and requirements, and complete an annual declaration in that regard.

The council is also required to set and promote standards for the safe and effective practise of pharmacy at registered pharmacies and the council must set standards for the carrying out of a retail pharmacy business. It is also required to establish an inspectorate and make provision in rules relating to the intervals at which premises must be inspected, and the circumstances in which inspections are to be carried out. An inspector may enter a pharmacy at any reasonable hour upon production of evidence of their identity and appointment. If they have reason to believe there is a failure in connection with the carrying out of a retail pharmacy business, or to meet with the standards and conditions of a registered pharmacy, the inspector may serve an improvement notice on the person carrying out the pharmacy business. This notice may be appealed to a sheriff, who may either cancel the notice or confirm it with or without modification.

Similarly, persons may be appointed by the council to visit places of education and places where examinations or tests of compliance are held. Those visitors are selected with regard to the profession on which they are to report, with at least one such visitor already having been entered in a part of the Register which relates to that profession. Visitors are to report on the nature, quality and content of the instruction given at the place visited. The council must send a copy of that report to the institution visited and allow a period of time within which that place may make observations on the report.

It is an offence to make a false representation as to being entered on any of the registers or to use the title 'pharmacist' or 'pharmacy technician', or to display a fraudulent certificate or purport to hold a certificate of registration. Proceedings under this offence must be started within six months beginning with the date on which, in the opinion of the council in England and Wales or the prosecutor in Scotland, there is sufficient evidence to justify a prosecution. The offence carries a penalty of a fine of up to level 3 on the standard scale (£1,000).

2.9.1.2 Business and premises

Only registered pharmaceutical chemists (and registered medical practitioners, dentists and veterinary surgeons) may carry on a retail pharmacy business – that is, in the retail sale of medicinal products other than those which are on the general sales list. The business may be carried out by individuals, partnerships or bodies corporate. If conducted by an individual, the business must be under the 'personal control' of a registered pharmaceutical chemist (as considered in *Pharmaceutical Society of Great Britain* v *Boots Cash Chemists (Southern) Ltd* (1953)). The name(s) of the chemist(s) must be prominently displayed. Partnerships must be under the personal control of one of the partners. Further conditions apply to bodies corporate, such as the requirement that a registered pharmaceutical chemist must manage the corporation and act in the capacity of 'superintendent' in personal control of the retail outlets. Certificates must be prominently displayed there too. Those carrying on a retail pharmacy business must submit an annual return to the Registrar and pay an annual retention fee. Failure to do so is an offence, and failure to pay the retention fee may result in deregistration of the premises. If the Registrar is satisfied that the conditions exist for premises to be entered in the register, then the Registrar has a duty to enter those premises in part 3 of the register. Temporary registration and annotations may be made to the register in the case of emergencies involving loss of human life or human illness.

Further statutory offences exist in the Medicines Act 1968, as amended, relating to fraudulent use of the titles of 'pharmaceutical chemist', 'pharmaceutist', 'pharmacist', 'Member of the Pharmaceutical Society' and 'Fellow of the Pharmaceutical Society' and to conducting a pharmacy business unlawfully. These carry penalties of a fine of up to level 3 on the standard scale (£1,000).

2.9.1.3 Professional discipline

The council must set standards relating to conduct, ethics and performance to be expected of registrants, and make provision in respect of the criteria according to which the Fitness to Practise Committee will decide whether a registrant's fitness to practise is impaired. Any such failure is not in itself proof of misconduct, but is to be taken into account in any misconduct proceedings. Where such an allegation is made to the council, the Registrar must refer the allegation to the Investigating Committee, or where the rules so indicate, directly to the Fitness to Practise Committee.

If the Investigation Committee decides that the allegation need not be considered, then it may give a warning or advice to the person concerned. If the allegation is referred to the Fitness to Practise Committee, then it must be investigated. If either the Fitness to Practise or the Investigating Committee considers that the council should exercise its powers to bring criminal proceedings, it must notify the Registrar accordingly. Decisions of the Fitness to Practise Committee are appealable to the Court of Session, which may dismiss or allow the appeal, or substitute the direction with a different one; the court may also remit the case to the Registrar or the Fitness to Practise Committee for disposal in accordance with the court's decision.

Under Art 51 of the Pharmacy Order 2010 (SI 2010/231), a person's fitness to practise is regarded as 'impaired' only by reason of the following:

a) misconduct;

b) deficient professional performance (which includes competence);

c) adverse physical or mental health which impairs their ability to practise safely and effectively;

d) failure to comply with a reasonable requirement imposed by an individual assessor or an assessment team;

e) conviction of a criminal offence in Great Britain;

f) conviction of a criminal offence elsewhere, which would also be an offence in the UK;

g) an order under section 246(2) or (3) of the Criminal Procedure (Scotland) Act 1995(2) discharging the person absolutely (admonition and absolute discharge);

h) having accepted a conditional offer under section 302 of the Criminal Procedure (Scotland) Act 1995(3) (fixed penalty: conditional offer by procurator fiscal);

i) having agreed to pay a penalty under section 115A of the Social Security Administration Act 1992(4) (penalty as alternative to prosecution);

j) a police caution in the British Islands;

k) having agreed to be bound over to keep the peace by a magistrates' court in England or Wales;

l) a determination of unfitness to practise made by a regulatory body in the United Kingdom responsible for the regulation of a health or social care;

m) the Independent Barring Board including the person in a barred list and

n) the Scottish Ministers including the person in the children's list or the adults' list (within the meaning of the Protection of Vulnerable Groups (Scotland) Act 2007(7)).

If the Fitness to Practise Committee finds the person's fitness to practise to be impaired, it may:

- direct that the person's name be removed from the register;

- direct that entry of the person's name in the register be suspended for up to 12 months;

- direct that the person's entry in the register be rendered conditional upon that person complying, within up to three years, with the requirements specified in the direction as the Committee thinks fit to impose in the interests of the public;

- issue a warning to the person concerned and record the details in the register in connection with any matter arising out of, or related to, the allegation and give a direction that details of the warning be recorded in the Register or

- advise any other person or body involved in the investigation of the allegation, and of any issue arising out of, that allegation.

2.9.2 Opticians

The profession is controlled by the General Optical Council, under the Opticians Act 1989, as amended by the Health Care and Associated Professions (Miscellaneous Amendments) Order 2008, SI 2008/1774. The Council comprises six registrant members and six lay members. They are all appointed by the Privy Council, which also appoints a chair from among the lay members. The over-arching objective of the Council is the protection of the public. The Council may make rules for the conduct of dispensing opticians and optometrists. It may also make rules for the carrying on of an optometry business and its employees. The Council approves training and qualifications required for registration. The Privy Council has the power to monitor the exercise of the Council's functions.

2.9.2.1 Registration and discipline

The Council maintains registers of optometrists, dispensing opticians (persons who fit and supply optical appliances) and bodies corporate engaged in either business. It also maintains a register of those training as optometrists or dispensing opticians. Registrants must hold qualifications approved by the Council, based on completing a course from an approved institution. Practical experience is also required, as is adequate insurance, under SI 2014/1887. For registration purposes, the Council comprises the Registration Committee (for advice and assistance to the Council) and the Registration Appeals Committee (to determine appeals against a decision of the Registrar refusing registration) Separate provision is made under the Recognition of Professional Qualifications and Implementation of International Recognition Agreements (Amendment) Regulations 2023, SI 2023/1286, in the case of a person whose qualification is a specified state qualification. That applies to a qualification as an optometrist or dispensing optician granted in one of the states specified in those regulations.

By virtue of the Opticians Act 1989, as amended by the Health and Social Care (Safety and Quality) Act 2015, two committees drawn from the membership of the Council ensure the fitness to practise of the profession. The Investigation Committee investigates allegations of impaired fitness to practise. It refers appropriate matters to the Fitness to Practise Committee. The Council may issue guidance on fitness to practise and on document disclosure for the purpose of investigation, and has a duty to make information available to specified state professionals, that is, those holding specified state qualifications. That information deals with applicable laws, processes and procedures, as well as principles of discipline and documentation required.

The Fitness to Practise Committee has the power to order the erasure from the register, suspension or conditional registration of a registrant whose fitness to practise is impaired. It may also impose a financial penalty. If it finds fitness is not impaired, it may still issue a warning. A right of appeal lies to the Court of Session or in some circumstances the sheriff court.

2.9.3 Osteopaths

The profession is controlled by the General Osteopathic Council under the General Osteopathic Council (Constitution) Order 2009, which replaced the Osteopaths Act 1993. The council comprises four committees, as constructed under SI 2009/468 (as amended):

1. the Education Committee;
2. the Investigating Committee;
3. the Professional Conduct Committee and
4. the Health Committee.

As with the General Optical Council, the over-arching objective of the General Council in exercising its functions is the protection of the public. The council itself comprises five registered members and five members as appointed by the Privy Council which also determines the term of appointment of each of the members. The Privy Council also appoints a chair for a term of office determined by the Council. No member may hold office for more than eight years on aggregate during any period of 20 years. There are various grounds for disqualification, including conviction of an offence involving dishonesty or deception, or removal from the office of charity trustee.

2.9.3.1 Registration

The Registrar maintains a register of osteopaths. Registration may be full, conditional or provisional, depending on conditions satisfied as set out by the Council. These conditions deal with holding a recognised qualification, or since 2023 holding a 'specified state qualification' which is not a recognised qualification and has met the requirement specified in relation to the person, is of good character and good physical and mental health and the payment of a fee. 'Specified state qualification' has a similar meaning as applies to opticians, that is, a qualification in osteopathy granted in one of the states specified in SI 2023/1286. The council has a duty to make information available to specified state professionals, that is, those holding specified state qualifications. That information deals with applicable laws, processes and procedures, as well as principles of discipline and documentation required.

Conditional registration may be open to those without formal qualifications who meet the other criteria and can demonstrate that, for at least four years (continuous or not), they have spent a substantial part of their working time in the lawful, safe and competent practice of osteopathy. In such cases, the person may be required to conform to rules made by the Council, pass a prescribed test of competence and give the required undertaking (e.g. to undertake further training). It may be possible, on fulfilling certain conditions, to convert provisional to full registration.

The Council may make rules that some or all applicants be registered initially with provisional registration and provide for the conversion to full registration, subject to conditions. A provisionally registered osteopath may practise only under the supervision of a fully registered and approved osteopath. The council has made rules requiring all practising osteopaths to have indemnity arrangements in place, that cover specified risks at a minimum level of cover.

2.9.3.2 Proficiency and discipline

The Council must determine and publish the required standard of proficiency as well as a code of practice. This code should set out standards and offer advice. It must be kept under review and may be varied by the Council. An allegation of a failure to comply with its provisions will not in itself be sufficient to amount to unacceptable professional practice, but will be taken into account in any subsequent proceedings under the 1993 Act. Under an amendment made to the 1993 Act, by the Recognition of Professional Qualifications and Implementation of International Recognition Agreements (Amendment) Regulations 2023 (SI 2023/1286), the General Council must also make information about certain matters available to those specified state professionals mentioned above.

The Investigating Committee, Professional Conduct Committee and Health Committee undertake disciplinary roles. If there is a case to answer and in the interests of public protection, the Investigating Committee may order the Registrar to suspend the osteopath's registration. This may happen where preliminary investigations indicate any of the following:

1. conduct falling short of the standard required of a registered osteopath;
2. professional incompetence;
3. conviction (at any time) of a criminal offence or
4. seriously impaired ability to practise due to physical or mental condition.

An allegation may be referred to the Professional Conduct or Health Committees, which may impose an interim suspension order.

Appeals lie to His Majesty in Council on a point of law only, but in future will lie to the Court of Session.

It is an offence falsely to hold oneself out as registered as any of the categories of osteopath. Under certain circumstances, it is an offence to fail to comply with a requirement imposed by the Professional Conduct Committee, the Health Committee or an appeal tribunal hearing an appeal. On summary conviction this offence carries a penalty of a fine of up to level 5 on the standard scale (£5,000).

2.9.4   Chiropractors

Regulation of the profession is provided by the General Chiropractic Council (Constitution) Order 2008, which replaced the Chiropractors Act 1994 under which the General Chiropractic Council and its four statutory committees were established:

1.   Education Committee;

2.   Investigating Committee;

3.   Professional Conduct Committee (PCC) and

4.   Health Committee.

As with osteopaths and opticians, the over-arching objective of the General Council in exercising its functions is the protection of the public.

The Council may establish further committees and appoint a Registrar. The Council sets the standards required for full or conditional registration as a chiropractor and makes rules for provisional registration for one year. Rules may dictate how conditional registration can be converted to full registration, before which the registrant may practise only under supervision. Any person who satisfies specified conditions will be entitled to be registered as a conditionally registered osteopath, including payment of a prescribed fee and submission of a prescribed completed form. They need to satisfy the Registrar that they are of good character and enjoy good physical and mental health, and have been practicing osteopathy for four years. They must also hold a recognised qualification, or a specified state qualification which is a recognised qualification and has met the requirement specified in relation to the person. 'Specified state qualification' has a similar meaning as applies to opticians, that is, a qualification in osteopathy granted in one of the states specified in SI 2023/1286. That information deals with applicable laws, processes and procedures, as well as principles of discipline and documentation required.

The Council determines and publishes required standards of proficiency and approved qualifications, with the approval of the Privy Council, and may require further continuous training of chiropractors. The Council may require a specified state professional wishing to be registered to practise as an osteopath to demonstrate that they possess the language skills necessary to do so.

Following consultation with practitioners' representatives, the Council must prepare a code of practice. This should set out expected standards of conduct and practice and give advice.

Allegations of unacceptable professional conduct or professional incompetence must be referred to the Investigating Committee. If there is a case to answer, it will be referred to the PCC or the Health Committee. On the basis of public protection, any of those three committees may then order interim suspension of registration. Following further consideration, the practitioner may be admonished, have their registration suspended, be removed from the register or have a *conditions of practice order* made. The decision may be appealed.

The Council may also make rules requiring proper practice insurance, which it did under the Health Care and Associated Professions (Indemnity Arrangements) Order 2014.

2.9.5   The Health and Care Professions

The Health and Care Professions Council was established by s 214(2) of the Health and Social Care Act 2012 (c 7), which amended the Health and Social Work Professions Order 2001, by renaming the Health Professions Council. The council sets standards of education, training, conduct and performance for a number of health professions. These include:

- arts therapists;
- chiropodists;
- clinical scientists;
- dieticians;
- medical laboratory technicians;
- occupational therapists;
- orthoptists;
- paramedics;
- physiotherapists;
- prosthetists and orthotists;

- radiographers and
- speech and language therapists.

The council itself comprises both registrant and lay members, all appointed by the Privy Council, which also appoints a chair. At any one time there must be at least one council member who lives or works wholly or mainly in each of England, Scotland, Wales and Northern Ireland. The council comprises the following four committees:

1. Education and Training Committee;
2. Investigating Committee;
3. Conduct and Competence Committee and
4. Health Committee.

The Council directs the performance of the committee functions. Further functions may be conferred on the Council by the Privy Council, which must be consulted annually by the Health and Care Professions Council.

The Council must keep registers of the different professions under their various professional titles. It is an offence falsely to hold oneself out as registered under any of the professions supplementary to medicine.

Those seeking registration must satisfy the Council of their education, training and qualification, or satisfy the education and training committee that they have passed an aptitude test or successfully completed an adaptation period pursuant to the provision relating to specified state professionals. As with other professions discussed above, since 2023 such a professional will hold a 'specified state qualification' which is a qualification in one of the relevant professions awarded in one of the states specified in the Recognition of Professional Qualifications and Implementation of International Recognition Agreements (Amendment) Regulations 2023. The council has a duty to make information available to specified state professionals, that is, those holding specified state qualifications. That information deals with applicable laws, processes and procedures, as well as principles of discipline and documentation required.

The Council must establish and keep under review required standards of conduct, performance and ethics. These are to be designed around public protection.

Allegations of impaired fitness to practise made against a registrant are first considered by the Investigating Committee or by 'screeners' (individuals specially appointed under SI 2002/254, art 23). If it appears that there is a case to answer, the matter is considered by the Conduct and Competence Committee or the Health Committee. They have the power to strike off or suspend the registrant from the register. Appeals are to the Court of Session. A person struck off may apply for reinstatement, but only after five years. No more than one such application may be made in any 12-month period.

In any event, the council requires each practicing registrant to hold appropriate indemnity cover for practising as a member of the relevant profession in question, without which they will not be admitted to the register of practitioners.

Essential facts

Statutory control

- The medical profession is regulated by a large body of statute and is an area "reserved" to Westminster under the Scotland Act 1998.
- The Professional Standards Authority for Health and Social Care is a body corporate overseeing the activities of the profession in the public interest.
- The other regulatory bodies are required to co-operate with the Authority, which may report on those bodies and may refer to the court disciplinary cases made by those bodies.

Medical practitioners

- The General Medical Council regulates the training in and practice of medicine, under the Medical Act 1983.
- Only registered medical practitioners may practise under that title; otherwise, an offence is committed.
- The GMC Registrar must maintain and publish registers of general practitioners and specialist practitioners.
- Registration is open to those who have completed particular qualifications, and to non-EEA practitioners if their qualifications are seen as equivalent.
- Training, qualifications and experience are supervised by the GMC itself. Practitioners must have a primary qualification and a qualification of practical experience in a resident capacity.
- Licence to practise may be obtained once registered and this is regulated by the GMC.
- Misconduct leading to the harm of a patient may leave the practitioner open to civil or criminal liability as well as professional sanction.

- The Investigation Committee, the Interim Orders Tribunals and the Medical Practice Tribunal Service deal with allegations of misconduct of practitioners.
- Responsible Officers are appointed by specified bodies such as NHS Trusts to ensure regular appraisal of medical practitioners.
- Allegations of professional misconduct must be investigated and may be passed on to one of the panels if there is a case to answer. Panels may direct that the person's name be erased from the register. Certain decisions may be appealed to the Court of Session.
- Grounds on which fitness to practise may be impaired are misconduct, unethical behaviour, sexual involvement with a patient, neglect of duty and advertising and dishonesty.
- Responsible officers may be appointed by health boards ensure regular appraisal of medical practitioners.

Dental practitioners

- The dental profession is regulated by the Dentists Act 1984 under the General Dental Council.
- The GDC comprises six registrant and six lay members, appointed by the Privy Council, and a chair elected from that membership.
- The GDC also contains six committees: the Professional Conduct Committee, the Health Committee, the Investigating Committee, the Professional Performance Committee, the Interim Orders Committee and the Registration Appeals Committee.
- The GDC Registrar must keep a register of those whose qualifications entitle them to practise dentistry.
- The GDC regulates and supervises admissible qualifications and experience, including compatible overseas qualifications.
- Dentistry is run as a business in the United Kingdom. Separate provisions apply to partnerships and bodies corporate.
- Insurance is required of dentists in practice.
- Allegations that fitness to practise is impaired are investigated by the Investigation Committee and may be referred to the Interim Orders Committee while an investigation is ongoing.
- The Registrar refers allegations of professional misconduct to the Investigation Committee and, if appropriate, the Interim Orders Committee. If there is a case to answer, the matter is referred to one of the Practice Committees.

- The grounds on which fitness to practise is considered 'impaired' include misconduct, deficient professional performance, adverse physical or mental health and conviction of a criminal offence.
- In certain circumstances a person's name may be erased from the register – if it was fraudulently entered or following a finding of serious professional misconduct. Under certain conditions it may be reinstated.
- Dental care professionals (dental hygienists and dental therapists) are also regulated by the GDC. Similar provisions apply to registration, training and insurance as apply to dentists.

Nurses, midwives and health visitors

- The Nursing and Midwifery Council was established by the Nursing and Midwifery Order 2001.
- The Council comprises six registrant and six lay members, with one from each of the constituent nations of the United Kingdom.
- The Council has two 'practice committees': the Investigating Committee and the Fitness to Practise Committee.
- The Council maintains a register of nurses and midwives and makes rules as regards training sufficient for registration; it also makes and keeps under review standards and codes of conduct.
- The Investigating Committee and the Fitness to Practise Committee may order that a person be struck off the register.
- The same registration provisions apply to EEA members as apply to UK membership following Brexit.

Other health care professionals

- Other health care professionals are regulated by individual regulatory bodies having similar roles to the General Medical Council and the General Dental Council as regards qualifications, registration, conduct and discipline.
- The Councils regulating the various health care professions also comprise appropriate committees for conduct, registration, discipline and investigation, similar to those regulating medicine and dentistry. They may also impose sanctions on practitioners for misconduct.
- Councils must also determine and publish the required standards of proficiency and codes of practice.

- Pharmacists are regulated by the General Pharmaceutical Council and its Investigating Committee and Fitness to Practise Committee, charged with the promotion of standards of practice and professional discipline.
- Further provisions apply to pharmacists, pharmaceutical chemists and businesses and bodies corporate relating to the role of superintendents, for example.
- Statutory offences including fraudulent use of various titles applied to pharmacists. Similar offences apply to the other health care professions.
- Opticians are regulated by the General Optical Council under the Opticians Act 1989.
- Hearing aid dispensers are regulated by the Hearing Aid Council established by the Hearing Aid Council Act 1968.
- Osteopaths are regulated by the General Osteopathic Council under the Osteopaths Act 1993.
- Chiropractors are regulated under the Chiropractors 1994 Act by the General Chiropractic Council and its four statutory committees.
- The Health Professions Order 2001 brings together and allows regulation by the Health Professions Council of arts therapists, chiropodists, clinical scientists, dieticians, medical laboratory technicians, occupational therapists, orthoptists, paramedics, physiotherapists, prosthetists and orthotists, radiographers and speech and language therapists.
- The Health and Care Professions Council was established in 2012 to set the standards of education, training and professional conduct of a range of professions, including arts therapists, chiropodists, clinical scientists, dieticians, medical laboratory technicians, occupational therapists, orthoptists, paramedics, physiotherapists, prosthetists and orthotists, radiographers and speech and language therapists. It comprises registrant and lay members and its functions are discharged by its four committees.

Essential cases

Younghusband v Luftig (1949): the accused had not claimed one of the qualifications mentioned in the legislation, by using the designation 'MD Berlin' to denote his degree from that university.

Wilson v Inyang (1951): it will be a defence that the accused held a genuine belief of entitlement to hold himself out as a doctor.

R v General Medical Council, ex p Virik (1996): in determining whether to grant full registration to a doctor with acceptable overseas qualifications, the GMC need not make a comparison with a hypothetical EU equivalent applicant.

R (Kuzmin) v General Medical Council (2019): tribunals may draw adverse inferences were the person charged with breaches to remain silent.

Ogunsanya v General Medical Council (2021): the question of impairment is not limited to conduct in a specific capacity.

Lanford v General Medical Council (1990): in allegations of misconduct by a medical practitioner, the onus and standard of proof required are those of the criminal law.

Daly v General Medical Council (1952): the Chief Executive, who was also a practitioner, had a duty in both capacities.

Roylance v General Medical Council (No 2) (2000): a Chief Executive was found guilty of serious professional misconduct for failing to act over high infant mortality rates and on those grounds to prevent the surgery of a child who later died.

De Gregory v General Medical Council (1961): if a practitioner has used a professional position to gain access to family confidences, the same standard must be maintained if or when the practitioner befriends the family.

Bhattacharya v General Medical Council (1967): whether the conduct brings the profession into disrepute will differ from case to case.

R v Richardson (1998): an unregistered dentist treating a patient may be negligent, but that will not amount to a criminal assault.

Felix v General Dental Council (1960): to ensure a finding by the GDC of infamous and disgraceful conduct in a professional respect for wrongfully claiming fees, it is necessary to prove moral turpitude, fraud or dishonesty, or persistent recklessness such as to amount to dishonesty.

Professional Standards Authority for Health and Social Care v Nursing and Midwifery Council (2017): the perceived need for a penalty did not mean that a finding of current impairment had to be made, which depends on the merits of each case.

3 FERTILITY, GENETICS AND REPRODUCTION

3.1 INFERTILITY

3.1.1 Rights and definitions

Infertility may be defined in several ways, and has been by the World Health Organization and the Human Fertilisation and Embryology Authority (HFEA). For present purposes it is considered to be the inability to conceive despite unprotected sexual intercourse for a period of time.

The right to found a family is guaranteed under Art 12 of the European Convention on Human Rights (ECHR). This may have implications for the provision of fertility services. Indeed, in *R (on the application of Assisted Reproduction and Gynaecology Centre) v Human Fertilisation and Embryology Authority* [2002] EWCA Civ 20, the court assumed that Art 8 (on respect for private and family life) and 12 (the right to found a family) apply to keeping embryos outside the body.

Treatment for infertility may involve one or more of the following techniques: *in vitro* fertilisation, artificial insemination, donated gametes (sperm and eggs) and surrogacy. Where medical technology is employed, the terms of the Human Fertilisation and Embryology Act 1990 come into play. The Act regulates the storage, use and creation of human embryos and the licencing of clinics engaged in those activities.

3.1.2 *In vitro* fertilisation

3.1.2.1 *Human Fertilisation and Embryology Act 1990*

The Warnock Report of 1984 recommended that there should be statutory regulation of this aspect of medical practice. The Report was prompted by concerns that increasingly available reproductive technology might be open to abuse. The statutory regulation came in the form of the Human Fertilisation and Embryology Act 1990 (the '1990 Act'). Its terms are reserved to Westminster under Head J3 of Sch 5 to the Scotland Act 1998. As a result, all subordinate legislation and the subject-matter of the 1990 Act are not within the legislative competence of the Scottish Parliament. For this reason, the case law of England and Wales, as well as that of Scotland, will be referred to.

The areas covered by the 1990 Act are:

- Access to treatment;
- Licensing of practices offering treatment;

- Consent to use of genetic material;
- Control of information;
- Conscientious objection of medical practitioners and
- Status of children born as a result of infertility treatments.

The 1990 Act regulates infertility treatment, and research on and storage of human embryos. It covers only embryos created and stored outside the body. Section 1 of the 1990 Act describes an 'Embryo' as a live human embryo and does not include a human admixed embryo. References to an embryo include an egg that is in the process of fertilisation or is undergoing any other process capable of resulting in an embryo.

Significant amendments were made to the 1990 Act by virtue of the Human Fertilisation and Embryology Act 2008. In terms of definitions, s 1 of the 2008 Act allows the Secretary of State, should they deem it appropriate in light of developments in science and medicine, to make regulations providing that 'embryo', 'eggs', 'sperm' or 'gametes' will include things specified in the regulations which would not otherwise fall within the definition in question. An exception exists in terms of anything containing nuclear or mitochondrial DNA that is not human in origin. It is likely that this has to do with research on the use of embryonic stem cells in infertility treatment, but the Explanatory Notes are not clear on that point.

Under the 1990 Act '*In vitro* embryo creation' refers to fertilisation outside the body, even if fertilisation was not completed there; the 2008 Act is more specific insofar as it now also refers to any other process by which an embryo is created outside the body.

'Treatment services' refers to medical, obstetric or surgical services open to the public to assist women to carry children. A woman is said to be carrying a child only once the embryo has become implanted in her womb.

3.1.2.2 The Human Fertilisation and Embryology Authority

The Human Fertilisation and Embryology Authority (HFEA) was created by the 1990 Act, and amended by the 2008 Act, providing in particular that the crown may modify its functions, as well as those of the Human Tissue Authority, or indeed transfer any of those functions to an eligible person. An eligible person is defined under s1(3) of the Public Bodies Act 2011. The list includes ministers in the devolved governments as well as other categories of individual, including 'any other person exercising public functions'.

The HFEA is a corporate body with a Chair, deputy and members appointed by the Secretary of State, most of whom must be neither doctors nor scientific researchers. The Chair and deputy must not be scientists either. The HFEA must publish an annual report and maintain a code of practice.

It is also required to keep certain matters under review, such as information on the development of human embryos, and to perform those functions set out in regulations. These are found in various statutory instruments subordinate to the 1990 Act, such as the Human Fertilisation and Embryology Act 1990 (Amendment) Regulations 2006. Under the 2008 Act the HFEA is obliged to carry out its responsibilities effectively, efficiently and economically, while also having regard to best regulatory practice principles. Some of those more administrative or technical functions may be carried out under contract with other authorities, as holders of public office.

The activities of the HFEA are required to be publicised and publicity material must offer advice to those seeking the services that fall under the purview of the HFEA. Section 66 of the 2008 Act provides that the HFEA may charge a fee for any advice provided under the 1990 Act. It is required to maintain a statement of general principles it feels should be followed in carrying out activities under the 1990 Act.

3.1.2.3 Licencing by the Human Fertilisation and Embryology Authority

Crucially, the HFEA grants licences under the terms of the 1990 Act, as amended by the 2008 Act and the Human Fertilisation and Embryology (Quality and Safety) Regulations 2007; 'licence' means one granted under the 1990 Act. Three general situations are envisaged:

1. The HFEA grants licences for otherwise illegal activities that are capable of licensing under the 1990 Act. This means that licences may not be granted for illegal activities (such as human cloning) which the HFEA does not have authority to license under the 1990 Act. An example of this category of licence is for the creation and storage of embryos.

2. The HFEA does not grant licences for legal activities not requiring licences, such as artificial insemination using donor sperm.

3. The HFEA cannot grant licences for activities specifically prohibited under the 1990 Act, such as:

    •   use for reproduction of eggs from a foetus or embryos created using those eggs. Research using foetal gametes is permitted, however;

    •   keeping an embryo beyond the 'primitive streak', that is, up to 14 days from the day on which the process of creating the embryo began, under s 3(4);

    •   human cloning.

It is permissible under the 2007 Regulations to keep and process – though not store – an embryo destined for human application subject to a third-party agreement, that is, an agreement between a license holder and a third party, whose role is set out in the terms of the licence. By extension, no person may procure, test, process or distribute any gametes intended for human application, without a licence or third-party agreement.

Licences may be issued by the HFEA for gamete storage and embryo research. The procedure for issuing licences is set out in the 1990 Act. It is undertaken by the Licence Committee of the HFEA, which also has the role (under s 9) of variation, suspension and revocation of licences. That committee was constituted under the Human Fertilisation and Embryology (Licence Committee and Appeals) Regulations 1991, and more recently the Human Fertilisation and Embryology (Appeals) Regulations 2009, SI 2009/1891 provides for an appeals committee to reconsider licensing decisions made by the HFEA.

Licences are issued for specific purposes, to the person responsible for those activities. That person will be the clinician, or the nominal licensee in the case of a manager or administrator of a clinic. Further conditions apply to that person, for example the requirement to keep records of the activities undertaken and provisions as to consents to the use of embryos and gametes, or storage of gametes, embryos or human admixed embryos. A consent to the use of any human admixed embryo must specify the intended uses, research projects and other conditions subject to which the human admixed embryo may be so used.

A licence may be granted in respect of infertility treatment, storage and research, but only to be carried out on the premises to which the licence applies. The HFEA may enter and inspect the premises. The activity may not be supervised by more than one person or carried out in more than one place. Certain activities may not be undertaken except in pursuance of the terms and conditions of a licence. These categories (under s 3 and Sch 2) are research, treatment and storage.

3.1.2.3.1 Research licences

A licence for research may be granted to a single person, to authorise activities as part of a single research project over up to three years. This may include *in vitro* creation and subsequent storage of embryos for research. Research licences may not authorise those activities specifically prohibited as set out above. Section 15 and Para 3 of Sch 2 to the 1990 Act, as amended by the 2008 Act, set out specific conditions that apply to research licences. The HFEA must be satisfied that the activities are necessary or desirable for:

a) increasing knowledge about a serious diseases or medical conditions;

b) developing treatments for serious diseases or medical conditions;

c) increasing knowledge about causes of congenital diseases or medical conditions that do not fall within head a) above;

d) promoting advances in the treatment of infertility;

e) increasing knowledge about the causes of miscarriage;

f) developing more effective contraception techniques;

g) developing methods for detecting the presence of gene, chromosome or mitochondrion abnormalities in embryos before implantation or

h) increasing knowledge about the development of embryos.

For the HFEA to grant a research license it must be satisfied that the proposed use of embryos or admixed human embryos is required for the purposes of the research. The Authority may issue a research license subject to particular conditions. Under the 2008 amendments to the 1990 Act, a research license may authorise:

1. creating, keeping or using *in vitro* embryos for a research project specified in the license;

2. mixing human sperm with the egg of an animal for the purpose of developing effective techniques for determining fertility or normality of human sperm, but only where anything that forms is destroyed once the research is complete, and no later than the two-cell stage or

3. *in vitro* creation of human admixed embryos and keeping or using such embryos, for the purposes of a research project as specified in the licence.

3.1.2.3.2 Infertility treatment licences

Conditions applicable to treatment licences are contained in s 18 and Sch 2 of the 1990 Act. Such licences may be granted for up to five years, to authorise activities in the provision of treatment services. Examples of such activities include the creation of embryos *in vitro*, or the procuring, keeping, testing, processing or distributing embryos and procuring, testing, processing, distributing or using gametes. Such licences also apply to the placing of an embryo in a woman and determining the suitability of so doing. They may also be granted for the use of embryos for the purpose of training persons in embryo biopsy, embryo storage or other embryological techniques, but those embryos may not be used for the provision of treatment services.

It is permitted to mix sperm with the egg of an animal in order to determine normality or fertility, but the product must then be destroyed. The treatment licence may not authorise altering the nuclear or mitochondrial DNA of a cell while it forms part of an embryo, except for the purpose of creating something that will be a permitted embryo.

Aside from the general conditions that apply to licences as set out above, and those that apply to consent, there are conditions specific to treatment licences. These relate to the requirements on the HFEA to record the services provided, the persons treated and the persons whose gametes are retained for the creation of embryos. Information necessary to facilitate the traceability of gametes and embryos and relating to the quality or safety of gametes or embryos is to be recorded and provided to the HFEA if requested.

Records should retain details of any child who appears to have been born as a result of treatment. The welfare of the child is paramount in the provision of treatment services under the 1990 Act. Treatment may be provided only if this has been taken into account, as has the welfare of any child who may be affected by the birth of a child as a result of infertility treatment. Welfare considerations include the need for supportive parenting. Treatment may not proceed unless the woman and any man or woman who is to be treated together with her have been given proper counselling about the implications of the treatment services being provided, and have been provided with such relevant information as is proper. Account should be taken of any agreed fatherhood conditions that have been made under the 2008 Act.

3.1.2.3.3 Storage licences

S 171 and Sch 17 of the Health and Care Act 2022 made provision for a new scheme for storage of gametes. It allows for all patients to store gametes or embryos for up to 55 years, although their consent needs to be renewed every 10 years. This is an advance on the previous scheme which limited storage facilities to those who had been declared prematurely infertile or likely to become so.

Sch 3 of the 1990 Act still applies in respect of different conditions for gametes, embryos taken from a woman and embryos the creation of which has been brought about *in vitro* otherwise than in pursuance of a licence. A maximum storage duration of 55 years applies. That time limit applies to embryos and gametes stored for treatment purposes. A ten-year time limit applies to embryos kept in storage for research or training purposes. The same time limit applies to human admixed embryos.

Neither an embryo created *in vitro* nor a person's gametes may be stored without the effective consent of that person or each relevant person, and an embryo taken from a woman must be stored with the consent of that woman. Not only must it be in writing, it must also specify the maximum storage period if less than the statutory 55-year maximum. As if learning from the case law considered below, the new scheme requires that the written consent specify what should be done with the embryos or gametes in the event of the donor's death, or their incapacity that prevents them from varying their consent.

Further specific conditions apply to storage licenses:

- gametes or embryos may be stored only if acquired from a person to whom a licence or third party agreement applies;

- an embryo created *in vitro* not in pursuance of a license may be stored only if acquired from a person to whom a licence or third party agreement applies;

- stored gametes or embryos may be supplied only for the purpose of providing treatment services or to a person to whom a licence applies;

- gametes or embryos kept in storage pursuant to a license must be removed and disposed of once they may no longer be lawfully kept;

- no information may be removed from records once the legal storage period has expired.

Further detailed provisions relating to consent have been set out under the new scheme. These include provisions in relation to renewal, variation and withdrawal, and requirements that the person keeping embryos in storage must, after each ten-year consent period, request that the consent to storage is renewed by the person whose embryos are being stored.

3.1.2.3.4 Embryo testing and sex selection

Under Sch 2 of the 2008 Act, embryo testing and sex selection under the terms of a treatment licence may take place only for the following purposes:

1. establishing the presence of a gene, chromosome or mitochondrion abnormality that may affect its capacity to result in a live birth;

2. where there is a risk that the embryo may have any gene, chromosome or mitochondrion abnormality, establishing whether it has that abnormality. For this to be allowed the HFEA must be satisfied that there is a significant risk that any person born with that abnormality will develop a serious physical or mental disability, a serious illness or any other serious medical condition;

3. establishing the sex of an embryo when there is a particular risk that any resulting child will have or develop a gender-related serious

physical or mental disability. This requires that the HFEA is satisfied that the condition affects only one sex, or indeed affects one
sex significantly more than the other;

4. establishing the compatibility of any resulting child, where a sibling
   who is the child of the persons whose gametes are used to bring
   about the creation of the embryo suffers from a serious medical
   condition which could be treated by the tissue of any resulting
   child, not including any whole organ of the child and

5. where there is uncertainty in establishing whether the embryo is
   one whose creation was brought about by using the gametes of
   particular persons.

3.1.2.3.5 Pre-implantation genetic diagnosis licences

The technology behind pre-implantation genetic diagnosis (PGD) allows
the screening of embryos for genetic characteristics, including sex selection
which is contrary to the HFEA Code of Practice. PGD requires a licence. It
involves selecting those embryos that are implanted in the uterus.

While screening out embryos on the basis of sex alone is contrary to
the Code, certain so-called X-linked hereditary conditions that are suffered
only by members of a particular sex may be screened out. Examples include
Duchene muscular dystrophy, which is a debilitating condition suffered by
males.

In *R (Quintavalle)* v *Human Fertilisation and Embryology Authority* (2005),
sex selection was allowed using PGD, to ensure that the child born would
be a suitable bone marrow donor for his brother, who had a genetic form of
anaemia. The family also sought a child who would not inherit the condition. The HFEA was prepared to grant a licence only for the diagnosis of the
genetic condition, rather than for the tissue typing, which is the assessment
of tissue from separate sources for immunological compatibility.

Under judicial review of that decision, the House of Lords held that
the case hinged on the meaning of 'suitability' under s 2(1) of the 1990 Act.
Tissue typing through PGD and IVF may allow a woman to be less inhibited
about bearing children; the Act therefore allowed the HFEA to grant such a
licence. The HFEA subsequently amended its Guidelines.

3.1.2.3.6 Non-medical fertility services licences

In provisions added to s 3 of the 1990 Act by the Human Fertilisation
and Embryology (Quality and Safety) Regulations 2007, the HFEA may
grant five-year term licences for non-medical, surgical or obstetric services.
These include any non-medical services that are provided, in the course
of the running of a business, for the purpose of assisting women to carry

children, as well as the procurement and distribution of sperm. Such licenses may not authorise storage, procurement, testing, processing or distribution of embryos unless so doing is compliant with requirements of European Directive 2004/23 on quality standards and safety.

As well as the general conditions that apply to all licenses, further conditions apply to non-medical services licenses, such as provisions relating to the information necessary to facilitate the traceability of gametes and embryos, and the recording of information on the person being treated, the services provided for them and any child that appears to have been born as a result. Further provisions require providing the opportunity for the woman to take up proper counselling around the implications of the proposed steps being taken.

3.1.2.4 Consent

Consent is fundamental to the storage and use of gametes and embryos, particularly with regard to the concept of being 'treated together', which is discussed further below. Schedule 3 to the 1990 Act sets out what is required for consent to be valid, and applies to both donors and recipients of genetic material. These requirements do not apply in relation to the use of gametes in the course of providing basic partner treatment services, that is, services provided for a woman and a man treated together, without using donated or stored gametes, or gametes created outside of the woman's body.

The consent requirements are more stringent than common law provisions as to consent of donors and recipients of genetic material. An example of the greater stringency is in the requirement to provide counselling services. Amendments to Sch 3 by the 2008 Act and the Health and Care Act 2022 created an exception to consent requirements insofar as human cells can be used without the consent of the person providing them in particular cases. These include cells taken from children, from adults who lack capacity or from existing cells or cell lines. Provisions for the application to store or use gametes without the adult's consent are provided in section 84A and 84B of the Adults with Incapacity (Scotland) Act 2000 (asp 4).

The HFEA Code of Practice gives some guidance but does not carry the force of law, but under the 2008 Act the HFEA is required to take into account any failure to abide by the code when considering a failure to observe the conditions of a licence already granted.

The consents required under s 25 of the 1990 Act for licensing, storage and use ensure that legal control of the genetic material remains with the suppliers of that material. Gametes may be used only for the purposes to which consent was given when the gametes were procured. This applies to those who make use of gametes and to the provisions for storage.

In general, there must be written consent to the use of the embryo, specifying that its use is for the provision of treatment services to the consenting party. The consent must specify that use is for the person treated as specified in the treatment licence, or that person and another specified person treated together. Alternatively, the consent may specify that the infertility treatment licence is for providing treatment services to persons not including the person giving consent, i.e. in the case of donated gametes. The records that are required to be kept in providing treatment services must contain details of the consent given.

There is case law in which the HFEA was found to have erred in citing lack of effective consent as a ground for refusing to allow the export of the deceased donor's eggs, for donor fertilisation and later implantation in her mother's womb in America. In *R (M)* v *Human Fertilisation and Embryology Authority* (2016), the court found that Sch 3 said only that a person had to receive 'such relevant information as is proper', and that this recognised that information is variable according to the circumstances of a case. Neither did the Committee adequately explain why the Appellant needed to be given the information which was allegedly lacking.

As is the case with consent to medical treatment generally, consent here should not be given under undue influence. Although there is no Scottish case law in point, this area was considered by the High Court in England in *Centre for Reproductive Medicine* v *U* (2002). That case involved the use of sperm after the donor's death. It had been surgically removed while U was alive, as he had previously had a vasectomy. Proper consent to retrieval and storage of the sperm had been given and counselling provided. Although provision existed for use of the sperm after U's death, the Centre for Reproductive Medicine had indicated on the form that posthumous conception would not be in the interest of the child born as a result and was unethical. The Centre had agreed to store the sperm only during U's life, yet on a different form U had specified that it should still be stored for use after his death. He subsequently altered the form at a follow-up appointment with a specialist nurse, specifying that the sperm should be allowed to perish. It was common ground that the nurse had asked Mr U to change the form, yet Mrs U argued that Mr U changed it reluctantly and under the authority of the nurse.

Three embryos were created *in vitro*, two of which were implanted in Mrs U. A pregnancy was not successful and the third embryo was stored. Mr U subsequently died. The Centre argued that the third embryo should be allowed to perish, on account of Mr U's withdrawal of consent to the storage of his sperm after his death, which would make its continued storage thereof a criminal offence.

On the one hand, the HFEA is on record as discouraging posthumous conception; the 1990 Act specifies that in those circumstances a person in U's position would not be treated as the father of the chid and that treatment services should not be provided unless the welfare of the child has been taken into account. On the other hand, Mrs U's case was based on misrepresentation, undue influence and duress. The Centre sought the guidance of the court. The case law on undue influence was not helpful to the court, as the Centre would gain nothing through the alteration made to the form. The court found that Mr U did not make the changes under any compulsion and the question remained whether effective consent had been given by Mr U to the storage and use of the third embryo. The court found no reason to believe that Mr U had not intended to make the alteration he had made, and the cells should be allowed to perish.

3.1.2.5 Case law on storage and being 'treated together'

R v Human Fertilisation and Embryology Authority, ex parte Blood (1997) (the 'Blood case') and U v W (1998) dealt with storage, licensing, consent and 'treatment together' under the 1990 Act.

In the Blood case, Mr Blood died following meningitis. Sperm was taken and stored without his express consent before his death, while he was unconscious. His consent therefore did not specify what should be done with the sperm in the event of his death. The HFEA refused a treatment licence, on the ground of lack of consent, although Mrs Blood argued that her husband had given his consent in informal discussion and that an export licence to Belgium should be granted. The court found that this should be granted under the EC Treaty on free movement of goods and services, as, without it, Mrs Blood would be denied treatment in a European Member State.

However, this left the matter of storage, which cannot be done without written consent of both parties. Yet, given that the sperm had already been stored, the question of treatment, too, remained. A treatment licence was refused, as the Bloods had not been treated together. Under judicial review of that decision it was held that the clinic had acted unlawfully in storing the sperm without consent (it was not prosecuted as storage had occurred while the case was under way). With the taking and storage being unlawful, and treatment therefore refused, conception by artificial insemination depended on the export of the sperm to Belgium, which was permitted.

The court in U v W had the benefit of the decision in the Blood case. U had been successfully treated in Rome, using sperm donated by W. The couple had separated after the birth of twins and U sought a declaration of W's paternity. This would be possible only if the couple were deemed to have been 'treated together'. The court found that they had been so treated and that the terms of the 1990 Act effectively restricted U's access to services under the EC Treaty. Yet U lost her case, on the ground that the clinic in Rome was not a licence holder under the 1990 Act.

It has been held in subsequent cases that the right to family life under Art 8 of the European Convention on Human Rights does not override withdrawal of consent by one of the parties formerly 'treated together' with the other. See *Evans* v *Amicus Healthcare Ltd*; *Hadley* v *Midland Fertility Services Ltd* (2003).

3.1.2.6 Serious adverse events and serious adverse reactions

The HFEA is under a duty to investigate such events that have been defined under the 2007 Regulations as any form of embryo or gamete misidentification. It must also investigate any 'untoward occurrence' associated with procurement, testing, processing, storage or distribution of gametes or embryos intended for human application, that may lead to transmission of a communicable disease, death or disabling condition, illness or hospitalisation. In that investigation the HFEA must, where appropriate, arrange for and report on an inspection of the premises where the adverse event took place.

3.1.2.7 Cloned embryos

Following the decision in *R (Quintavalle)* v *Secretary of State for Health* (Pro-Life Alliance) (2003), the 1990 Act was deemed to apply to cloned embryos, despite the argument by a pro-life group that it did not. The rationale of the decision was that Parliament would not have intended to differentiate on the basis of the method of the creation of an embryo. In the spirit of the law, cloned embryos fall within the definition of 'embryo' under the 1990 Act, despite fertilisation not having taken place as a matter of science.

3.1.2.8 Offences

Under s 3 of the 1990 Act, it is an offence to place non-human embryos or gametes inside a woman. The penalty is up to ten years in prison or a fine, or both (see s 41). Since the 2008 Act it has been an offence to place inside a woman an embryo other than a permitted one, or any gametes other than permitted eggs or permitted sperm. A 'permitted egg' and 'permitted sperm' will have been produced by and extracted from the ovaries or testes of a woman or man whose DNA had not been altered. A 'permitted embryo' is one created by the fertilisation of a permitted egg by a permitted sperm, no mitochondrial DNA has been altered, and no cell has been added other than by the division process of the embryo's own cells. An exception applies under the mitochondrial donation Regulations (2015) in respect of donated mitochondria in assisted conception as a treatment.

It is not permitted to keep an embryo after the appearance of the 'primitive streak' (14 days). This offence carries the same penalty.

Lesser offences are committed by doing those things requiring a licence, but doing so without that licence having been granted, or a third party agreement (as the case may be). These offences attract a penalty of two years' imprisonment on indictment and six months' imprisonment on summary conviction.

Under s 41 of the 1990 Act, no money or benefit may be received in respect of the supply of gametes or embryos. It is an offence for any person to whom a licence applies to accept such money or benefit. This attracts a penalty of up to six months' imprisonment on indictment or a fine of up to level 5 on the standard scale (£5,000), or both.

3.1.2.9 Genetic material not of human origin

It is an offence to place a non-human embryo or gametes, or a human admixed embryo, in a woman. Without a licence it is also an offence to mix human and animal gametes to bring about a human admixed embryo, or to keep or use such an embryo. Yet such a licence cannot authorise keeping such an embryo after the primitive streak, or a period of 14 days from the date on which the creation process began, whichever is earlier. Neither can such a licence authorise placing a human admixed embryo in an animal.

Specifically under s 4 of the 2008 Act, without a licence it is an offence to:

- use female germ cells from an embryo or foetus;
- use embryos created for fertility services for a woman;
- place in a woman a human admixed embryo, any other non-human embryo, or any gametes other than human gametes;
- mix human gametes with animal gametes, to bring about the creation of a human admixed embryo; or
- keep or use a human admixed embryo.

This offence attracts the same penalty as above, that is, a ten-year custodial term or a fine, or both. It is also an offence to place sperm and eggs inside a woman without a licence, even where a licence would have been permitted but was nonetheless not obtained. The same is true of procuring or distributing an embryo intended for human application and of procuring, testing, processing or distributing any gametes intended for human application, except in pursuance of a licence or a third party agreement.

3.1.2.10 Donor anonymity, maternity and paternity

A list of 'identifiable individuals' whose gametes have been stored or used and those who have been treated must be maintained by the HFEA. Anonymity of those who made donations before April 2005 must be preserved, although information on their genetic health and ethnic origin may be passed on where a child was born as a result, but only after that child becomes 18. On the other hand, where a donor-conceived person ('the applicant') attains the age of 16, they may request from the HFEA information about their donor, as well as the number, sex and year of birth of their donor-conceived half-siblings.

The donor's identity may be divulged where the donation was made after April 2005, under the Human Fertilisation and Embryology (Disclosure of Information) Act 1992. This information may also be available under Art 8 of the ECHR. A court may order this where there is a dispute as regards parentage or in connection with a congenital disability, once the implications of disclosure have been explained to the donor.

The 1990 Act was updated by s 37 of the 2008 Act to include agreed fatherhood provisions and those applicable to types of marriage and partnership, and makes provision as to those who will be regarded as the parents of a child born as a result of treatment under that Act. After 2009 they no longer applied in relation to children carried by women as a result of the placing in them of embryos or of sperm and eggs, or their artificial insemination.

None, one or both of the parties treated together may be the biological parents of the child, depending on the technique used. The rules set out in the 1990 Act can not be rebutted; they do not, however, apply to the transfer of titles or honours.

The woman carrying the child is considered the mother, regardless of the genetic provenance of the child she carries and regardless of where the woman was treated. Her consent to a subsequent adoption order and the granting of that order would change this position. If the woman carrying the child was married at the time of treatment, her husband is treated as the father of that child. Again, this presumption is regardless of whether it was his sperm that contributed to the embryo she carried until birth. The exception to this rule is where the husband did not consent to the sperm of another man being used, although he will bear the onus of establishing lack of consent. If the couple is not married, but were treated together under the 1990 Act, the man treated with the mother of the child is regarded as the child's father.

3.1.2.11 Control of information

In Chapter 6 we turn to confidentiality and justification for breaches of medical confidentiality. Some parallels can be drawn at this stage with the 1990 Act as amended by ss 33-47 of the 2008 Act. In addition, information held by the HFEA may be obtained under the Data Protection Act 2018 (c 12) which provides a new legal framework for data protection, in conjunction with the United Kingdom General Data Protection Regulation ('UK GDPR'), which was the assimilation of European Parliament and Council (EU) Regulation 2016/679.

The HFEA is required to keep a register of information that contains information relating to any identifiable 'relevant individual' born as a result of the procurement or storage of embryos or gametes under the terms of those activities. A 'relevant individual' is one who was or may have been born in consequence of treatment services under the Act.

An 'applicant' aged 16 or older may by notice to the HFEA require the Authority to comply with their request to provide information on whether a donor, or any other person, might be their parent. Compliance is subject to the applicant having been given suitable opportunity to receive proper counselling about the implications of compliance with their request. A donor-conceived person is entitled to information on whether they are related to a person whom they propose to marry or enter into a civil partnership or intimate relationship. The HFEA may inform the donor of these requests for information. Further provisions apply to the provision of information on the existence of genetic siblings that exist as a result of services provided under the legislation. These relate to the number, sex and year of birth of those siblings, and on condition that both relevant individuals (i.e. potential siblings) are over 18, and been offered appropriate counselling. A voluntary contact register may be held by the HFEA containing details of persons who have expressed their wish to receive information about any person to whom they are genetically related. If the HFEA decided to not set up such a register, it may provide financial assistance to any person who does so, and impose conditions with which such a person must comply. The HFEA has a range of discretionary functions such as determining criteria for inclusion in the register, the analysis of DNA samples at the request of those listed, and other conditions it sees fit to impose on those seeking sibling-related information.

The HFA must keep a register recording the grant, suspension or revocation of every treatment and storage licence as discussed above, and of serious adverse events and reactions, also considered earlier.

3.1.2.12 Access to treatment

The 1990 Act does not place restrictions on access to treatment, although the HFEA is required to take into account the welfare of any child to be born as a result of treatment. HFEA guidance sets out conditions to be taken into account, including the need of that child for supportive parenting, and the interests of an existing child in deciding whether to provide treatment. This followed the case of *R (Quintavalle)* v *Human Fertilisation and Embryology Authority* (2005) in which sex selection was allowed using PGD, to ensure that the child born would be a suitable bone marrow donor for his brother. Decisions to refuse a treatment licence may be judicially reviewed. This has happened, for example, where treatment was refused to a 37-year-old woman where the HFEA cut-off age was set at 35. In *R* v *Sheffield Health Authority, ex parte Seale* (1994), the court found that in making its decision, it was not *Wednesbury* unreasonable for the HFEA to consider the likely effectiveness of treatment.

Under s 38 of the 1990 Act, no person may be compelled to participate in any of the activities regulated under the Act. This allows a medical practitioner to conscientiously object to all or part of the regulated activities.

3.2 SURROGACY

As is the case with human fertilisation and embryology, the subject-matter of surrogacy is reserved to Westminster (Scotland Act 1998 Sch 5 Head J3). As we will see, however, there are relevant statutes that are specific to the law in Scotland, even although the main subject-matter remains reserved. That is why the law commissions of Scotland and of England and Wales undertook joint work on reforming the current law. This led to a proposed bill, but at time of writing this has not been introduced to the Westminster Parliament. Among the recommendations are those relating to payment and around how parenthood is transferred, and that surrogacy arrangements should remain unenforceable.

There are two statutes regulating surrogacy. These are the Surrogacy Arrangements Act 1985 (the '1985 Act'), unless the pregnancy was medically assisted, in which case the 1990 Act comes into play (e.g. donor insemination). Under the 1985 Act the 'surrogate mother' arranges to carry a child and give it up after its birth to the person with whom the arrangement was made. She may or may not be the genetic mother, depending on the method of conception used.

3.2.1   Commerce and regulation

The arrangement made between the surrogate mother and the commissioning couple may be informal or formalised and subject to the controls in the 1985 Act. Financial arrangements or 'baby selling' are prohibited under the Adoption and Children (Scotland) Act 2007 and the Children's Hearings (Scotland) Act 2011. The 1985 Act also prohibits financial transactions in respect of surrogacy arrangements made. Nor is any arrangement made enforceable.

Section 2 of the 1985 Act prohibits actions done on a commercial basis, such as acting as an agent in a surrogacy agreement or knowingly causing another person to do so, although surrogate mother and commissioning father will not be subject to criminal liability. This was amended by the Human Fertilisation and Embryology Act 2008, such that a non-profit making body may receive reasonable payment for providing some surrogacy services. And although under the 1985 Act it is an offence to advertise surrogacy services, under 2008 Act amendments, this does not apply to advertisements placed by such a non-profit making body. That is the case, as long as the advertisement relates only to those acts of the non-profit body that themselves do not contravene s 2(1) of the 1985 Act, even if done on a commercial basis.

In 2023 the Law Commission of England and Wales and the Scottish Law Commission jointly published *Building Families through Surrogacy: A New Law*, which considered the issue of payments in some detail, as well as pathways to legal parenthood. It also published a draft Bill on Regulated Surrogacy Agreements, Parental Orders, and Payments in Relation to Surrogacy, which sets out 'permitted costs' in the context of a general prohibition. Lack of parliamentary time did not allow for these proposals to be taken forward.

As the law currently stands, payment made for the benefit of the surrogate mother is not excluded by the 1985 Act. This begs the question of what amounts to 'reasonable expenses'. In *Re an Adoption Application (Surrogacy)* (1987), the court found that £5,000 did not amount to profit and the adoption order was granted. It also begs the question of enforceability. In the Scottish case of *C and C v GS* (1996), the mother decided not to give up the child. The court found that the £8,000 paid to her was paid in expectation that a parental order would follow. On the ground of the security of the child, an adoption order was granted. In the interests of the child, a payment may be authorised after the fact even if it breached the prohibition against commercial transactions. In *Re C, Application by Mr and Mrs X under s 30 of the Human Fertilisation and Embryology Act 1990* (2002), it was held that £12,000 was not unreasonable and could be authorised retrospectively when the parental order is made. Reasonable expenses can include loss of earnings and loss of income support.

In *XX* v *Whittington Hospital NHS Trust* (2021) the Supreme Court found that a woman rendered infertile due to medical negligence may claim for the costs of commercial services abroad as part of actionable damages. This indicates a policy shift in the law insofar as it was found by the majority that awarding such damages was no longer contrary to public policy. It did however go on to rule that the damages would be limited to what treatments were reasonable for the claimant to seek, and that it needed to be reasonable for the claimant to seek a foreign commercial arrangement as opposed to making an equivalent arrangement within the United Kingdom. The costs themselves required also to be reasonable.

It is noteworthy that an increasing number of cases involving the reasonableness of payments have also involved surrogacy services abroad. See for example *Re A* (2021), *Re X* (2021), *Re A-B* (2020), and *Re A & B (Children) (Surrogacy: Parental orders: time limits)* (2015). This may change should the proposed bill be passed in coming years.

3.2.2   Status of the child

In keeping with the common law position, the surrogate is the mother of the child. Although this was restated in the 1990 Act, since 2009 and following s 57 of the 2008 Act, those provisions do not have effect in relation to children carried by women as a result of the placing in them of embryos or of sperm and eggs, or their artificial insemination. It is noteworthy that if maternity is disputed, it needs to be proven as a matter of fact through recourse to evidence from those present at the birth. The joint Law Commission Surrogacy Bill proposes a 'new pathway', by which the intended parents will be the legal parents at the birth of the child.

A parental or adoption order is required because the surrogate mother, being the birth mother, is the legal mother of the child and her husband is presumed to be the father. However, if the commissioning father's sperm was used and the birth mother was unmarried, he will be considered the father but will not bear parental responsibilities. Where artificial means of reproduction was used, the 1990 Act comes into play, as will the issue of whether the couple was 'treated together', as discussed earlier. Otherwise the matter will be regulated under the Children (Scotland) Act 1995, as amended by the Human Fertilisation and Embryology Act 2008. The 2008 Act s 54 and 55, significantly extended the categories of couples who can apply for a parental order. It also allows one applicant to apply for a parental order, where a child has been conceived using the gametes of at least one member of the couple, or the applicant, and has been carried by a surrogate mother.

It is possible that none of the participating parties wants the child, as might be the case where the child is born with a disability. The surrogate mother will not be able to dispense with responsibility, but a court may be called upon to arrange for the child's residence and care in the child's best interests.

If an adoption or parental order is granted, it can specify that parental duties have been surrendered. Applications must be made to the court between six weeks and six months after the child's birth. The child must, at the time of the application, be living with the commissioning couple.

Section 36 of the 1990 Act, read in conjunction with s 54 of the 2008 Act, provides for parental orders to be made where the surrogacy arrangement has been made. A parental order will give legal effect after the fact to the surrogacy arrangement. Under the HFEA Code of Practice, in order for the order to be granted the child must be genetically related to one of the commissioning parents and the surrogate parents must give their consent. They remain the legal parents until the order is granted, at which point the birth certificate must be changed. In Scotland a copy of the original may be provided to the child once they reach the age of 16.

In *Re Q (parental order)* (1996), the surrogate was single, the egg came from the commissioning mother and the sperm from a donation. The commissioning father was therefore not the biological father and the couple could not therefore be considered to have been 'treated together'. It was held that no man could be treated as the father for the purposes of giving consent to the making of a parental order and the commissioning couple would have to apply for an adoption order.

3.3 CONTROL OF FERTILITY

The control of fertility may be concerned with attempts to prevent conception, or methods of ending a pregnancy. Other medico–legal issues associated with the control of fertility apply when something has gone wrong, be it due to imperfect consent or negligence in carrying out a contraceptive procedure. It may, for example, be the case that an action is brought in negligence on the ground that, had a sterilisation been carried out properly, a pregnancy and birth would not have resulted. A claim may be based on 'wrongful pregnancy' or 'wrongful birth'; these will be discussed below. The issue of the control of fertility also raises questions surrounding the rights of the foetus and foetal research.

3.3.1   Contraception

The legal controls in place regarding contraception relate to several areas
of medical law, including negligence, consent and products liability. Much
depends on the method of contraception used, be it through medication, a
device or surgery. If the method used is pharmaceutical or a medical device,
recourse might be had to the Consumer Protection Act 1987, which will be
discussed in Chapter 4 on negligence. It may also, or in the alternative, be
a question of negligence in prescribing, or in the provision of warnings of
side-effects. This, too, is covered in Chapter 4 and in Chapter 5 on consent.
The provision of contraceptive advice and information may raise issues of
consent and capacity, including the provision of contraceptive advice to the
mature minor (as defined in the Age of Legal Capacity (Scotland) Act 1991)
or the adult who lacks legal capacity by virtue of their mental health. This is
also discussed in Chapter 5.

Of interest here is the issue of post-coital contraception using, for example, the so-called 'morning after pill' or through an intra-uterine device
(IUD or 'coil'). The English case of *R* v *Dhingra* (1991) concerned the inser-
tion of an IUD after intercourse. This led to a pregnancy being aborted
and raised questions as to whether there had been a contravention of the
Offences Against the Person Act 1861 by procuring a miscarriage. It was
held in that case where the IUD was inserted 11 days after intercourse, the
woman could not have been pregnant in the sense of implantation having
taken place. Strictly speaking, the 1861 Act does not require an actual pregnancy; the intention is sufficient. By contrast, in Scotland, where the 1861
Act does not apply, the common law crime of abortion requires the presence
of a pregnancy.

The court has considered whether the 'morning after pill' is an abortifacient and hence that its administration and over-the-counter supply amount
to an offence. Following *R* v *Dhingra*, it was held in *R (on the application of
Smeaton)* v *Secretary of State for Health (morning after pill and abortion)* (2002)
that it was not an abortifacient because, to be effective, it must be taken
before implantation.

3.3.2   The foetus

The foetus is a human organism after it is considered an embryo – that is,
from around eight weeks after conception until it is born. It is not legally
protected unless and until it is born alive. This is important in respect of
injuries sustained before birth (discussed later in this chapter) and in respect
of research on foetal tissue, which is not regulated under the Human Tissue

(Scotland) Act 2006, and the Human Tissue (Scotland) Act 2019 (see Chapter 7). Research licences have been discussed earlier in this chapter.

The foetus is protected in England and Wales by the Offences Against the Person Act 1861, insofar as procuring a miscarriage by the pregnant woman or a third party are offences, if the foetus was 'capable of being born alive' (a presumption at 28 weeks' gestation), or by the offence of 'child destruction' under the Infant Life Preservation Act 1929. The latter carries the statutory defence of having been 'done in good faith for the purpose only of preserving the life of the mother' as upheld and extended in *R* v *Bourne* (1938).

In Scotland such protection lies in the common law offence of procuring an abortion. Prosecutions remain unlikely as they require proof of pregnancy. The offence also relies upon wickedness of intent, which in turn distinguishes the therapeutic from the criminal as far as *mens rea* is concerned. This means that therapeutic abortion of a non-viable foetus was not a crime until the passage of the 1967 Act, just as was the case in England under the statutory defence in that jurisdiction. There is a greater distinction between the jurisdictions as far as a viable foetus is concerned. Whereas in Scotland such a foetus may be aborted as long as there is no wicked intent, this is not the case under the 1929 Act. The 28-week presumption was carried over to the 1967 Act for England and Wales, as the 1929 Act had never applied in Scotland, whereas under the 1967 Act as passed, abortion carried no time limit in Scotland. Change for both jurisdictions came with s 37 of the Human Fertilisation and Embryology Act 1990, that amended s 1(1) of the 1967 Act to apply a 24-week limit to the third and fourth ground listed below, that is, to prevent a risk to the mother's life or to avoid giving birth to a child with a disability.

3.3.3   Abortion

The law on abortion in the United Kingdom is set out in the Abortion Act 1967 (the '1967 Act'). Its subject-matter was reserved to Westminster under section J1 of Sch 5 to the Scotland Act 1998, but this was repealed by s 53 of the Scotland Act 2016, despite not being recommended by the Smith Commission final report in 2014. That means that the subject-matter of the Abortion Act 1967 falls within the legislative competence of the Scottish Parliament. In the absence of any legislative activity north of the border – apart from the introduction of the Member's Abortion Services (Safe Access Zones) (Scotland) Bill aimed at protecting service users from intimidation by anti-abortion groups around clinics, and a petition in 2022 to 'amend the law to fully decriminalise abortion in Scotland' – the following paragraphs will confine themselves to the United Kingdom legislation.

The 1967 Act presumes abortion to be a criminal act, and provides defences to what amounts to the Scots common law crime of procuring an abortion – that is, destroying the life of a foetus. The crime cannot be committed if the woman is not pregnant. Until it was judicially established that impossible attempts could be criminal, attempted abortion was not a crime either. Note however that under s 294 of the Criminal Procedure (Scotland) Act 1995 an attempt to commit any indictable crime is itself an indictable crime.

Under the 1967 Act, procuring an abortion is not a common law offence under certain circumstances. The 1967 Act was amended by the 1990 Act, and by the Human Fertilisation and Embryology Act 2008 in respect of the lawful grounds for performing an abortion. The effect was that of the four grounds for legal abortion, three can be performed at any stage of the pregnancy. In any event, the termination must be performed by a registered medical practitioner, although s 4 of the 1967 Act as amended allows for conscientious objection.

The validity of a conscientious objection is subject to a proximity test. It is valid only among those who are directly connected to the medical termination of pregnancy itself. A claim to conscientious objection was rejected by the Supreme Court in *Doogan* v *Greater Glasgow and Clyde Health Board* (2015), for midwives whose primary role involved coordination of activities on the labour ward. Under this rule it is doubtful whether the pharmacist would be able to conscientiously object to the provision of medication, but this is covered by professional guidance rather than law.

The 1967 Act requires two registered medical practitioners to certify that the ground relied upon as a defence applies in the circumstances.

Four defences are available up until the end of the 24th week of pregnancy. After that, the first ground ceases to be available. The grounds are:

1. a risk to the mental or physical health of the mother or to existing children in the family;

2. a risk of grave permanent injury to the mother's mental or physical health;

3. to prevent a risk to the mother's life; and

4. to avoid the risk that the child will suffer from serious physical or mental handicap.

That the grounds under the final [disability S 1(1)(d)] criterion include Down's syndrome, and that this inclusion does not run contrary to the European Convention on Human Rights, was confirmed in the English

High Court judgment in *Crowter and Others* v *Secretary of State for Health and Social Care* (2022).

Abortion serves a key pinch point in other areas of medical law. Just as the terms of the Age of Legal Capacity (Scotland) Act 1991 allow the young person to be prescribed contraceptive medication without parental knowledge or consent, so too will it permit them to access abortion services. Confidentiality is also a right as between spouses, on the basis that there is no right of veto in the Abortion Act 1967. We also find the issue discussed in wrongful life jurisprudence where – as happened in *McFarlane* v *Tayside Health Board* (2000) – arguments may be presented as to whether the failure to undergo an abortion constituted a *novus actus interveniens*, breaking the chain of causation between the negligent omission to inform and the harm caused by that omission.

3.3.4   Ante-natal injury

Under Scots common law, legal personality is attained at birth. There is in general no delictual claim for injuries sustained before birth unless and until the child is born alive. This is the *nasciturus* principle which states that a child is deemed to have been born when it would be to that child's advantage in private law. While the foetus has rights upon birth, this does not mean that it has rights in the womb, so long as the terms of the Abortion Act 1967 have been complied with.

In *Kelly* v *Kelly* (1997) the father of a foetus sought to prevent his estranged wife from undergoing an abortion. The interdict was refused on the ground that rights accrue only upon birth and a father may bring an action only where the abortion would itself be a legal wrong.

Since the 1967 Act there has been an evident trend towards greater recognition of foetal rights, though any legal action still depends on the foetus being born alive. In *McCluskey* v *HM Advocate* (1989), a foetus was recognised as a person when criminally injured in terms of the Road Traffic Act 1972, and in *Re T (adult: refusal of treatment)* (1992) the court commented obiter that a competent adult's right to refuse treatment may be affected if a foetus is involved. In *Watson* v *Fife Health Board* (1993) it was confirmed that a child has an action against its mother, and the health board, for injuries sustained before birth. Damages are available under the terms of the Damages (Scotland) Act 2011. On the other hand, in the English case of *CP (a child)* v *First-tier Tribunal (Criminal Injuries Compensation)* (2015) the child was born with foetal alcohol spectrum disorder as a direct result of her mother's excessive drinking during pregnancy. She was unsuccessful in the compensation claim for her injuries, because the court found that the foetus did not constitute 'any other person', under the Offences Against the Person Act 1861. This was a matter of statutory interpretation of an Act that does not extend to Scotland. It is likely however that under Scots law the outcome would be the same, with reference to Institutional writers such as Hume, who considered the foetus as a *pars viscerum matris*, that is, an integral part of the mother to be. Accordingly Scots law does not criminalise procuring an abortion, as the foetus is part of the woman's body. Rather, Scots law criminalises intentionally or recklessly carrying out an unsafe termination. This may form the basis for the lack of criminal charges against women for procuring an abortion, as doing so would be considered self-harm, which is not unlawful.

3.3.5   Wrongful life and wrongful birth

Following a failed sterilisation operation, an action may be raised that argues that, but for that wrong, a child would not have been conceived and born. The case may also involve the allegation that, but for a lack of information on the risk of failure, the pursuer would not have become pregnant and given birth. Such cases may be further complicated depending on whether the child born suffers a disability that sterilisation may have set out to avoid.

Sterilisation itself refers to ending permanently a person's ability or capacity to conceive. This may be accomplished through a hysterectomy or tubal ligation in women or a vasectomy in men. In the case of a tubal ligation or vasectomy the woman or man is not strictly speaking 'sterile', but they will be unable to conceive a child. As with other medical procedures, there are risks. One such risk may be that it fails to produce permanent sterility, leading to conception, birth and the costs involved in bringing up a child. That would be the legal harm, although an important factor will be whether the child is born with a congenital disability or not.

The legal actions available are the following:

1. *wrongful conception* or *wrongful pregnancy*: the action is brought by the parents in negligence for failure to prevent the pregnancy;

2. *wrongful birth*: the claim is brought by parents for negligent failure to terminate a pregnancy;

3. *wrongful life*: this involves either of the above two claims, but brought by the child, who is usually congenitally disabled. The claim is for the negligent failure to prevent the pregnancy that led to their birth or the negligent failure to terminate the pregnancy that led to their birth.

3.3.5.1 Wrongful pregnancy

3.3.5.1.1 The healthy child

McFarlane v *Tayside Health Board* (2000) raised questions around whether damages could be claimed where negligence in performing a sterilisation operation led to the birth of a healthy child and, if so, under what heads of damages. The case followed *Allan* v *Greater Glasgow Health Board* (1998), where it was found that there was no reason not to be able to claim for the upkeep of the child, although the decision in *McFarlane* reversed that Outer House ruling. This form of potential delictual liability would be Aquilian, which requires evidence of wrongful conduct that caused a legally recognised patrimonial (monetary) harm (*damnum*).

The McFarlanes had four children. Mr McFarlane subsequently underwent a vasectomy and at a follow-up appointment was told that his sperm count was negative and alternative means of contraception could be avoided. Mrs McFarlane subsequently became pregnant and the couple brought an action in wrongful pregnancy, claiming pain and suffering and distress at the outcome, as well as the cost of bringing up the child and moving to a bigger house.

The case for the cost of upbringing turned on the manifestation of a legal wrong – that is, the invasion of a legally recognised interest. It also considered whether the couple's failure to undergo an abortion constituted a *novus actus interveniens* breaking the chain of causation between the wrong and the harm. The House of Lords upheld Mrs McFarlane's claim for *solatium* associated with her pregnancy and her patrimonial claim for the expenses associated with that pregnancy.

It was held that the couple's failure to undergo a termination did not constitute a *novus actus interveniens*.

However, the House rejected the parents' claim for the cost of bringing up a healthy child. The decision was based on the societal interest in balancing the increased cost against the parental benefit of a healthy child and on distributive justice. It was not considered reasonable for the duty of care of a health authority to include liability for the cost of bringing up a child. It was considered morally wrong to regard the birth of a healthy child as a legal wrong. Here it is important to distinguish *solatium* and damages: claims under both forms are available under an action for *damnum injuria datum*, while *solatium* claims may arise under the *actio iniuriarum*. The former refers to a delictual Aquilian loss caused by a legal wrong; the latter applies to infringement of personality interests. In *McFarlane* the claim succeeded in the action for *damnum injuria datum*, but the quantum of damages did not include the costs of raising a healthy child.

The legal policy founded in *McFarlane* and *Rees* was considered in a wrongful birth claim founded on a breach of contract, as opposed to clinical negligence. In *ARB* v *IVF Hammersmith Ltd (R, third party)* (2020), the IVF clinic was in breach of an express term not to thaw and implant an embryo without the father's consent. This was done without ARB's written or informed consent to do so when they did (2010), despite the fact that the couple had separated, and ARB's former wife had used a forged pre-signed consent form. That led to the thawing and implantation of a stored embryo, and the subsequent birth of a daughter. That birth constituted a legal loss that arose from the breach of contract; it was considered equivalent to the same loss in tort law, which would be disallowed for policy reasons based on *McFarlane* and *Rees*.

3.3.5.1.2 The disabled child

There have been cases in which negligence led to the birth of a disabled child. The parents have claimed for the difference in cost between raising a healthy child and of bringing up a disabled child.

In *McLelland* v *Greater Glasgow Health Board* (2001), the expectant mother had a family history of Down's syndrome that was known to the health board, who failed to carry out an amniocentesis to diagnose the condition in her unborn child. The pursuer underwent a non-diagnostic screening test which proved negative and so did not have an abortion. Upon the birth of their son with Down's syndrome, the couple successfully claimed damages for the increased costs of bringing up a child with a disability. The court found that the duty of care in this instance included averting the consequences of the increased costs of bringing up a child with Down's syndrome – a case of pure economic loss. It was also pointed out in the judgment that while *McFarlane* was a wrongful pregnancy case, *McLelland* was a claim for wrongful birth.

In the English wrongful pregnancy case of *R (on the application of Smeaton)* v *Secretary of State for Health (morning after pill and abortion)* (2002) *University Hospital NHS Trust* (2001), a negligently performed sterilisation operation led to the birth of an autistic child. It was held that the Trust was liable in damages for the additional cost of upkeep of the child until its majority.

The effect of these decisions, and of that in *McFarlane*, is that there is no claim for the cost of bringing up a healthy child, but *additional* costs associated with bringing up a disabled child can be claimed under the heads of wrongful pregnancy or wrongful birth.

3.3.5.1.3 The disabled parent and the healthy child

In *Rees* v *Darlington Memorial Hospital NHS Trust* (2003), a healthy child was born to a visually impaired woman after a failed sterilisation. She sued for the cost of upkeep of the child. The House of Lords followed *McFarlane* and held that the costs of bringing up a healthy child could not be claimed, as the health board had not caused the disability which led to the increased costs. To allow such a claim would lead to a slippery slope in admitting a plethora of similar claims. In any event, there is public provision for meeting the consequences of disability. The claimant was, however, awarded a 'conventional sum' of £15,000 in recognition of the legal wrong suffered, which was in effect an award for *solatium*. In Scotland this would, in principle, be covered as *solatium* arising from *damnum injuria datum* where the action is based on *culpa*, rather than the *action iniuriarum*. This *actio* is discussed elsewhere, in particular in Chapter 6 on confidentiality and invasion of privacy and in Chapter 7 on the ownership and control of human tissue and the 'organ retention' cases.

3.3.5.2 Wrongful life

The wrongful life action is brought by the child born following a legal wrong such as a failed sterilisation or the failure to perform an abortion. The philosophical conundrum is that the child is in effect claiming a preference for non-existence over the disabled existence into which they have been born. The argument would be that had their parents known of an inherent risk or had the treatment not been negligently performed, the child would not have been brought into existence. A further problem is that of proof of causation: it is difficult to see how defective counselling would have caused the defect itself, that is, the child's disability.

In the English case of *McKay* v *Essex Area Health Authority* (1982), the child was born suffering from congenital rubella syndrome. His mother alleged that a blood test had been performed negligently. The court, however, found that there was no cause of action, as the child was alleging not that they had been born, but that they had been born with a disability. An obligation to abort would amount to placing a lower value on a child with a disability and a higher value on non-existence. Yet, because the court found there was no duty of care, it did not need to compare existence with non-existence. According to *P's Curator Bonis* v *Criminal Injuries Compensation Board* (1997), this decision would be followed in Scotland.

3.3.6   Non-consensual sterilisation

Sterilisation without consent amounts to an assault. This possibility will be elided by consent in broad terms, causing the action to be in negligence, as discussed in Chapter 4. The situation is more complicated where the adult lacks capacity to consent by virtue of their mental incapacity. In this instance, the 'best interests' test should be applied.

However, the 'best interests' test was excluded from Part 5 of the Adults with Incapacity (Scotland) Act 2000. Under s 47, the medical practitioner primarily responsible for the care of the adult with incapacity has the power to decide what is reasonable for the promotion of the physical and mental wellbeing of the patient. This can be done only after the person's guardian or proxy has been consulted. The adult must not oppose the proposed treatment.

This position should be seen in light of the case law prior to passing the 2000 Act. In *L, Petr* (1996), the power was granted to the curator *ad litem* to consent to the surgical sterilisation of the *incapax*. The *incapax* suffered from autism and opposed the petition. The 'best interests' test was applied and the risk of the *incapax* engaging in sexual intercourse was weighed against the risks involved in the operation. On this basis, the petition was granted.

3.4   GENETICS

One of the effects of study into human genetics is increased knowledge of characteristics that can be passed on through reproduction. It raises questions surrounding information provision and consent, as well as questions surrounding the standard of care, privacy, confidentiality and, of course, human cloning. Questions are also raised regarding the operation of the European Convention on Human Rights, as the right to one's genetic identity is asserted there. The issue of genetics and data protection are reserved to Westminster under head J2 of Sch 5 to the Scotland Act 1998.

3.4.1   Therapy

Two types of therapy are possible. Somatic gene therapy aims to correct a condition in the person treated. This is done by adding genetic material to the pre-embryo. Germ line therapy, on the other hand, corrects a condition in a person's genetic make-up, with the aim of preventing that person's children inheriting a gene, but will not affect the person treated. This type of therapy is regulated by protocol rather than law, because of fears that the technique amounts to a form of eugenics.

3.4.2   Genetic information

The discussions in Chapter 5 on information disclosure and consent and in Chapter 6 on confidentiality and privacy are relevant here. In so far as genetic information is a factor in confidentiality, privacy and consent, the same general principles apply as apply in those areas of medical law. Indeed, the Human Genetics Commission has recommended against legislation in this area.

3.4.2.1 Civil law and human rights

Cases may be brought in the civil law of negligence, based on an alleged failure to provide a piece of genetic information. For example, *Anderson v Forth Valley Health Board* (1998) dealt with a failure to provide such information, leading to the birth of a child with muscular dystrophy. This fell within the law of negligence. And in the English wrongful pregnancy case of *Parkinson v St James and Seacroft University Hospital NHS Trust* (2001), discussed above, the court found that disability arising from genetic causes, and which are not *novus actus intervenientens*, will be sufficient to found a claim in negligence.

Genetics and human rights will also play a part in the civil law, in particular Art 8 ECHR on the right to family life. In *Re J (adoption: contacting father)* (2003), the mother did not want to tell the father of a child with cystic fibrosis of that child's existence. The court held that it was not in the child's best interests for the father to be informed, hence there was no right to family life in that situation and the child could be placed for adoption.

Further case law concerns paternity more directly, as establishment of genetic paternity will have a bearing on legal paternity. In *R (on the application of Rose) v Secretary of State for Health* (2002), the issue was the point at which Art 8 was engaged where a child was conceived using artificial insemination by donor. The claimants sought information about the donor. The court found that everyone has the right to information as to their genetic identity, thus, Art 8 was engaged.

Other areas of the civil law affected by genetic information are insurance, employment and discrimination law, under the Equality Act 2010. These fall outwith the scope of this book.

3.4.2.2 Criminal law

Genetics in the criminal law is important in expert evidence. For example, the case of *R v Cannings* (2004) concerned sudden infant death syndrome. Three of the Cannings' children had died without explanation. Expert evidence was led on the probability of three such deaths occurring in a single family. Mrs Cannings was convicted of murder. Her conviction was quashed on appeal once the expert evidence given at trial was undermined. Further evidence suggested a real possibility of a family disposition to the syndrome. Other similar convictions that had been based on the same evidence were also subsequently quashed.

A further use the criminal law has for genetics is in DNA evidence. This has led to cases being re-opened after many years because of scientific advances. This evidence was found admissible in *R* v *Hanratty* (2002) in the (albeit unsuccessful) attempt to reverse a capital murder conviction from 1961.

Essential facts

Infertility

- Infertility is the inability to conceive despite unprotected sexual intercourse for a period of time.
- The right to found a family is guaranteed under Art 12 of the European Convention on Human Rights.

In vitro fertilisation

- *In vitro* procreation refers to procreation outside the body, even if fertilisation is not completed there. It is regulated by the Human Fertilisation and Embryology Acts 1990 and 2008, which established the Human Fertilisation and Embryology Authority (HFEA).
- The HFEA issues licences for certain activities regulated under the 1990 Act, including licences for research, treatment, storage and pre-implantation genetic diagnosis.
- There is a procedure by which the licensing decision of the HFEA may be appealed.
- Research licences must be necessary or desirable to promote advances in treatment for infertility, to increase knowledge of congenital disease or causes of miscarriage, to develop more effective methods of contraception or methods for detecting genetic abnormalities, to develop methods for detecting the presence in embryos of certain genes, chromosomes or mitochondrial abnormalities, or to increase knowledge of the development of embryos.
- Treatment licences require the consent of the parties treated. Records must be maintained by the HFEA of any child born as a result of treatment. The future child's interests must be taken into account in deciding whether to grant a treatment licence, and such licences will not be issued to a man and woman 'treated together' if they have not been offered appropriate counselling.
- The HFEA may not grant licences for illegal activities such as human cloning, unless this is done for research purposes and the product is destroyed within the earlier of either 14 days, or the appearance of a 'primitive streak'.

- Storage licences may be granted for a range of time periods, which may be increased in certain circumstances such as the health of the donor of the gametes. Gametes or embryos may be stored for up to 55 years and consent must be renewed every 10 years. A ten-year time limit applies to embryos stored for research or training purposes.
- Embryo testing and sex selection under a treatment licence may take place only for specific purposes that relate to risks to the child that would be created through treatment under that licence, such as the risk of genetic disease.
- Consent is a fundamental requirement for the storage of gametes and embryos; there are exceptions to this requirement such as where cells are taken from someone who lacks capacity.
- If a couple has been 'treated together' under the 1990 Act, the consent of both parties to storage and subsequent use of gametes is required.
- Offences are set out in the 1990 and 2008 Acts. These include keeping an embryo beyond the 'primitive streak' of 14 days and engaging in an activity requiring a licence, but doing so without a licence. Specific offences relate to using female germ cells or mixing human and animal gametes without a licence. Offences attract a jail term of up to ten years, or a fine, or both.
- Donor anonymity is maintained in respect of donations made before April 2005. After that the identity of the donor may be divulged to a child born as a result of that donation once they turn 18. A 'donor-conceived' 16-year-old may request from the HFEA information about their donor, and the number, sex and year of birth of their donor-conceived half-siblings.
- The HFEA is required to maintain a register of information to which donor-conceived persons are entitled.
- The legal mother is the birth mother; the father is her husband or the man with whom she was 'treated together', unless 'agreed fatherhood' provision has been made.

Surrogacy

- Surrogacy is regulated under the 1990 and 2008 Acts and the Surrogacy Arrangements Act 1985.
- Arrangements between the surrogate mother and the commissioning couple may be informal or formalised; they may not be commercial, although payment is allowed for reasonable expenses.

- Surrogacy arrangements will be sanctioned after the fact by virtue of an adoption order.
- The birth mother is the mother of the child, until that child is adopted by the commissioning couple. The same is true of the husband of the surrogate mother.
- The 2008 Act extended the categories of couples, or individuals, that may apply for a parental order following surrogacy.

Control of fertility

- Contraception raises issues in negligence, information disclosure and consent, as well as products liability, depending on the contraceptive method used.
- Since 2016, abortion has been devolved to the Scottish Parliament.
- Procuring an abortion is a common law crime. Statutory defences are: (1) risk to the mental or physical health of the mother or to existing children in the family; (2) risk of grave permanent injury to the mother's mental or physical health; (3) to prevent a risk to the mother's life; and (4) to avoid the risk that the child will suffer from serious physical or mental abnormality, including Down's syndrome.
- A medical practitioner may conscientiously object to carrying out a termination of pregnancy, but the validity of a conscientious objection is subject to a proximity test.
- Wrongful conception or wrongful pregnancy is a claim brought by the parents in negligence for failure to prevent a pregnancy.
- Wrongful birth claims are brought by parents for negligent failure to terminate a pregnancy.
- Wrongful life actions involve either of the above two claims, but brought by the child, who is usually congenitally disabled.
- Courts will allow claims in respect of disabled children to the extent of *solatium* for pain and distress as a result of pregnancy and birth.
- Courts will allow claims for the increased cost of bringing up a disabled child, but not for the costs of bringing up a healthy child.
- Legal personality is attained at birth. There is no claim for injury before birth unless and until the child is born alive.
- Non-consensual sterilisation of an incompetent adult is an assault but this is elided by certification by the person primarily responsible for the care of the adult that their wellbeing will be preserved by the procedure.

Genetics
- Genetic information raises civil law questions of information disclosure and consent, as well as confidentiality, privacy and human rights.
- In the criminal law, genetic information is useful in expert evidence.

Essential cases

R (on the application of Assisted Reproduction and Gynaecology Centre) v Human Fertilisation and Embryology Authority (2002): Arts 8 and 12 of the ECHR apply to keeping embryos outside the body.

R (M) v Human Fertilisation and Embryology Authority (2016): information required in the consent process is variable according to the circumstances of a case.

Centre for Reproductive Medicine v U (2002): the case law on undue influence was not helpful to the court, as the Centre would gain nothing through an alteration made to a consent form. That alteration withdrew consent to posthumous use of gametes, which is in any event discouraged by the HFEA and may be contrary to the best interests of a resultant child, which, under the 1990 Act, must be taken into account.

R (Quintavalle) v Human Fertilisation and Embryology Authority (2005): sex selection and tissue typing were allowed, using pre-implantation genetic diagnosis, to ensure that the child born would be a suitable bone marrow donor for his brother, who had a genetic form of anaemia. Because the techniques may allow a woman to be less inhibited about bearing children, the Act allowed the HFEA to grant such a licence.

R v Human Fertilisation and Embryology Authority, ex parte Blood (1997): express written consent of both parties is required under the 1990 Act for storage and use of gametes where the couple is 'treated together'. Export of gametes was permitted under the EC Treaty articles on the free movement of goods and services.

U v W (1998): the couple was deemed to have been 'treated together' under the 1990 Act, yet the clinic they used in Rome was not a licence holder under the 1990 Act and hence the claim failed.

Evans v Amicus Healthcare Ltd; Hadley v Midland Fertility Services Ltd (2003): the right to family life under Art 8 of the ECHR does not override withdrawal of consent by one of the parties.

R (Quintavalle) v Secretary of State for Health (Pro-Life Alliance) (2003): the 1990 Act applies to cloned embryos despite fertilisation not having taken place.

R v Sheffield Health Authority, ex parte Seale (1994): it was not *Wednesbury* unreasonable for the HFEA to consider the likely effectiveness of treatment when considering an application for a treatment licence.

Re an Adoption Application (Surrogacy) (1987): £5,000 paid to a surrogate mother did not amount to profit under the 1985 Act and the adoption order was granted.

C and C v GS (1996): in the interests of the child, a payment may be authorised after the fact, even if it breached the prohibition against commercial transactions.

XX v Whittington Hospital NHS Trust (2021): a woman rendered infertile due to medical negligence may claim for the costs of commercial services abroad as part of actionable damages.

Re C, Application by Mr and Mrs X under s 30 of the Human Fertilisation and Embryology Act 1990 (2002): £12,000 was not an unreasonable payment for a surrogacy arrangement and could be authorised retrospectively when the parental order was made. Reasonable expenses can include loss of earnings and loss of income support.

R v Dhingra (1991): where an IUD was inserted 11 days after intercourse, the woman could not have been pregnant in the sense of implantation having taken place and hence the Offences Against the Person Act 1861 had not been breached.

R (on the application of Smeaton) v Secretary of State for Health (morning after pill and abortion) (2002): the 'morning after pill' is not an abortifacient because, to be effective, it must be taken before implantation.

Doogan v Greater Glasgow and Clyde Health Board (2015): validity of a conscientious objection is subject to a proximity test. It is valid only among those who are directly connected to the medical termination of pregnancy itself, not to midwives whose primary role involved coordination of activities on the labour ward.

R v Bourne (1938): killing a foetus capable of being born alive amounted to the offence of 'child destruction' under the Infant Life Preservation Act 1929 but carries the statutory defence of having been 'done in good faith for the purpose only of preserving the life of the mother'.

McFarlane v Tayside Health Board (2000): following a failed vasectomy, damages were allowed for *solatium* associated with pregnancy and for the patrimonial claim for the expenses associated with that pregnancy, but the House of Lords rejected the parents' claim for the cost of bringing up a healthy child.

McLelland v Greater Glasgow Health Board (2001): the couple successfully claimed damages for the increased costs of bringing up a child with a disability, following a failure to diagnose Down's syndrome when it was known the pursuer had a family history of the condition. The case was one of pure economic loss.

Rees v Darlington Memorial Hospital NHS Trust (2003): *McFarlane* was followed in awarding no damages in respect of the cost of bringing up a healthy child born to a disabled woman after a failed sterilisation.

B v IVF Hammersmith Ltd (R, third party) (2020): the legal policy founded in McFarlane and Rees was adopted in a wrongful birth claim founded on a breach of contract, as opposed to clinical negligence.

McKay v Essex Area Health Authority (1982): there was no cause of action for wrongful life where a child was born suffering from congenital rubella syndrome following an allegedly negligently performed blood test.

P's Curator Bonis v Criminal Injuries Compensation Board (1997): the decision in *McKay* v *Essex Area Health Authority* (1982) would be followed in Scotland.

Anderson v Forth Valley Health Board (1998): failure to provide genetic information, leading to the birth of a child with muscular dystrophy, falls within the law of negligence.

Watson v Fife Health Board (1993): a child has an action against its mother, and the health board, for injuries sustained before birth.

CP (a child) v First-tier Tribunal (Criminal Injuries Compensation) (2015): unsuccessful claim by the child born with foetal alcohol spectrum disorder as a direct result of her mother's excessive drinking during pregnancy as child isn't 'any other person' under the Offences Against the Person Act 1861.

Re J (adoption: contacting father) (2003): it was not in the best interests of a child with cystic fibrosis that the father be informed of her existence; hence there was no right to family life in that situation.

R (on the application of Rose) v Secretary of State for Health (2002): Art 8 of the ECHR was engaged where the parents of a child conceived using artificial insemination by donor sought information about the donor, as there is a right to information as to one's genetic identity under Art 8.

R v Cannings (2004): a conviction was quashed on appeal once the expert evidence given at trial was undermined. Further genetic evidence suggested a real possibility of a family disposition to sudden infant death syndrome.

R v Hanratty (2002): DNA evidence was found to be admissible in an attempt to reverse a capital murder conviction from 1961.

4 NEGLIGENCE AND CIVIL LIABILITY

The law on medical negligence arguably forms a core element of medical law because, as we will see, the judicial tests for medical negligence are applied to all facets of medical practice. Liability in negligence *per se* falls within the civil law. It is therefore significant that, because civil law was allowed to develop separately following the Union of the Parliaments of Scotland and England in 1707, medical negligence is in some way devolved to Scotland insofar as it has been allowed to develop separately for 300 years. Even so, it is also the case that there are arguably no significant differences between the law in England and Wales and that in Scotland. The reason for this may well lie in the policy considerations that fall in favour of substantially similar regimes north and south of the border.

The law on medical negligence draws on principles from the law of negligence generally and professional negligence in particular. This lies within the law of delict where, in the medical professional context, there may be liability for an act or omission of a medical professional, to the injury of a patient. The burden of proof is on the pursuer to establish that a duty of care was owed, that it was breached by the medical professional's failure to achieve the requisite standard of care and that the breach caused the patient a legally recognised injury.

4.1 THE BASIS OF LIABILITY – CONTRACT OR DELICT?

The conduct of the medical practitioner has long been subject to the law of obligations. There is some debate as to the various roles of the law of contract and the law of delict. Although some institutional writers considered the importance of the principle of lack of skill amounting to *culpa*, Bell's *Principles* considered liability to lie in the implied terms of a contract (e.g. for the hire of a surgeon). Even some early 20th-century claims lay in contract.

The law in England began to move away from this position in the 19th century, arguably influenced by the fact that a wife had no capacity to contract on her own behalf. This movement towards founding a claim in negligence was followed by the Scottish courts in *Edgar* v *Lamont* (1914). In that case the pursuer injured her finger while gardening. A medical practitioner was called out. The pursuer later sued for negligent treatment and amputation. The defender argued that the action lay in contract and the contract was with the pursuer's husband and hence that, in sending for the doctor, the pursuer had acted as his agent. The court found that liability lay in negligence, regardless of who called the doctor or who the parties to any contract were. As such, liability lies in the breach of a duty of care.

Where there is a contract between the doctor and the patient, a contractual remedy may be sought, although in the context of the National Health Service in Scotland (NHSiS), such a contract can be said to amount to no more than a social contract. The great majority of patients in the National Health Service in Scotland will not have a contract with the medical practitioner.

The terms of the relationship between doctor and patient in the context of the NHS are covered by a plethora of statutory provisions. Claims based on the law of contract will generally be available only to private patients but, for the most part, claims will lie in contract with an additional or alternative claim lying in delict, based on the same set of facts. In *Dow* v *Tayside University Hospitals NHS Trust* (2006) the court found that a contractual relationship could exist in addition to the statutory one, but only where it was clear the doctor was exceptionally entering into such a contract, demonstrating the intention to create additional liability. Conversely, and underlining the importance of precision in pleadings, in *McCallum* v *Morrison* (2023) the appellant did not include in their pleadings any of the implied contractual terms that were alleged to have been breached. They therefore failed to advance a relevant contractual case in the pleadings. They did not advance any evidence of the existence of a contract, and the court was not prepared to draw any inference of its existence.

According to *Roe* v *Minister of Health* (1954), the standard of care in both branches of the civil law is that of reasonableness. According to s 13 of the Supply of Goods and Services Act 1982, contracts for the supply of services contain an implied term to the effect that the supplier will carry out the service with reasonable care and skill. Even so, a doctor may – possibly unwisely – make promises as to the results of, for example, cosmetic surgery. This happened in *Hsuing* v *Webster* (1992). In such a case, a higher standard may apply.

Where there is an available contractual claim, the same levels of damages can be expected and the same rules of prescription and limitation will apply. In both cases the pursuer will need to prove causation.

4.2 LIABILITY AND INDEMNITY

That there has in recent years been an increase in medical negligence claims is not disputed. Neither is the fact that the growth in claims is progressing at a marginally slower rate in Scotland than in England. Although a claim in medical negligence – whether successful or not – can harm the career of a medical practitioner, it is not the practitioner as an individual who will defend the action or pay the damages. This is because of vicarious liability and NHS indemnity respectively. Liability may also be joint and several and licenced medical practitioners are required to have an indemnity arrangement in force, under s 44C(1) of the Medical Act 1983.

4.2.1   Joint and vicarious liability

Joint liability may arise where the acts of different parties contribute to the actionable wrong, provided that they are connected. In successful claims the court may apportion damages *pro rata*, although in practice this does not happen. Although direct liability is possible, in an NHS context liability tends to be *vicarious*, that is, a third party will be held liable for the wrongs of the medical practitioner. Generally health boards will be liable for the wrongful conduct of hospital staff and visiting consultants.

As long as the employee is acting within the scope of their employment, it is the contract of employment between the health service and the medical practitioner that gives rise to the possibility of vicarious liability (*respondeat superior*). The patient may sue the employer or the employee or both, jointly or severally. The NHS will not, however, be held vicariously liable where a doctor carries out private work within the NHS hospital. In such circumstances, liability would be direct.

There is also a case for action against scientists who carry out testing on behalf of a health board. *S* v *Lothian Health Board* (2009) was an action brought by the mother of a child born with cystic fibrosis. It was brought on the basis of alleged negligence by the scientists who performed a test for the cystic fibrosis gene. It was allowed to proceed to proof before answer, despite the scientists not having been employed by the hospital. The test was whether or not the hospital assumed responsibility for the wellbeing of the patient, rather than whether the defenders had control over the work carried out.

General practices and dental practices are independent contractors rather than employers. As such, claims are brought against individuals.

In *Bonthrone* v *Secretary of State for Scotland* (1987), a brain-damaged boy had received the whooping cough vaccine. His parents argued that the vaccine had caused his brain damage. Damages were claimed from the Secretary of State for Scotland (now Scottish Ministers) as vicariously liable for the acts of the general practitioner under the National Health Service (Scotland) Act 1972. The pursuer argued that general practitioners provided services under the Act, which services it was the duty of the Secretary of State to provide. The court rejected this argument and found that the Secretary of

State was vicariously responsible for the treatment of NHS hospital patients in hospital, but not for their treatment by general practitioners who should be regarded as independent contractors. However, the pursuer's alternative claim was that the health board (second defenders) were both directly liable and vicariously liable for the conduct of general medical practitioners. The court found that vicarious liability applies only in the context of a contract of employment and hence that vicarious liability did not apply in the case at hand. Neither was the health board directly liable, as it was the general medical practitioner who had administered the vaccine. The meaning and implication of these principles is that employers in a general practice may be vicariously liable.

General practices may be partnerships. As such, the partnership may be vicariously liable for the acts and omissions of its partners. Liability is joint and several for actions within the normal course of the business of the partnership, which means that *all* partners in a GP partnership will be liable, jointly and severally, as will be the partnership itself.

4.2.2   Indemnity

Under the 2018 General Medical Services Regulations, NHSiS general medical services contracts require that 'the contractor must at all times have in force in relation to it an indemnity arrangement which provides appropriate cover'. The obligation to provide clinical services may not be sub-contracted, unless the contractor has satisfied itself that the sub-contractor holds adequate immunity arrangements. 'Indemnity arrangement' means an insurance contract or other arrangement made for the purpose of indemnifying the contractor for liabilities that may be incurred in the performance of clinical services under the contract.

Since 2002, regulations have established the Clinical Negligence and Other Risks Indemnity Scheme for health boards administered by Scottish Ministers. The scheme provides for the pooling of risks to meet liabilities and does so through members' contributions. It applies to liability for clinical risks in respect of personal injury resulting from diagnosis, care or treatment by act or omission of an employee of a scheme member. Members are not medical practitioners, but the health boards, the State Hospitals, the Scottish Ambulance Service Board, the NHS Education Board for Scotland, the Common Services Agency and the Scottish National Blood Transfusion Service.

The immunity provision that applies to NHS employees does not apply to general medical practitioners, as they are independent contractors. As discussed in Chapter 2, they are still required to take out appropriate indemnity in order to be represented legally at fatal accident inquiries, disciplinary hearings or, indeed, allegations of medical negligence.

4.3 DUTY OF CARE

Even before the House of Lords in *Donoghue* v *Stevenson* (1932) cogently set out the standard of care in negligence, Scots law had a mechanism for considering such matters. This was grounded on the neo-Aquilian action based on *culpa* or fault. This form of delictual liability has its basis in the Roman *actio legis Aquiliae*. It refers to wrongful or unreasonable conduct which causes patrimonial (monetary) harm to a natural person, which is also referred to as *damnum injuria datum*. The 1795 case of *Gardner* v *Ferguson* arguably gave rise to the Scots law of actionable *damnum* being predicated upon *culpa*, in the form of harm to free persons, as distinguished from *contumelia*, or 'insult'.

The harm (*damnum*) itself needs to be legally recognised, and should be distinguished from cases in which the *damnum* is not recognised as a national policy. This has occurred for example in wrongful birth cases such as *McFarlane* v *Tayside Health Board* (2000), discussed in Chapter 3, in which the courts did not consider the costs of raising a healthy child to be recognised *damnum*.

Aquilian liability is distinguished from the other two pillars of the delictual liability in the *actio iniuriarum* (injury) and the action for *solatium* (pain and suffering), which are considered in greater detail in the Chapter 5 on consent. Any of these pillars can be found within the doctor-patient relationship, depending on the specific facts that arise.

The fact that the doctor owes the patient a duty of care is not a matter of dispute, provided that there is a doctor–patient relationship in existence.

Once the proximity of a doctor-patient relationship been established, the enquiry moves on to the standard of care: that is, what duties of care are owed within the doctor–patient relationship.

Although rare, it has been held that a duty of care has been found not to exist, on the ground of legal policy. Examples include 'wrongful birth' and 'wrongful life' claims discussed in Chapter 3. Where there is no legal interest to be protected, no duty of care will arise.

Neither will a duty of care arise for 'pure' omissions, such as in the so-called 'good Samaritan' or 'duty to rescue' cases. As indicated in *Morrison* v *Forsyth* (1995), there is no duty on a doctor to rescue or attempt to rescue a person where the doctor–patient relationship has not already been established and where contact occurs in that context. This is different from the doctor's relationship with his or her patients, where the relationship sets up a duty of care between doctor and patient. Where that duty of care exists, there may be a duty of rescue, for example where a patient suffers from a psychiatric illness manifesting itself in the tendency towards self-harm. This may give rise to a duty of affirmative action.

The notional duty of care concerns the question of whether the patient's or pursuer's interest that has been invaded is a legally recognised and protected right, as opposed to a social or moral interest. The duty operates on a threshold basis: the duty not to infringe the patient's recognised interests. An actual duty arises where the doctor-defender owed the patient-pursuer a duty to not infringe those interests in the actual circumstances. For a duty of care to exist, the prerequisite of 'foreseeability' must be satisfied: that is, the proximity between the doctor and patient gives rise to foreseeability of harm occurring.

According to the judgment in *Fairlie* v *Perth and Kinross Healthcare NHS Trust* (2004), in general, the duty of care is owed only to a doctor's patients (see discussion of the *ABC* decision in Chapter 6). This includes circumstances in which a patient's psychiatric injuries are caused by abuse by a third party. The court rejected the argument of a father that he was owed a duty of care for the distress suffered when he was accused of abusing his daughter, after she had undergone psychiatric treatment. The father's case failed because the conduct of the physician treating his daughter was too remote from his distress.

Circumstances may arise, however, in which one person is medically examined for another person's benefit. This may happen where a person is medically examined in order to gain employment. A negligent diagnosis or examination would have consequences for both the patient and the prospective employer.

The fulfilling of a statutory duty can give rise to a common law duty of care. This may happen in the context of a hospital accident and emergency service or an ambulance service, both of which operate on a statutory basis. A problem exists insofar as the pursuer may have suffered injury before the service took over their care, but the statutory duty brings the parties into a proximate relationship with one another. In the English case of *Kent* v *Griffiths* (2000) it was held that the duty arises in the case of an ambulance service when the call is accepted. The same appears to be true in Scotland, where *Aitken* v *Scottish Ambulance Service* (2011) was allowed to go to proof. That case found the Scottish Ambulance Service owed a duty of care to cause an ambulance to attend at the pursuer's house following an emergency call.

4.4   STANDARD OF CARE

In all negligence actions the requisite standard of care is that of reasonable-ness. In medical negligence cases it is the same, with the important difference that the requisite 'normal and usual' practice is assessed by expert evidence which itself must be reasonable. This is the case because of the specialised nature of medical practice and the fact that judges, lawyers and lay persons are not able to reach a decision as to reasonable care without recourse to medical evidence. The practice of medicine is also an art form rather than a pure science. As such, there is scope for different opinions of good medical practice. The requisite standard is that level of care exercised by the compe-tent medical practitioner acting in the class of practitioners usually occupied by the defender practitioner. There are no 'degrees of negligence', but a sin-gle standard of care that is to be applied to all circumstances.

4.4.1   Historical development

The principle imputing wrongfulness from acting with a lack of skill in a professional capacity comes from the Roman law: *spondet peritiam artis, et imperitia culpae adnumeratur* translates as 'he is responsible for skill in his pro-fession, and want of such skill is regarded as a fault'. That principle was cited with approval in *Gerrard* v *Royal Infirmary of Edinburgh NHS Trust* (2005), coming, as it did, half a century after the landmark judgment in *Hunter* v *Hanley* (1955). But before that, and until the early 20th century, the principle applied in the context of contract, as its application in the Roman law was in Aquilian liability in respect of damage to one's slave (Justinian), which amounted to damage to property as opposed to personal injury.

Reported cases of actions for medical negligence first appeared in the late 19th and very early 20th centuries. *Dickson* v *Hygienic Institute* (1910) dealt with the conduct of a dental practitioner. The court found that where a person holds themselves out as having a high degree of skill carrying out treatment under contract, the required degree of skill is that of other mem-bers of his profession.

It is this expectation of a high degree of skill that led to the apparent approval of a test for 'gross negligence' as appropriate in cases of medical neg-ligence. This position was settled in the watershed case of *Hunter* v *Hanley* in 1955, in which it was found that in civil liability for medical negligence there is no room for gross negligence. Indeed, there are no 'degrees of negligence', but a single standard that must be applied to all medical claims.

4.4.1.1 The test in Hunter v Hanley

In the benchmark case of *Hunter* v *Hanley* (1955), the plaintiff had received a series of intra-muscular injections of penicillin in her hip. The needle broke and remained embedded. Further surgery did not remove the needle. She sued on the ground that a doctor with an average knowledge ought to have known to use a stronger needle. This raised the question of what was the normal practice as to the type of needle to use. Lord President Clyde set out a general test: to succeed in a negligence action in medical negligence in diagnosis or treatment, it must be established that the doctor is guilty of a failure that no doctor of ordinary skill would make if acting with ordinary care.

The Lord President went on to note that deviation is not in itself evidence of negligence; if it was, it would impede medical progress and innovation. In deviation cases, he required three elements to be proven. These were that:

1. there is a usual and normal practice;

2. the defender did not adopt that practice and

3. 'the course the doctor adopted is one which no professional man of ordinary skill would have taken if he had been acting with ordinary care'.

Crucially, it is insufficient to prove that the pursuer's injury is caused by the defender's deviation. It must be established that the deviation was negligent.

This tripartite test applies to *deviation* cases. If there is no usual practice, or if the usual practice was not followed, the more general test applies. This general test is the one set out above: that is, whether the doctor has been proven guilty of such failure as no doctor of ordinary skill would be guilty of if acting with ordinary care. It was found in *Dougan* v *Lanarkshire Acute Hospitals NHS Trust* (2001) that the absence of a standard practice does not affect the continued applicability of the test in *Hunter* v *Hanley* because the question of the doctor's conduct remains the same.

In England the test was set out in *Bolam* v *Friern Hospital Management Committee* (1957). In that case the plaintiff underwent electro-convulsive therapy for depression but was not given relaxant medication. He suffered fractures to his skull. His case in negligence alleged a negligent failure to give him the drugs, to restrain him and to warn him of the risks inherent in the procedure.

The evidence was to the effect that some practitioners would have given drugs or employed greater restraints in the absence of medication, while others would not have done so. The test in *Hunter* v *Hanley* was altered slightly and expressed as follows: 'A doctor is not guilty of negligence if he acted in accordance with a practice accepted as proper by a responsible body of

medical men skilled in that particular art'. NcNair J argued that the difference was only a matter of expression, but that did not stop commentators
arguing that there was a different test in Scotland from that in England and
Wales. It was later held in *Maynard* v *West Midlands Regional Health Authority*
(1985) that where a defendant acted in accordance with one of two opposing schools of practice, negligence could not be found. In the English case
of *Muller* v *King's College Hospital NHS Foundation Trust* (2017) the court
distinguished cases of 'pure treatment' from those involving 'pure diagnosis',
in this case as to whether or not a biopsy in fact revealed a malignant mela-
noma, rather than whether to undertake the biopsy at all, as in *Maynard*. The
diagnosis is either correct, or it is not, therefore it would be either negligent,
or not, and the *Bolam* test would not be relevant. This finding is in contrast
to that in *Gordon* v *Wilson*, discussed below.

The *Bolam* test was criticised as being determinative to the extent that
the court simply approved medical expert opinion. But in *Bolitho* v *City and
Hackney Health Authority* (1998), the House of Lords found that it is for the
court to determine whether the body of medical opinion relied upon is
itself reasonable. In that case the medical practitioner failed to attend and to
intubate a two-year-old boy with respiratory problems. It was found that he
would not have died had the omission not taken place. The court found that
despite a body of professional opinion sanctioning the defendant's conduct,
the defendant may still be found liable. This is because the body of opinion
relied upon must, in the court's opinion, be reasonable and responsible.

There has been considerable debate in both academic and judicial circles
as to the differences between the tests in *Hunter* v *Hanley* and *Bolam/Bolitho*.
Lord Caplan said in *Moyes* v *Lothian Health Board* (1990) that *Bolam* had
'amplified' *Hunter*, but that in the end 'the appropriate tests in medical negligence cases are to be found in *Hunter* v *Hanley* and *Bolam*'. What is clear
is that British courts will to some extent defer to the views of the medical
profession.

4.4.2 Normal or usual practice

As indicated above, where negligence is alleged, there may be a normal practice (which either was or was not adhered to) and there may not be such a
normal practice.

Where it is alleged that the defender did not adhere to an established
normal practice, the burden of proof on the pursuer will be considerable.
However, once the deviation has been established, the burden shifts to the
defender to justify that deviation. Although this is consistent with the law
in England set out in *Clark* v *McLennan* (1983), it is inconsistent with the

Scottish case of *Devaney* v *Glasgow Health Board* (1987). In *Devaney*, the pursuer had surgery to his aorta but suffered a cardiac arrest and paralysis after the operation. He argued that the surgeon had employed the incorrect technique. Although the evidence as to the risks involved was divided, the court found that the defender does not bear the onus of justifying the technique used. With the evidence split, it was not proven that the surgeon had acted in a way in which no other surgeon would have acted, and hence no negligence was found.

Following normal practice may still amount to negligence if, in the opinion of the court, the practice followed is found to be neither reasonable nor responsible. This follows the judgment in *Bolitho* in England. In the Scottish judgment of *Gordon* v *Wilson* (1992), the court found that where there are two bodies of conflicting but reasonable medical evidence, the court is powerless to prefer one over the other. The court can, however, prefer one professional interpretation of medical *facts* over another and can test the credibility and reliability of expert witnesses.

In *Gordon* v *Wilson*, the pursuer alleged negligence in failing to diagnose a brain tumour at an early stage and sued in respect of the resultant nerve damage caused by the delay. Two experts were heard, to the effect that it was unusual for a general practitioner to encounter a brain tumour and that very few tumours were meningiomas, as was the case in the defender's instance. One expert felt that an urgent referral to a specialist should have been made, while the other felt it unjustified in the circumstance. Both experts were considered credible and reliable. Lord Penrose drew on the *Maynard* judgment to find that preference for one body of opinion was not enough to establish negligence. This stance has been upheld in *Beasley* v *Fife Health Board* (2001) and *Honisz* v *Lothian Health Board* (2006).

Several cases have left open the possibility in Scots law of the court rejecting expert evidence. For example, in *Phillips* v *Grampian Health Board* (1991), Lord Clyde found that evidence of a body of opinion opposing the pursuer's case will be fatal to that case unless it is entirely rejected by the court. And the judgment in *Bolitho* has been cited with approval in Scottish courts, although without holding that the evidence in question was in fact illogical or unreasonable. In *Duffy* v *Lanarkshire Health Board* (2001), the court found that decisions of medical professionals must be 'capable of withstanding logical analysis, and be seen as reasonable and responsible'.

The tripartite test for deviation cases as set out in *Hunter* v *Hanley* (1955) requires the establishment of a normal practice, but the general test caters for situations in which there is no normal practice. Yet there is case law to the effect that the tripartite test applies only where a deviation from normal practice is alleged, but that failure to establish that there is a usual practice (the first leg of the tripartite test) may not be fatal to the case. In such situations, the only question for answer will be whether the defender is guilty of a failure that no doctor of ordinary skill would make if acting with ordinary care. This was the case in *Gerrard* v *Royal Infirmary of Edinburgh NHS Trust* (2005).

4.4.3   Medical risks and benefits

Of primary importance when the medical practitioner is making any calculation of medical risks and benefits that the practitioner must make is that their judgement will, in all facets of medical care, be subject to the test set out in *Hunter* v *Hanley* (1955). This includes whether a risk ought to have been taken, whether it should not have been taken when it was taken and whether a patient should have been informed of a risk inherent in the procedure.

The case law is clear that negligence will be found if a practitioner knowingly takes an easily avoidable risk. In *Hucks* v *Cole* (1993), the defendant failed to administer penicillin and septicaemia set in. Where, on the other hand, there is a high risk of the patient dying or their condition worsening, that factor may be weighed against the side-effects of the treatment. In *Duffy* v *Lanarkshire Health Board* (2001), the pursuer had had a bone marrow transplant to treat aplastic anaemia which she alleged she had contracted as a side-effect of the drug chloramphenicol. The Extra Division of the Inner House, Court of Session, found that the doctor was not negligent in weighing the possible side-effects against the fatal nature of aplastic anaemia, as five different courses of antibiotics had not treated the pursuer's underlying pathology.

4.4.3.1 Inexperience

A medical practitioner must act responsibly within their scope of experience, but inexperience is no excuse in a negligence action. The maxim *imperitia culpae adnumeratur* is applied, as discussed above. In *Steward* v *Greater Glasgow Health Board* (1976), the pursuer alleged negligence in failing to assess a mother's condition properly at the time of her daughter's birth, leading to brain injury to the daughter. Negligence was also alleged in the carrying out of the delivery by vacuum suction. The defenders were absolved because the practitioners had acted according to accepted practice in an emergency situation. But Lord Keith also said that negligence could be established where a practitioner failed to seek help when required and where circumstances allowed and where injury could have been avoided thereby. Yet seeking advice may itself be insufficient. In *Andrews* v *Greater Glasgow Health Board* (2019) it was held that a junior doctor had been negligent in their failure to advise a patient who subsequently died that she should be admitted to hospital; the junior doctor had not discharged his duty of care by seeking advice from a senior colleague.

In the English case of *Wilsher* v *Essex Area Health Authority* (1988), the court found that inexperience is no excuse. In that case the plaintiff suffered from several conditions caused by his prematurity, including oxygen deprivation. He went on to contract retrolental fibroplasia and consequent blindness caused by a catheter having been inserted into a vein rather than an artery, resulting in him receiving excess oxygen on two occasions. The defendant health authority argued that inexperience should result in a lower standard being applied to the conduct of the junior doctor in question. This argument was rejected by the court, which found that all medical staff must meet the standard of competence and experience expected of those holding such posts.

4.4.3.2 Negligent treatment and errors of judgement

All areas of medical practice are subject to *Hunter* v *Hanley* (1955), but the main areas considered by the courts are diagnosis and treatment. Negligent treatment cases can arise in any medical scenario, including during and following childbirth. Negligence was found in *Hunter* v *Glasgow Corporation* (1971), for example, where midwives failed to remove the afterbirth completely, causing sepsis necessitating surgery. The exploratory operation was performed unskilfully, causing organ damage and necessitating a hysterectomy. Statistically speaking, however, most allegations fail to prove negligence.

The question arises whether errors of judgement can amount to negligence. According to the English case of *Whitehouse* v *Jordan* (1980), they can – although Lord Denning in the court below had initially argued that they did not. In that case, a senior hospital registrar attempted a forceps delivery. He pulled six times to no effect, as the child had become impacted, and a caesarean section was performed. However, the impaction had led to oxygen deprivation. The evidence turned on the professional judgement of whether the defender had 'pulled too long and too hard' on the forceps, leading to the impaction. In the House of Lords' judgment, the court found that errors may or may not be negligent, depending on whether the error does or does not pass the test in *Bolam* in England and Wales or in *Hunter* v *Hanley* in Scotland.

The decision in *Whitehouse* was relied on in Scotland in *Phillips* v *Grampian Health Board* (1991), which found that it is not enough for a pursuer to establish an error of judgement; it must also be established that the error was one that no doctor of ordinary skill would make. On this point reference should be made to the discussion of the English case of *Penney* v

East Kent Health Authority in *Muller* v *King's College Hospital NHS Foundation Trust* (2017) where the court (reluctantly) concluded that even in pure diagnosis cases, it may not prefer one expert to another, and that this requires in any event to be viewed through the lens of the *Bolitho* exception.

4.4.3.3 Criminal negligence in the medical context

Although this chapter is nominally concerned with civil liability, in recent years criminal law has come into play in respect of medical negligence. Although there is no Scottish jurisprudence on the issue, Lord Russell had observed in *Hunter* v *Hanley* that,

> in relation to criminal responsibility flowing from negligence, the words 'gross negligence' are not uncommonly used to denote the very high standard of negligence or recklessness required to establish criminal responsibility – a degree which goes beyond the mere case of compensation between the subjects in a civil claim, and is higher than ordinary negligence or culpa.

English courts have ruled on the issue of criminal negligence, and while Scottish courts may be able to learn from those decisions, it is likely that Scottish jurisprudence will follow a different course. Questions are raised in both jurisdictions around whether it is appropriate to criminalise the conduct of health care professionals.

   R v *Bawa-Garba* (2016) involved the death of a six-year-old patient in the care of junior doctor Hadiza Bawa-Garba, who had recently returned from maternity leave, and two nurses who were also prosecuted. She was convicted of gross negligence manslaughter after Jack Adcock died following cardiac arrest occasioned by her failure to diagnose septic shock that was a result of his pneumonia. Dr Bawa-Garba confused Jack with another patient who had a 'do not resuscitate' order in place, and fatally interrupted resuscitation attempts. The jury found that Dr Bawa-Garba's conduct had met the threshold for criminal liability set out in *R* v *Adomako* (1995). The jury in such cases is required to decide 'whether the extent to which the defendant's conduct departed from the proper standard of care incumbent upon him, involving as it must have done a risk of death to the patient, was such that it should be judged criminal'. This is based on the judgment in *R* v *Bateman* (1925) that defined the offence as conduct that 'showed such disregard for the life and safety of others as to amount to a crime'. There was no clear definition given of what amounts to 'gross'.

   It is doubtful whether a similar conclusion would have been reached in a Scottish court. That is because the test for criminal liability in culpable homicide is less vague than it is in gross negligence manslaughter. The offence is committed when death is caused by the improper conduct of a person, that does not amount to murder, but meets the standard of 'wicked recklessness'. There is a robust jurisprudence in cases such as *Transco Plc* v *Her Majesty's Advocate* (2004) on what amounts to such recklessness, being 'wicked' or showing 'complete indifference' to the consequences of one's actions, to fulfil the *mens rea* requirements of the offence. This requires the subjective fault of the accused; it also requires the Procurator Fiscal to meet a 'public interest' test in order to bring the prosecution. Taken together, similar prosecutions of health care professionals are less likely in Scotland than they are in England and Wales.

4.4.3.4 Diagnosis

In *Moyes* v *Lothian Health Board* (1990) the patient underwent an angiography, which is a diagnostic procedure carrying a risk of stroke, which the patient suffered. In *Gordon* v *Wilson* (1992) (discussed above), the pursuer sued for the failure to diagnose a tumour earlier. In both cases – and in subsequent case law – it was held that the test in *Hunter* v *Hanley* applies to diagnosis as well as treatment. Further, if symptoms should cause a competent doctor to investigate further, failure to do so may amount to negligence. In *Johns* v *Greater Glasgow Health Board* (1989), the patient had a fall and went to hospital. Her swollen wrists were overlooked; hence an X-ray was not ordered and fractures were not diagnosed. Negligence was found.

4.4.3.5 Emergencies

As indicated above, defenders must act according to accepted practice in an emergency situation (*Steward* v *Greater Glasgow Health Board* (1976)). This is also the position in England. In *Kent* v *Griffiths* (2000) it was held that in the case of an ambulance service, a duty arises when the call is accepted. In *Barnett* v *Chelsea and Kensington Hospital Management Committee* (1968), three night-watchmen became ill after drinking tea. They were taken to the casualty department where they were told to go to their own doctors. One of the men subsequently died of arsenic poisoning following a negligent failure by the casualty officer to examine him properly. However, while it was found that the *Bolam* standard applies to emergency situations as well as diagnosis and that by that standard the defendant was found negligent, the plaintiff failed to establish causation and so did not win the case.

In *Darnley* v *Croydon Health Service (NHS) Trust* (2018) the Supreme Court considered the scope of the duty to take reasonable care not to act in a way that could cause a patient presenting at A&E to sustain physical injury.

That duty was owed by medically qualified personnel as well as administrative staff. The patient was incorrectly told he would need to wait 4–5 hours before being seen, rather than the conventional 30 minutes. On the basis of this misinformation he decided to leave the hospital, and that caused him to suffer permanent brain damage, which would have been avoided had he been seen in a timely manner.

4.5   CAUSATION

The general rule is that negligence is said to have caused injury if, but for the negligence, the patient would not have suffered the injury. Conversely if – as was the case in *Barnett* v *Chelsea and Kensington Hospital Management Committee* (1968) involving arsenic poisoning – the injury would have occurred regardless of the proven negligence, causation is not established. This is the 'but for' or *sine qua non* test. This test covers simple issues of cause and effect. However, in some circumstances several agents may contribute to the injury, in which case a test that establishes a material contribution will be required. In other cases, a pursuer may have been exposed to a harmful agent, in which case a test for a material increase in risk will be required.

Among other things, the judgment in *Fairchild* v *Glenhaven Funeral Services Ltd* (2002) looked at the extent to which causation is a question of fact. Lord Hoffmann found that it was, because rules of law set out particular requirements which determine the scope of liability (legal causation). The question of fact is whether the rules of liability have been satisfied (factual causation).

4.5.1   The 'but for' test

Generally, where a legal injury would *not* have occurred but for the negligence of the defender, causation will be established and the pursuer's case won. This must be established in both general and individual terms.

This may be a matter of medical fact, as was the case in *Kay's Tutor* v *Ayrshire and Arran Health Board* (1987). In that case it was established that a penicillin overdose – albeit negligently administered – does not, as a matter of fact, cause deafness. The deafness was caused by the child's underlying meningitis. Damages were, however, awarded for *solatium* – for the temporary suffering of the child as a result of the overdose.

A different facet of causation is exemplified in *Kenyon* v *Bell* (1953). That case indicated a more individualistic approach to the 'but for' test, which takes into account the particular circumstances of the patient and their pathology. A child was injured in a car accident, receiving a cut to her eye. Her eye had to be removed. Despite proof of negligence, the court rejected the pursuer's claim, on the medical evidence that the particular patient would have lost her eye anyway.

The general rule is a doctor will not be liable to a patient where the 'but for' cause of an injury falls outside of the scope of the doctor's duty. In other words the doctor is not liable for injuries unrelated to duty. This was demonstrated (obiter) in *Moyes* v *Lothian Health Board* (1990). In that case it was observed that the failure to warn about the risks involved in diagnostic treatment which was negligently performed would not have made any difference to the pursuer's case if the risk which eventuated was not one that the doctor had a duty to disclose. In *Meadows* v *Khan* (2011) the medical practitioner negligently failed to refer a patient for the appropriate test for the haemophilia gene. A child was subsequently born with both haemophilia and autism. They would not have been born but for the negligence. The Supreme Court held that the scope of duty included the haemophilia tests but not that for autism, as it was only the former that the defendant had undertaken. Therefore the autism could not form part of the claim, as the defendant had not undertaken responsibility for the progression of the pregnancy.

4.5.2   Material increase in risk

Arguably the strictness of the 'but for' test has been relaxed by judicial acknowledgement of the sufficiency of material increase in risk as establishing causation. In the classic case of *McGhee* v *National Coal Board* (1973), the pursuer was employed in a brick works. No washing facilities were provided. He had to cycle home without showering first, and suffered dermatitis. It was found that the failure to provide washing facilities was negligent. The House of Lords found that there was no real difference between saying that the omission had led to a material increase in risk and saying that there had been a material contribution to that injury.

The *McGhee* judgment has served as authority in the medical negligence field. In the case of *Wilsher* v *Essex Area Health Authority* (1988) (discussed above in respect of the negligent administration of excess oxygen), the excess oxygen could have caused the blindness suffered, but the retrolental fibroplasia that led to the blindness could also have been caused by one of four other conditions from which the plaintiff already suffered (iatrogenic injury). The House of Lords held that, following a finding of negligence, the onus lay on the plaintiff to show that the negligence had caused the injury. The plaintiff had not discharged this burden.

Fairchild v *Glenhaven Funeral Services Ltd* (2002) was an industrial disease case involving the asbestos-related illness mesothelioma. The employers were negligent in not providing protection from inhaling asbestos dust. The House of Lords adopted a modified approach to causation that became known as the '*Fairchild* exception'. This exception allows a departure from the 'but for' test in material contribution cases. The court in *Fairchild* found that the court in the *McGhee* judgment had applied a less stringent 'but for' test that equated material contribution with factual causation. The extent to which these judgments might apply to medical negligence cases remains unclear.

Even so, there is the suggestion in *McGhee* that because the defenders materially increased the risk of the pursuer contracting dermatitis, the onus shifted to the defender to show that whatever caused the illness, it was not the extra time required before the pursuer was able to wash the dust off his skin. Yet attempts in *Wilsher* and in *Craig* v *Glasgow Victoria and Leverndale Hospitals Board of Management* (1976) to use Lord Wilberforce's judgment in *McGhee* to shift the burden of proof in medical negligence cases were rejected by the court.

The doctrine of *res ipsa loquitur* ('the thing itself speaks') has not generally found favour in Scottish courts, although it has done so in some commonwealth jurisdictions. It applies in situations in which the facts indicate an act is so obviously negligent that the burden of proof is reversed, so as to require the defender to rebut that contention through effective use of the standard in *Hunter* v *Hanley*. The doctrine applies only where there is no evidence of why or how the harm occurred; it is a harm that would not normally occur in the absence of negligence; and the defender has control of the circumstances in which it occurred. For example, in *Gillespie* v *Grampian Health Board* (1997) a surgical repair to the pursuer's middle finger led to a permanent disfigurement to her upper arm, most likely from the tourniquet. It was held that the doctrine did apply. Conversely, in *Gill's Curator Bonis* v *Grampian Health Board* (1995) the doctrine did not apply because the pursuer failed to satisfy the first criterion, i.e. that there was no evidence of why or how the harm occurred. In that case there was a clear reason why she might attempt suicide given her surveillance in a mental hospital.

4.5.3   Loss of chance and loss of opportunity

Correctly diagnosing a condition should lead to an outcome more favourable than incorrectly diagnosing the condition. The purpose of the civil law and the law of delict is to restore the pursuer to the position they would have been in but for the negligence. This leads to arguments on the loss of chance to make a complete recovery, because of negligent misdiagnosis.

In Scotland it is not possible to claim for the loss of the chance for a better medical outcome. In *Kenyon* v *Bell* (1953), a six-month-old girl was found lying on the kitchen floor, bleeding from a cut to her eye. The casualty doctor instructed a nurse only to put drops in the eye and to apply powder. The parents were told it would not be necessary to see their family doctor. It was later found that there was internal haemorrhaging to the eye as well as a detached retina, necessitating the removal of the eye. The pursuer's main argument was for the loss of the eye; failing that, the pursuer claimed loss of a material chance that the eye could be saved. The court found that unless there could be drawn a reasonable inference that the eye could have been saved had the defender exercised proper care, the claim must fail. Similarly, if the cause of losing the eye were uncertain, the pursuer's claim would fail.

There are some subtle differences south of the border. In the English case of *Hotson* v *East Berkshire Area Health Authority* (1987), the court found that it could not rule that in no circumstances could a plaintiff succeed by proving loss of chance of a complete recovery. In that case a 13-year-old boy fell out of a tree. The hospital failed to diagnose a fracture to his knee. A correct diagnosis was made five days later, by which time lack of blood supply had led to permanent disability. The defendant argued that the fall was the sole cause of injury. The plaintiff argued that the delayed diagnosis led to the loss of the chance of a complete recovery (there was a 25 per cent chance of a complete recovery had the correct diagnosis been made). The Court of Appeal awarded 25 per cent of the damages the boy would have received had he proven his case completely, but the House of Lords reversed this decision because the judge's decision amounted to a finding of fact which had not been established.

On the other hand, in *Wright* v *Cambridge Medical Group* (2011) a general practitioner delayed referring a patient to hospital was found liable for the permanent injury that was a result of that delay. It was considered fair, just and reasonable under the *Caparo* test that the scope of the GP's duty should extend to the permanent injury suffered. It was for the GP to rebut the presumption that had the claimant been timeously referred she would not have suffered the injury. In fact the delay had led to less time for the hospital to reach the proper diagnosis and give appropriate treatment, which were causative of her loss.

Loss of chance of a better medical outcome is different to the 'loss of opportunity' cases. Scottish courts have considered the 'loss of opportunity' caused by misdiagnosis in cases in which, for example, there was the loss of the opportunity to terminate a pregnancy because of misdiagnosis of Down's syndrome in the foetus. This was the case in *McLelland* v *Greater Glasgow Health Board* (1999). The defenders admitted negligence and the court had to rule on damages for *solatium* and for the cost of the child's care. Damages were implicitly awarded for loss of opportunity, because all heads of damages flowed from the finding that had the pursuer known that trisomy 21 existed, she would have terminated the pregnancy.

In the not dissimilar case of *Goorkani* v *Tayside Health Board* (1991), the pursuer succeeded in establishing negligence (albeit in treatment). Yet he failed to prove that had he known of the risk of sterility from taking a particular drug, he would not have taken the drug. He failed to discharge this burden of proof of causation because he would have gone blind without the drug. However, the court awarded him damages for *inter alia* loss of the opportunity to become accustomed to his pending infertility (see Chapter 5 on consent, for further discussion).

4.5.4   Factual and legal causation

Legal causation considers those facts that should be used to establish causation and the use of causal language to do so. This may be by way of the *sine qua non* ('but for') test, which is a test for the chain of causation between the negligence and the injury. That chain may be broken by an intervening act of a third party or the pursuer themselves, known as a *novus actus interveniens*. In such a circumstance, causation is not established. For example, in *McFarlane* v *Tayside Health Board* (2000), a child was born following a failed sterilisation operation the risks of which were not adequately explained to the pursuer. On policy grounds, the court found that the pursuer's failure to have an abortion or to give the child up for adoption could not constitute a *novus actus interveniens*. This is similar to the position taken in *Emeh* v *Kensington and Chelsea Area Health Authority* (1984).

However, a different position was taken in *Sabri-Tabrizi* v *Lothian Health Board* (1998) in which a failed sterilisation led to a pregnancy. The pursuer had an abortion but continued to have sexual intercourse with her husband, leading to a further pregnancy and delivery of a stillborn child. The House of Lords found that she should have known, following her pregnancy and abortion, that there remained a residual risk of pregnancy and that in the circumstances to have sexual intercourse without contraception constituted a *novus actus interveniens*.

For further discussion of the relationship between causation and the test for breach of the duty of care, see Chapter 5 on causation in information disclosure cases, in particular the judgment in *Chester* v *Afshar* (2004).

4.6   DEFENCES

Defences to allegations of medical negligence may be either complete or partial. Complete defences include statutory limitation and partial defences include contributory negligence. In the former case, the defender is absolved, while in the latter case the award of damages is apportioned.

4.6.1 Limitation

This is the most commonly invoked defence. It applies under the Part II of the Prescription and Limitation (Scotland) Act 1973. Under s 17, in actions for personal injuries, a claim must be brought within three years (the triennium) of the date when the injuries were sustained or where there has been a continuing act or omission, within three years of the date on which the act or omission ceased, whichever is the later. A continuing act or omission may occur in drug prescription cases. For example, in *Kennedy* v *Steinberg* (1998) the pursuer alleged ongoing negligence in prescribing the depression medication Equanil, to which she had become addicted. The court found that the triennium ran from the date on which, in the opinion of the court, it would have been reasonably practicable for the pursuer in all the circumstances to be aware that:

1. the injuries were sufficiently serious to justify bringing an action of damages;

2. they were attributable to an act or omission and

3. the defender was a person to whose act or omission they were attributable.

It is not sufficient for the pursuer to argue that they were not aware of the limitation period or that they failed to see a solicitor until after the triennium had expired.

Reasonable impracticality can be inferred from circumstances and is to be distinguished from reasonable excuse. Reasonable excuse amounts to averments such as those made in *Mackay* v *Lothian Health Board* (2001) in which the pursuer said that there was nothing to prompt him to question the defenders' conduct. Courts would not side with the pursuer in such circumstances. According to *Elliot* v *J and C Finney* (1989), a reasonable excuse for not raising the question is if gathering sufficient information on which to base the question would entail excessive time and money.

In *Phillips* v *Grampian Health Board* (1991), the pursuer was admitted to hospital in 1978, with a swollen testicle. No biopsy or surgical exploration was carried out. Although gonorrhoea was diagnosed, the medical report did not exclude tumour. More than a year later, the patient was referred to a urological unit and testicular cancer was diagnosed, with a secondary cancer in his lungs. Subsequent treatment proved unsuccessful; he died seven years later, of lung failure. In the meantime, in 1985 he had commenced a negligence action, which was continued by his wife. The court found that it had been reasonably practicable for him to discover before July 1982, that his cancer was due to the delay and that the delay had been caused by the hospital's error.

Lord Clyde had observed in the *Phillips* case that, under s 19A of the 1973 Act, there is an unfettered judicial discretion to allow an action to be brought, notwithstanding the provisions in the Act. This discretion is exercised sparingly, sometimes after a preliminary proof on limitation. Where factors in favour and factors against prejudice to the pursuer in not allowing the claim are equally balanced, the court must refuse to exercise its discretion in favour of the pursuer. The weight attributed to each factor is determined by the Lord Ordinary and can be set aside by a higher court only if there has been an error of law.

Where the failure was due to the solicitor's negligent failure to bring the case within the triennium, the pursuer's action is against the solicitor rather than the medical practitioner (*Leith* v *Grampian University Hospital NHS Trust* (2005), citing *Forsyth* v *A F Stoddart & Co Ltd* (1985)). The same standard of professional negligence applies to solicitors as applies to medical practitioners, although the pursuer will bear a double burden: proof that the solicitor was negligent in failing to being the case in time and proof that had the claim been brought within the triennium, the pursuer would have won that case. Otherwise the pursuer will have failed to prove causation in the case against the solicitor because, but for the solicitor's negligence, the outcome of the medical negligence case would have been unaffected.

4.6.2   Illegality

From the maxim *ex turpi causa non oritur actio* (no action arises from immorality) comes a theoretically possible but rare defence against a medical negligence obligation. *Clunis* v *Camden and Islington Health Authority* (1997) concerned the obligation on the health authority to prevent the patient from committing a crime. Following the patient's discharge, several appointments were missed and the plaintiff committed manslaughter, to which charge he pleaded guilty. He argued that the health authority had been negligent in preventing him from committing the offence. The court would not let itself be used to enforce obligations arising from illegal acts.

4.6.3   Therapeutic privilege

If a defender can prove that the patient would have suffered psychological disadvantage had the material information been given to him, the defence of therapeutic privilege would be established. This is discussed in Chapter 5 on consent.

4.6.3.1 Contributory negligence

Where damage is suffered in part caused by the conduct of the pursuer, fault may be apportioned between the litigating parties under the Law Reform (Contributory Negligence) Act 1945. Although there are no cases in which a finding of contributory negligence has been made in English or Scots medical law, such a finding is theoretically possible. In *Farquhar* v *Murray* (1901), for example, the doctor went on leave for nine days, leaving instructions for the patient to apply a poultice to his diseased finger. The patient failed to do so, necessitating an amputation. Although the pursuer failed to prove his case in negligence, the court observed that had the negligence been established, the case may have been one in which the patient might have been found to have contributed to his injury.

4.7 ALTERNATIVES TO *CULPA*

The existing system is based on fault, but there are from time to time moves to reform it in order to speed up the process, reduce damages payouts and the cost of litigation and even redress the balance between pursuer and defender. Some areas of law and medicine have been reformed. The Consumer Protection Act 1987 governs pharmaceutical injury and is operative in the area of private law. The Vaccine Damage Payments Act 1979 provides payments for damage suffered as a result of state-sponsored vaccination programmes and operates in public law terms a statutory system of state liability.

4.7.1 Products liability

Although the Consumer Protection Act 1987 protects the consumer, the purchaser of a drug has an arguably more effective remedy in the law of contract. This is because where a prescription is dispensed privately under a contract between pharmacist and patient, there is an implied term of the contract that the goods are of satisfactory quality. This remedy would not, however, be open to a patient on the National Health Service as there is no contract in existence.

In other circumstances, liability for injury by a pharmaceutical product may be in negligence or in contract under the product's warranty. A duty of care is owed to consumers by manufacturers of medicinal and other products. However, a system of strict liability was established by the Consumer Protection Act 1987, which was enacted under obligations flowing from the European Products Liability Directive and the Pearson Commission Report. It came into force on 1 March 1988. Its terms apply to the whole of the United Kingdom and are reserved to Westminster under Part 5 of the Scotland Act 1998.

Actions are often brought by a group of parties similarly injured by a medicinal product, including pharmaceutical products and medical devices (prostheses). Although the 'class action' is not allowed in Scots law, group actions do occur, with several 'lead cases' representing a group. This was the case in *A v National Blood Authority* (2001).

In bringing an action under the 1987 Act, a claimant must establish:

1. that the device or medicine in question falls within the definition of 'product';

2. the identity of the 'producer';

3. defect in the product and

4. injury and causation.

The defender may be able to make use of the statutory 'development risk' defence.

4.7.1.1 Product and producer

Other than saying that the definition includes products comprised within other products (e.g. a pump on a dialysis machine), there is no definition of 'product' in the Act. The Directive does, however, consider that all moveables fall within the definition. 'Producer' is defined as the person who manufactured, won or abstracted it (in the case of a substance that was not manufactured) or the person who carried out the process giving rise to the essential characteristics of the product (if it was neither produced nor won or abstracted, as would be the case for agricultural produce).

There has been speculation as to whether blood and blood products fall within this definition. Blood certainly falls within the definition of 'substance' under ss 1 and 45 of the 1987 Act. Considered along with the definition of 'producer', this would suggest that the blood transfusion authority would be considered the 'producer' of blood 'products'.

The English case of *A v National Blood Authority* (2001) involved six lead cases in which claimants had contracted hepatitis C from transfusions of blood or blood products. The question arose as to whether Factor VIII platelets constituted 'products' under the 1987 Act. The court found that they did.

The defender is the person who stands to gain from the marketing of the product and the person who creates the risk. Producers are, for the most part, manufacturers, although suppliers can fall within the definition. In the Act, 'producer' includes manufacturers, distributors, importers and the companies who brand the product. This definition includes the prescribing medical practitioner and pharmaceutical chemist, who should be able to identify the manufacturer in order to avoid liability.

4.7.1.2 Defect

Under s 3 of the 1987 Act, the definition of 'defect' is the failure to meet the standard that 'persons generally are entitled to expect'. This is a test very close to that of reasonableness in negligence, but is arguably tighter as it is about more than careless production, concentrating as it does on the quality of the product itself. The Court of Justice of the European Union held, in Joined Cases C-503/13 and C-504/13 *Boston Scientific Medizintechnik* v *AOK Sachsen-Anhalt* (2015), that if it is found that products belonging to the same group or production series (e.g. pacemakers) had a potential defect, the product could be classified as defective without the need to establish that the product had such a defect.

The 1987 Act contains a definition of 'safety' and elaborates on what persons generally are entitled to expect. Safety is defined relative to the risk of personal injury or death and account should be taken of the manner in which and the purposes for which the product has been marketed, its get-up, the use of any mark in relation to the product, or warnings with respect to doing or refraining from doing anything in relation to the product. This may have to do with the labelling of the product, packaging that will not allow access to children and so on.

In *A* v *National Blood Authority* (2001) the court referred to the Directive rather than the Act, but the definitions of safety and entitlement expectations are the same. It was found that persons generally are entitled to expect transfused blood to be infection-free. The first Supreme Court product liability case was *Hastings* v *Finsbury Orthopaedics Ltd* (2022), in which the appellant received an allegedly defective metal-on-metal hip replacement. The Outer House of the Court of Session had found that the claimant had not established the product as defective. Appeal to the Inner House was refused and the claimant appealed to the Supreme Court, by which point the claim had been narrowed to whether the claimant could rely on the *prima facie* grounds of defect alone. The parties agreed that the 'entitled expectation' test under s 3(2) was whether the safety of the product would be worse when measured against other non-metal-on-metal hip devices. Yet the claim failed because the available statistical data was inadequate to the establishment of 'defect'.

4.7.1.3 Causation

The onus is on the pursuer to prove causation of harm. The same rules existing in the law of negligence are to be applied under the Consumer

Protection Act 1987. This may be a problematic matter of scientific fact, particularly if it is required to separate the damage occasioned by the medicinal product from the damage caused by the disease itself (iatrogenic injury). In *A v National Blood Authority* (2001) the court found that 'the defect was the virus in the blood and the damage was the virus in the patient'. The causal link was in the science.

4.7.1.4   Prescription periods

The same triennium limitation period applies to actions under the 1987 Act as applies in cases of negligence. The consumer must bring a claim within three years of it being reasonably practicable for them to do so. There is, however, a prescription period of ten years. This means that the claim is extinguished ten years after the 'relevant period', being the supply of the product. This is governed by the Prescription and Limitation (Scotland) Act 1973, as amended by the Prescription (Scotland) Act 2018 (asp 15), which came into effect in February 2025.

4.7.1.5   The 'development risk' and other defences

Also known as the 'state of the art' defence, this applies where the state of scientific and technical knowledge among producers of similar products was not, at the time, such that the defect might be expected to be discovered. This is set out in the Consumer Protection Act 1987, s 1(1), as amended by the Product Safety and Metrology etc (Amendment etc) (EU Exit) Regulations 2019, which retained the terms of the European Directive.

That said, there is an arguable difference between the 1987 Act and the Directive insofar as reasonableness exists in the United Kingdom version. This was considered by the European Court of Justice in *European Commission v United Kingdom (re the Product Liability Directive)* (Case C–300/95) (1997). In that case the court found that the defence in the 1987 Act could be interpreted more broadly than in the Directive, but that it had not been shown that the United Kingdom had gone against the spirit of the Directive.

There are various reasons why a defect may not be known or knowable, including economic feasibility of discovery of the defect. These are tested along similar lines to a negligence enquiry – that is, through the use of reasonableness. A defect may also be either foreseeable or indeed known, but remain undiscoverable in practice; for example, unsafe only in a minority of cases that clinical testing will not reveal. Limited scientific and technical knowledge may obscure the defect from being discovered. An often-cited example is that of the drug thalidomide in the 1960s.

In *A* v *National Blood Authority* the defence was used, but the court found that the defence did not apply where the risk was, or ought to have been, known. Once a defect is identified, the defence cannot logically be used. This finding did not stop the court making an assessment of the state of scientific knowledge at the time.

While the partial defence of contributory negligence may apply, the 1987 Act sets out further defences, including compliance with existing European Community law – now referred to as 'retained law' following Brexit and under the 2019 regulations noted above – that the defender was not the supplier of the product or that certain facets of the claim are competently refuted.

4.8   VACCINE DAMAGE

Because vaccine programmes are promoted by the state, the Pearson Commission recommended strict liability compensation. This led to the Vaccine Damage Payments Act 1979, although there is case law in *Ross* v *Secretary of State for Scotland* (1990) in which it was argued that in promoting vaccination the Secretary of State had exercised its discretionary power irresponsibly and was negligent in the way it promoted the programme. The court found that attacks on the use of ministerial discretion must show bad faith.

As well as the Pearson Commission recommendation, scenarios giving rise to cases such as *Loveday* v *Renton and Wellcome Foundation* (1990) led to the 1979 Act. *Loveday* dealt with brain damage following administration of the pertussis (whopping cough) vaccine, although the plaintiff failed to prove causation and did not win his case.

The 1979 Act applies to the following vaccines: diphtheria, tetanus, poliomyelitis, tuberculosis, measles, smallpox, whooping cough (pertussis), rubella, haemophilus type B infection, meningococcal group C, mumps, pneumococcal infection and human papillomavirus, influenza caused by the pandemic influenza A (H1N1) 2009 virus, rotavirus, influenza (other than influenza caused by a pandemic influenza virus), meningococcal group B and meningococcal group W and COVID-19.

It provides lump-sum payments for death or severe disablement as a result of these vaccines. There is no need to prove fault or negligence. It is, however, necessary to establish causation, which is a considerable hurdle for claimants.

Under the Vaccine Damage Payments Act 1979 Statutory Sum Order 2007, this sum is up to £120,000. Claims are settled by the Department for Work and Pensions. If refused, there is a right of review by a tribunal constituted under the 1979 Act.

This area of law is devolved to the Scottish Parliament, yet, perhaps because the relevant departments in Scotland and in England consult with one another, statutory instruments are enacted on a national basis. The logic appears to be to ensure that the same regime exists north and south of the border.

4.9 BLOOD PRODUCTS LIABILITY: HIV AND HEPATITIS C

Over the years, various funds have been set up to compensate those who have contracted blood diseases through transfusions. The Macfarlane Trust was set up by the Haemophilia Society to administer government funds. *Ex gratia* payments of £20,000 were made to those infected, but not to partners. Family members of deceased patients also received payments. The Eileen Trust aimed to help non-haemophiliacs who also contracted HIV from blood products. It administers lump-sum settlements from Scottish Government funds. The Skipton Fund is a UK-wide scheme that also makes *ex gratia* payments, in this case to those who were infected with hepatitis C as the result of NHS treatment with blood or blood products. Payments ranged between £20,000 and £25,000, depending on the severity of the disease. In the unsuccessful challenge to the eligibility criteria of the Skipton Fund the court in *Fargie, Petr* (2008) found that the Scottish Government was entitled to select the cut-off date of 29 August 2003.

Following *A* v *National Blood Authority* (2001), the then-Scottish Executive decided to make payments along the lines of that judgment to patients in Scotland. However, claimants could not avail themselves of these terms because of when the Act came into force and the fact that liability prescribes within ten years. An expert group was set up under Lord Ross, on the recommendation of the Health and Community Care Committee of the Scottish Parliament, which recommended that *ex gratia* payments be made to those who contracted hepatitis C through blood transfusions.

Under s 28 of the Smoking, Health and Social Care (Scotland) Act 2005, Scottish Ministers may establish a scheme for making payments by them to persons who before 1 September 1991:

1. were treated with blood transfusions (blood, tissue or blood prod-
    ucts) anywhere in the United Kingdom under the NHS and who
    became infected with the hepatitis C virus and did not die before
    29 August 2003;

2. were infected with hepatitis C by one of the people in the above
    category and did not die before 29 August 2003. This category
    of person includes spouses, civil partners, cohabitants and certain
    blood relatives.

Those two categories were amended by the Patient Rights (Scotland) Act 2011 to make payments to persons who did die before 29 August 2003, by adding a third category, that of dependents of those falling within the first two categories. Dependent includes a partner of the infected person or a person living with the infected person as husband or wife in a relationship that has the characteristics of civil partnership.

There have been several judicial and other enquiries into the issue of HIV and hepatitis C infection as a result of treatment with blood or blood products in the NHSiS in the 1970s and 1980s. They did not seek to provide any level of compensation, but rather to enquire into the issue itself, including historic timelines, causes and extents. Examples include the inquiry chaired by the Lady Cosgrove in 2008, and the inquiry chaired by Lord Penrose in 2015.

There was however a UK enquiry which did lead to pay-outs in 2022, following the report of the inquiry led by Sir Brian Langstaff. £100,000 interim payments were made to beneficiaries and widows, widowers or long-term partners of an infected beneficiaries who had died.

These enquiries fall outwith the scope of this book.

The *Report of the Expert Group on Financial and Other Support* (the Ross Report) had a broader remit than hepatitis C. It was charged with considering clinical negligence from a wholly Scottish point of view, and making recommendations on the reform of the system, including the substantive law, procedure, legal aid, mediation and access to justice, as well as the possible introduction of no-fault compensation or strict liability. Consideration of the Ross Report also falls outwith the scope of this book.

The issue of unintended or unexpected incidents resulting from the provision of a health service is covered by the Health (Tobacco, Nicotine etc and Care) (Scotland) Act 2016 asp 14. It places a duty of candour on a responsible person, as defined in s 25 as a health board, local authority, or person providing care or social work services, among others. The duty is activated when the incident results in one of a specified number of outcomes that are directly linked to the incident, including death: permanent loss of bodily, sensory, motor, physiologic or intellectual functions; or one of a number of severe harms. The responsible person must follow the duty of candour procedures as set out by Scottish Ministers under SSI 2018/57, and that include an apology to, or meeting with, the relevant person to provide an account of the incident. 'Apology' means a statement of sorrow or regret in respect of the unintended or unexpected incident.

Essential facts

Liability

- The basis of liability lies in delict rather than contract.
- Liability is seldom borne by the individual doctor, as their employer will usually be vicariously liable. Liability may, however, be joint and several.
- An action may also lie against scientists who carry out testing on behalf of the NHS.
- An indemnity scheme is required for the health service and also operates for doctors working in the National Health Service.

The duty of care

- A duty of care exists by virtue of the doctor–patient relationship in respect of acts or omissions made in the context of that relationship.
- The existence of a duty of care is based on the principles of proximity (between the parties) and foreseeability (of harm).
- A duty of care may also arise between a doctor and a non-patient where a legally proximate relationship exists between them.
- A duty of care on the ambulance service will arise following an emergency call.
- The duty of care will not arise for 'pure omissions', as no duty to rescue is imposed on a doctor in the absence of a doctor–patient relationship.

The standard of care

- The standard of care required of medical practitioners is set out in *Hunter* v *Hanley* (1955).
- Practitioners must attain the level of care of the reasonable medical practitioner in their field.
- The expert evidence relied upon to justify the case for either pursuer or defender must itself be reasonable and responsible.
- Where deviation from usual practice is alleged, the tripartite test must be established, i.e., that there is a usual practice, that the defender did not adopt that practice and that 'the course the doctor adopted is one which no professional man of ordinary skill would have taken if he had been acting with ordinary care'.
- It is for the court to determine whether the body of medical opinion relied upon is itself reasonable.

- The burden of establishing that the duty of care was breached is on the pursuer.
- All facets of medical practice are subject to the test in *Hunter* v *Hanley* (1955), including diagnosis, treatment and information disclosure. It can also involve pure diagnosis.
- The absence of a standard practice does not displace the test in *Hunter* v *Hanley*.
- Inexperience is no excuse in a negligence action, and seeking advice may itself not discharge that duty.
- Errors of judgement may amount to negligence.
- Criminal negligence may take place and homicide charges will be founded on the test for 'wicked recklessness', whereas in England and Wales 'gross negligence manslaughter' is based on the defendant showing such a disregard for life and safety so as to amount to a crime.

Causation

- It is necessary for the pursuer to prove that the negligence caused the injury, which is a question of fact.
- Proof of causation is through the 'but for' test; that is, proof that but for the negligence, the pursuer would not have suffered the injury complained of.
- Where there are several causal agents, material contribution to the injury may amount to causation in law.
- There is no action for loss of the chance of a better medical outcome, but there may be an action for the loss of the opportunity to mitigate or avoid the damage suffered.
- The chain of causation may be broken by a *novus actus interveniens*.

Defences

- Defences may be complete or partial.
- Other than *novus actus interveniens*, complete defences include disproving part of the pursuer's case, the three-year statutory limitation period having expired, illegality or therapeutic privilege.
- An example of a partial defence is contributory negligence, which will lead to apportionment of the damages award.

Alternatives to culpa

- There has been piecemeal reform of the fault-based system from time to time.

- Reforms have led to the Consumer Protection Act 1987 which deals with products liability.
- Under the 1987 Act there is a requirement to prove that the damage was caused by a product made by a 'producer', as defined in the Act. There is a requirement to prove defect, but not fault.
- A product is 'defective' if it fails to meet the standards that persons generally are entitled to expect.
- The defender may have recourse to the 'development risk' defence, based on the state of scientific knowledge at the time.
- Other instruments include the Vaccine Damage Payments Act 1979 and various *ex gratia* schemes relating to blood products liability and HIV or hepatitis C.
- Under the Vaccine Damage Payments Act 1979 there is no requirement to prove causation. It is an example of strict liability.
- Other examples of compensation schemes not based on fault include the Skipton fund and other statutory schemes relating to hepatitis C and HIV from blood transfusions on the NHS.

Essential cases

Edgar v Lamont (1914): the existence of a contract for medical treatment by a doctor does not bar an action in delict by the patient against the doctor for personal injury arising from the treatment. A contract for medical or dental treatment raises a duty to take reasonable care, the breach of which is negligence, which founds an action based not on contract but on delict.

Dow v Tayside University Hospitals NHS Trust (2006): there can be a contractual relationship in addition to the statutory one between doctor and patient, but only where it was clear that the doctor concerned was exceptionally entering into such a contract.

Roe v Minister of Health (1954): the standard of care in contract and in delict is the same: that is based on reasonableness.

Bonthrone v Secretary of State for Scotland (1987): vicarious liability can exist only in the context of a contract of employment. General medical practitioners are independent contractors whose actions will not be defended by the National Health Service or Secretary of State.

S v Lothian Health Board (2009): action may be taken against a health board based on the work of scientists not employed by the hospital.

Morrison v Forsyth (1995): there is no duty on a doctor to rescue or attempt to rescue a person where the doctor–patient relationship has not already been established and where contact occurs in that context.

Fairlie v Perth and Kinross Healthcare NHS Trust (2004): in general, the duty of care is owed only to a doctor's patients.

Meadows v Khan (2021): the scope of duty included haemophilia but not the autism suffered by the child once born, as the defendant had undertaken only to test for the haemophilia gene, and not responsibility for the progression of the pregnancy.

Kent v Griffiths (2000): in the case of an ambulance service, a duty of care arises when the call is accepted.

Aitken v Scottish Ambulance Service (2011): the Scottish Ambulance Service owed a duty of care to cause an ambulance to attend at the pursuer's house following an emergency call.

Darnley v Croydon Health Service (NHS) Trust (2018): duty owed by medically qualified and administrative staff to take reasonable care not to act in a way that could cause a patient presenting at A&E to sustain physical injury.

Hunter v Hanley (1955): generally, a doctor is negligent if they have been proven guilty of such failure as no doctor of ordinary skill would be guilty of if acting with ordinary care, but the tripartite test applies to deviations from practice: that is, it must be established that there is a usual practice, that the defender did not follow it and that 'the course the doctor adopted is one which no professional man of ordinary skill would have taken if he had been acting with ordinary care'.

R v Adomako (1995): It is for a jury to determine whether a doctor's conduct meets the criminal threshold in cases of the death of a patient.

R v Bawa-Garba (2016): gross negligence manslaughter conviction due to failure to diagnose sepsis.

Transco Plc v Her Majesty's Advocate (No1) (2004): sets out the Scottish test for wicked recklessness in culpable homicide cases.

Bolam v Friern Hospital Management Committee (1957): 'A doctor is not guilty of negligence if he acted in accordance with a practice accepted as proper by a responsible body of medical men skilled in that particular art'.

Maynard v West Midlands Regional Health Authority (1985): where a defender acted in accordance with one of two opposing schools of practice, negligence cannot be found.

Gordon v Wilson (1992): preference for one body of opinion over an equally credible body of opinion is insufficient to establish negligence. The test in *Hunter* v *Hanley* (1955) applies to diagnostic procedures as well as treatment.

Bolitho v City and Hackney Health Authority (1998): it is for the court to determine whether the body of medical opinion relied upon is itself reasonable.

Moyes v Lothian Health Board (1990): 'the appropriate tests in medical negligence cases are to be found in *Hunter* v *Hanley* and *Bolam*'.

Muller v King's College Hospital (2017): the *Bolam* test did not apply to the accuracy of diagnosis in a so-called 'pure diagnosis' case.

Devaney v Glasgow Health Board (1987): the onus of proof is on the pursuer, throughout.

Phillips v Grampian Health Board (1991): evidence of a body of opinion opposing the pursuer's case will be fatal to that case unless it is entirely rejected by the court.

Duffy v Lanarkshire Health Board (2001): decisions of medical professionals must be 'capable of withstanding logical analysis, and be seen as reasonable and responsible'.

Hucks v Cole (1993; opinion delivered in 1968): negligence will be found if a practitioner knowingly takes an easily avoidable risk.

Duffy v Lanarkshire Health Board (2001): life-threatening delay should be weighed against the risk of harmful side-effects of the proposed cure.

Steward v Greater Glasgow Health Board (1976): acting in accordance with medical practice absolves the defender, but failure to seek help when required and where circumstances allow and injury could have been avoided thereby will amount to negligence.

Wilsher v Essex Area Health Authority (1988): all medical staff must meet the standard of competence and experience expected of those holding such posts. The onus of establishing causation rests on the plaintiff.

Andrews v Greater Glasgow Health Board (2019): a junior doctor did not discharge his duty of care by seeking advice from a senior colleague.

Whitehouse v Jordan (1980): errors of judgement can amount to negligence.

Phillips v Grampian Health Board (1991): it is not enough for a pursuer to establish an error of judgement; it must also be established that the error was one that no doctor of ordinary skill would make.

McLelland v Greater Glasgow Health Board (1999): damages may be awarded based on the loss of opportunity for a different outcome had diagnosis been made correctly.

Hotson v East Berkshire Area Health Authority (1987): court could not rule that in no circumstances could a plaintiff succeed by proving loss of chance of a complete recovery, though in this case it was not successful.

Wright v Cambridge Medical Group (2011): loss of chance: a general practitioner who delayed referring a patient to hospital was liable for the permanent injury that was a result of that delay.

Gill's Curator Bonis v Grampian Health Board (1995): the *res ipsa loquitur* doctrine did not apply because the pursuer did not satisfy the criterion that there was no evidence of why or how the harm occurred.

Fairchild v Glenhaven Funeral Services Ltd (2002): causation is a question of fact as to whether the rules of liability have been satisfied.

Kay's Tutor v Ayrshire and Arran Health Board (1987): causation must be established as a matter of medical fact in general scientific terms.

Kenyon v Bell (1953): causation must be established as a matter of medical fact as applied to the particular case. If the cause is uncertain, the pursuer's claim will fail even if there is a material chance that 'but for' the negligence the injury would not have been suffered.

Fairchild v Glenhaven Funeral Services Ltd (2003): causation is a question of fact. The "Fairchild exception" allowed a departure from the "but for" test in material contribution cases.

McFarlane v Tayside Health Board (2000): a child was born following a failed sterilisation operation the risks of which were not adequately explained to the female pursuer. On policy grounds, the court found that the pursuers' failure to have an abortion or to give the child up for adoption could not constitute *novus actus interveniens*.

Sabri-Tabrizi v Lothian Health Board (1998): continuing to have sexual intercourse without contraception constituted a *novus actus interveniens* where the pursuer knew there to be a residual risk of pregnancy.

Kennedy v Steinberg (1998): the triennium runs from the date on which it is reasonably practicable for the pursuer to be aware that the injuries are sufficiently serious to justify bringing an action of damages; that they are attributable to an act or omission; and that the defender was a person to whose act or omission they were attributable.

Clunis v Camden and Islington Health Authority (1997): the court will not let itself be used to enforce obligations that arise from illegal acts.

A v National Blood Authority (2001): Factor VIII blood platelets constitute 'products' under the Consumer Protection Act 1987: '[T]he defect was the virus in the blood and the damage was the virus in the patient'. The causal link was in the science. The development risk defence did not apply where the risk was, or ought to have been, known.

Hastings v Finsbury Orthopaedics Ltd (2022): product liability claim failed because the available statistical data was inadequate to the establishment of 'defect'.

5 CONSENT

As regards the legally competent adult patient, actions in consent follow a pattern common to common law countries and are litigated in negligence. There has been a rebuttable presumption of competence in adults since *Lindsay* v *Watson* (1843). Treatment without consent may be an assault, because the absence of consent forms part of the action in assault (the English law of trespassory touching does not form part of Scots law). Consent gives lawful justification to an overt physical act that would otherwise constitute an affront, and so render the *actio iniuriarum* available to the pursuer, as was observed in *McCallum* v *Morrison* (2023). The onus is on the defender to establish that consent was given by the pursuer. Where this burden is discharged by evidence of consent in broad terms, it may yet be alleged that consent was imperfect. If so, the case will be litigated under the law of negligence where damages will be sought for injuries caused – in the legal sense – by the doctor's failure to obtain complete or 'informed' consent.

This usually means the failure to warn of an inherent risk in the procedure, where the pursuer argues that had they been so warned, they would not have given their consent and would not have suffered the injury. Where Scots law differs is that a possible action for wounded feelings is built into the common law.

This area of law is based on the patient's right to self-determination within the law of delict, as well as within the European Convention on Human Rights. That the right of self-determination forms part of this area of Scots law was confirmed by Lord President Hope in *Law Hospital NHS Trust* v *Lord Advocate* (1996) in which he said that the right solves the problems of consent as far as the court is concerned. As he put it, 'consent renders lawful that which would otherwise be unlawful'. To that end, the defence of *volenti non fit iniuria* is applicable, as it means that a legal wrong is not done to someone who is willing and so voluntarily assumes the inherent risk.

By implication, it is for the patient to determine whether to take a particular risk. The right to consent carries with it a right to refuse treatment. The corollary of the right of the patient is the duty of the doctor. This implies a test for the duty of care which will, as suggested above, be subject to the test in *Hunter* v *Hanley* (1955): the duty to warn of inherent risks forms part of the doctor's duty of care. The failure to inform of a risk may constitute lack of reasonable care. The court in *Moyes* v *Lothian Health Board* (1990) saw it this way: 'Recognition by the doctor of the adult patient's right to make decisions about the risks he incurs is essentially an aspect of the duty to take reasonable care for his safety'.

In the case of adults who lack legal capacity by virtue of their mental incapacity, medical treatment will be justified where it is necessary, such as where the patient is unconscious and hence lacks capacity to consent. According to *Re F (mental patient: sterilisation)* (1990), the doctor may administer medical treatment where it is in the patient's best medical interests: that is, performed either to save their life or to improve their condition. The Scottish Law Commission has indicated that the decision would be followed in Scotland, even though the Court of Session has the option of appointing a tutor dative. Further provisions under the Adults with Incapacity (Scotland) Act 2000 and the Mental Health (Care and Treatment) (Scotland) Act 2003 apply to proxy decision-making by a guardian or welfare attorney with authority to act on the incapable adult's behalf.

Minors who lack capacity by virtue of their age are governed by the Children (Scotland) Act 1995, which confers on parents the general responsibility to safeguard their child's health and represent his interests in medical decision-making. Children reach capacity at the age of 16 in Scotland, but may be capable of medical decision-making before that age. So-called competent minors are governed by the Age of Legal Capacity (Scotland) Act 1991, which creates an exception to the general rule that children under 16 cannot validly consent to medical treatment on their own behalf. They may consent if, in the opinion of the medical practitioner treating them, they are capable of understanding the nature and possible consequences of the proposed treatment.

5.1   ASSAULT AND THE DEFENCE OF CONSENT

5.1.1   Assault

There are two common law categories of consent: to the medical intervention per se, and to the risks inherent in that intervention.

Unlike the English law of trespass to the person, in Scots law the intentional invasion of bodily integrity constitutes an *iniuria*, which is a form of liability in delict based on affront. The Sheriff Court case of *McCallum* v *Morrison* (2023) is illustrative in this respect. The case involved a dentist who had been removed from the Register by the General Dental for failing to comply with dental infection control procedures. The appellant in the Sheriff Court case was a patient at the Cumnock Practice. Following treatment at the practise he was among those who received a letter warning of a low risk of infection by blood-borne viruses. This caused him to become distressed, and later to be diagnosed with an acute stress disorder, due to a concern that he may have contacted a blood-borne virus and passed this on to members of his family. His condition improved following a negative blood test. While the primary focus of the judgment was on the duty of care, which was found not to have been breached, there was also a claim for assault under the *actio iniuriarum*. Although it was available in the circumstance, Sheriff Principal Ross observed that 'there are almost no modern instances of the *actio iniuriarum* being relied upon for a remedy', though it was applied in *Stevens v Yorkhill* (2006) in the absence of a duty of care. In *McCallum* v *Morrison* the sheriff found that the breach of professional guidelines was capable of amounting to an assault, where the affront threatens a person's bodily integrity. However, the case for assault still requires proof of an intention to do harm and a reasonable apprehension of that harm on the part of the victim.

Though not possible on the facts in *McCallum* because the risks were not reasonably foreseeable, Sheriff Ross did concede that intention can be inferred from recklessness, where a person acts in a way that shows indifference to a risk of injury that could have been foreseen. That would render the *action iniuriarum* available. On the facts of the case the court found that there had been consent to treatment at a time when the appellant had no apprehension of any harm, and had not in fact suffered from a blood-borne virus. There was therefore no basis for an action in assault. Even so, the court was reluctant in the absence of modern authority to 'cut across the developed law of negligence' and find civil liability on the part of a doctor for intentional injury to their patient.

While it may make no difference in practise, in the law of delict consent is not seen as a defence to assault, but rather the lack of consent is what constitutes the *iniuria*. This should be distinguished from findings from common law jurisdictions. In *Kelly* v *Hazlett* (1974), for example, the Canadian court found that a lack of proper information communicated by the medical practitioner can vitiate an apparent consent and constitute grounds for liability in battery.

Failure to properly advise can amount to negligence in the common law jurisdictions, as discussed later in this chapter. Indeed, there is English judicial authority in *Chatterton* v *Gerson* (1981) for the proposition that the tort of battery is appropriate where there has been no consent, but that the failure to disclose an inherent risk should be litigated in the law of negligence.

Scottish authority is for the most part confined to the institutional and textbook writers, but the Sheriff Court case of *Thomson* v *Devon* (1899) concurred with the position that treatment without consent constitutes an assault, where a prisoner was vaccinated without his consent. In the unreported case of *Craig* v *Glasgow Victoria and Leverndale Hospitals Board of*

Management (1976), the Court of Session was faced with a case of a man who had consented to exploratory surgery to investigate a swelling thought to be a cyst and to 'any operation the surgeon considers necessary'. In the event, the surgeon found and removed a carotid body tumour, but during the surgery the patient was deprived of oxygen and suffered brain damage. He brought a civil action in negligence and in assault. On the assault allegation, the First Division considered the word 'necessary' to include any operation the surgeon saw as necessary and rejected the further argument that permission was limited to the minor operation discussed before surgery. The case was distinguished from those in which a different operation is performed to correct a different condition from that originally complained of.

As pointed out above, Lord President Hope in *Law Hospital NHS Trust v Lord Advocate* (1996) said that 'consent renders lawful that which would otherwise be unlawful' and, by extension, elides the possibility of an action in assault. This was supported in *Bonthrone v Secretary of State for Scotland* (1987) in the Court of Session, in which the Lord Ordinary observed *obiter* that information to be provided to a patient by a doctor was governed by the normal test of professional negligence in *Hunter v Hanley* (1955).

If the assault is proven, the onus shifts to the defender to establish justification, for example by establishing that consent was given (*volenti non fit iniuria*). This might be contrasted with the English law in which it has been held in *Freeman v Home Office* (1983) that the onus of proving lack of consent in a battery case lies with the plaintiff. This case has, however, been criticised for being inconsistent with other English authority.

Rarely is it possible for a charge of criminal assault to be brought against a medical practitioner, because medical treatment is considered to be exempt, except in extreme circumstances. That is because the doctor is presumed to lack the requisite *mens rea* for the crime of assault. To attack a patient is antithetical to the practice of medicine. An example of conduct as sufficiently improper so as to not qualify as medical treatment is in *Hussain v Houston* (1995), where the doctor was convicted of the indecent assault of three female patients by touching their private parts in a way that was unconnected with their medical complaints.

5.1.2   Voluntary assumption of risk

The defence of voluntary assumption of risk (*volenti non fit iniuria*) is narrow in both English tort law and the Scots law of delict insofar as consent can be inferred from conduct – for example, the offering of an arm for taking blood pressure. This is the case only where there has been no misrepresentation on the part of the medical practitioner because, as a rule, consent must be freely and genuinely given. There is authority in the criminal law in *Hussain* v *Houston* (1995) to the effect that, in the instant case, consent was for a proper medical examination rather than what amounted to the indecent assault of three women patients (who were suffering from complaints unconnected with their genitalia). It remains the case in the civil law that a medical practitioner may not diverge from the treatment to which the patient has agreed to submit.

As *volenti* is a defence to a charge of assault, the burden of proof lies with the defender. In *Winnik* v *Dick* (1984), it was held that where there is a duty of care, successfully proving the maxim (*volenti*) means that the pursuer accepted the risk of the defender's negligence. This will absolve the defender from the consequence. The risk must, according to *Sabri-Tabrizi* v *Lothian Health Board* (1998), be assumed before or at the same time as the negligent omission.

It has, however, been argued that the *volenti* defence has no proper place in liability for the omission to provide information on attendant risks to medical procedures. This is because, the argument runs, the patient does not consent to negligence. Yet it is important to see such matters in the context of the voluntary assumption of risk. This, in turn, depends on the patient having been given adequate information on which to have freely based their consent to assume the risk, and indeed on the existence of a foreseeable risk. On that point it is noteworthy that in *McCallum* v *Morrison* (2023), noted above, the court found that the risk of physical or psychiatric injury was not foreseeable with what the court called 'substantial certainty'.

5.1.3   Criminal responsibility

While consent in broad terms elides the possibility of an action in the nominate delict of assault, further provisions apply to the crime of assault. When the court was considering the appropriate test for medical negligence, Lord Russell noted in *Hunter* v *Hanley* (1955) that 'gross negligence' would be required to denote the level of recklessness required for the criminal law to become involved. This indicated that a substantially higher standard would be required than that required of ordinary *culpa*. Negligence – as tested by the rules set out in Chapter 4 – is insufficient. Medical treatment is unlikely to comprise the level of attack necessary to the offence of the 'real injury' of assault. The contact between doctor and patient would require to be of such an order that it could not be defined as 'treatment'.

In *Hussain* v *Houston* (1995), discussed above, the doctor was convicted of indecent assault because the contact with his patients bore no relation to their actual medical complaints. And in the English case of *R* v *Melin* (2019) it was found that deception as to a person's status as a doctor could amount to deception as regards their identity, which would in turn be capable of vitiating consent.

5.2   NEGLIGENT FAILURE TO OBTAIN INFORMED CONSENT

The onus of establishing that there was a failure to disclose the risks of a medical procedure is borne by the pursuer. This is consistent with the law of damages in which the party bringing the case in negligence bears the burden of establishing the elements of the action, where *damnum*, or loss, is coincident with *iniuria*, or wrongfulness, as necessary elements of proof. It is necessary to prove that the omission to provide particular information was wrongful and that the omission caused or materially contributed to the pursuer's injury. This would be established where the pursuer proves that the omission caused them to not refuse treatment and hence to suffer the risk inherent in the treatment of which warning was not, in fact, given.

5.2.1   Standard of care and wrongfulness

That a duty of care exists between doctor and patient is seldom in doubt and has been considered in Chapter 4 along with the standard of care in negligence. As indicated above, in *Bonthrone* v *Secretary of State for Scotland* (1987) the Lord Ordinary had observed that information to be provided to a patient by a doctor is governed by the normal test of professional negligence set out in *Hunter* v *Hanley* (1955) (the *Bolam* test in England: established by *Bolam* v *Friern Hospital Management Committee* (1957)).

In information disclosure cases, the alleged negligence is not in the performance of the surgical or medical procedure, but in the omission to provide information on inherent risks that is material to the patient's decision whether or not to give their consent.

This means that the adequacy or not of medical information provided to the patient, on which consent was based, was assessed by the courts according to the medical professional standard. However, the debate has for many years been on the relative merits of that standard as contrasted with a standard based on more objective factors unique to the particular patient (see *Arndt* v *Smith* (1997)).

The doctrine of 'informed consent' was developed in the United States; it migrated to Canada, Australia and South Africa, but not until *Montgomery* v *Lanarkshire Health Board* (2015) did it find success as a doctrine in United Kingdom jurisdictions. This is because it holds that the standard of care under informed consent is that of the reasonable patient in the particular patient's position, and on that point UK courts had disagreed.

English law, in *Sidaway* v *Bethlem Royal Hospital Board of Governors* (1985), had found that the professional standard as set out in the *Bolam* judgment was appropriate to information disclosure cases. There was subsequently a trend away from a wholly medical professional standard. For example, in *Bolitho* v *City and Hackney Health Authority* (1998), the court required the medical opinion to be logical and coherent, so diluting the *Bolam* test to some extent. Over time, courts tended towards a less deferential attitude to the medical profession, and in favour of patients' rights. The finding in *Pearce* v *United Bristol Healthcare NHS Trust* (1998) suggested that the courts could be becoming more sympathetic to the view that doctors should disclose information to patients about significant risks, where 'significant' means knowledge that could affect the decision of a reasonable person whether or not to give their consent, which is a matter of causation considered later in this chapter. This trend culminated in the decision in *Chester* v *Afshar* (2005). In that case the House of Lords began with the presumption that standards of information disclosure had become patient-centred.

Until the decision in *Montgomery* there was a paucity of case law on the point in Scotland, but it did indicate a medical professional standard that could have followed the same trend as that in England. In *McLaughlin* v *Greater Glasgow Health Board* (1981), the Sheriff Court dealt with a case of failed sterilisation of a female patient. The pursuer admitted that she had been informed in broad terms, but alleged that she had not been informed of the full implications, to an extent sufficient on which to found her consent. She argued that *Hunter* v *Hanley* (1955) is applicable to the mechanics of the practice of medicine and that a different standard should be applied to information disclosure. The court held that there was nothing in the scope of professional duty that should not be assessed according to *Hunter* v *Hanley*.

The Court of Session considered the issue in *Moyes* v *Lothian Health Board* (1990), in which the patient had a stroke which was a known risk of an angiography diagnostic procedure. This risk was raised in the pursuer's case because of her history of migraine and her hypersensitivity to the contrast medium. There had been a failure to warn of this aggravated risk. The patient failed to prove a hypersensitivity to the contrast medium. She argued unsuccessfully that the test in *Hunter* had been amplified in *Bolam* and modified by *Sidaway* to the extent that a patient has a right to be informed of those risks that would alter their decision on whether or not to give consent. This would have been consistent with Lord Scarman's dissenting judgment in *Sidaway*. Even so, the judgment in *Moyes* did attempt to take a patient-oriented approach through reference to the adult patient's right of self-determination. However, the precedent of *Sidaway* (albeit in English law but heard by the House of Lords) meant that the matter should be assessed according to medical professional criteria. Although the decision in *Moyes* indicated a sympathy towards the patient's position, subsequent case law in Scotland did not initially move in the direction of a patient-centric approach, as was the case in England.

The line of case law from *Sidaway* through *Pearce* and *Bolitho*, came to its significant conclusion in the Supreme Court decision in *Montgomery* v *Lanarkshire Health Board* (2015), in which the court found the decision in *Sidaway* 'profoundly unsatisfactory'. Despite being heard by the United Kingdom Supreme Court, *Montgomery* is a Scottish case that was regarded as persuasive authority by English courts, before its ultimate reception into English law.

The case involved the failure to warn a pregnant woman of the increased risk of shoulder dystocia that could be suffered by the child she carried. That could lead to complications during its birth, including lack of oxygen (hypoxia). That risk was increased in cases of diabetic women who are statistically more prone to carrying larger babies and which, in turn, leads to a higher risk of shoulder dystocia if delivered vaginally. In fact Nadine Montgomery did express concern over the size of her baby, and the risk that it would be too big to deliver vaginally. Dr McLellan, a consultant obstetrician and gynaecologist employed by the Lanarkshire Health Board, did not mention the risk of dystocia and was not specifically questioned in that regard. The consequence was hypoxia and cerebral palsy in the child.

The *Montgomery* decision and its aftermath in effect reversed *Hunter* v *Hanley* and *Bolam* as regards the standard of information disclosure, and adopted Lord Scarman's dissent in *Sidaway*, which dissent ran along similar lines to the Australian decision in *Rogers* v *Whitaker*. Significantly, the decision reflected the then-current General Medical Council guidelines on information disclosure, which meant the law was in effect catching up with professional guidelines. The doctor was to provide such information as the reasonable patient in that patient's position would have required to properly inform their consent.

It is important to distinguish the standard for the duty to disclose from the standard of care in negligent clinical practice, where the latter still employs the test in *Hunter* v *Hanley*. A further distinction might be made on whether the same standard set out in *Montgomery* should also apply to information on alternative treatments. In *McCulloch* v *Forth Valley Health Board* (2023) the Supreme Court was asked to determine whether the test laid out in *Hunter* v *Hanley* was appropriate in respect of whether a particular alternative treatment should have been discussed with the patient. *McCulloch* involved whether a patient who had suffered a heart attack ought to have been advised of the option of a non-steroidal treatment such as ibuprofen. Lord Boyd's judgment in *AH* v *Greater Glasgow Health Board* (2018) was endorsed in *McCulloch*, in finding that the 'professional practice' test in *Hunter* v *Hanley* was appropriate, and the doctor was not under any obligation to discuss a treatment that they did not consider amounted to a reasonable alternative. In this way the court distinguished the patient-centric standard applicable to material risks under *Montgomery*, and the medical professional standard applicable to information on alternative treatments under *Hunter* v *Hanley*.

5.2.2 Causation

The finer points of factual and legal causation have been discussed in Chapter 4. As is the case with any claim in delict and negligence, it is necessary to prove that the legal wrong caused the pursuer's injury. In cases of consent based on information disclosure, there will have been a negligent omission to warn of a risk. The patient will have suffered that risk. To prove a causal link, the pursuer must prove that, but for the defender's omission, they would not have suffered the injury. To do this, the pursuer would need to assert that if they had been given information on the risk – that is, assuming that there had been no omission to provide that information – they would not have given their consent and hence not suffered the injury. It may, however, be sufficient that the pursuer is able to establish that they would not have undergone the procedure *at that time* or performed *by that defender*.

The court did not need to consider causation in *Moyes* v *Lothian Health Board* (1990), because the pursuer failed to establish negligence, although in *Goorkani* v *Tayside Health Board* (1991), the court did consider the test for causation. The pursuer had lost sight in one eye, through Behcet's disease. He had been treated with a drug to prevent blindness in the other eye. The drug carried with it the risk of infertility. It was held that failure to warn of the risk of infertility was negligent, but the pursuer failed to prove that – in weighing up blindness and infertility – he would have refused to take the prescribed medication. Interestingly, he was awarded £2,500 for loss of self-esteem, shock and anger at the discovery of his infertility and the shock the discovery brought to his marital relationship. (This is discussed further below.)

In the English case of *Chester* v *Afshar* (2005), the plaintiff was not warned of the risk of post-operative paralysis following elective surgery to her spine. This risk eventuated. Although she asserted that, with a warning, she would have sought advice on alternative procedures, the judge was unable to make a finding as to whether she would have consented or not. Even if she would have delayed surgery, the risk was a random one (1–2 per cent) and hence the defendant's negligence was not the legal cause of her injury.

Significantly, the court found that causation was to be assessed by reference to the doctor's duty. The injury was within the scope of the duty of information disclosure and was a result of the risk of which it was the doctor's duty to warn. The injury was therefore to be regarded as caused by the negligent omission. This was a departure from traditional causation principles as a matter of legal policy which indicated a move away from medical paternalism and towards patients' rights.

It is arguable that with the trend exemplified in *Chester* v *Afshar* and concluded in *Montgomery* being towards patients' rights, rights of personality should be included. This is supported by the fact that the court in *Moyes* found the position in Scottish information disclosure cases to be reflected in the judgment in *Sidaway*, which was overturned in *Montgomery*. This is reflected in the Scottish Government's partnership approach to consent (2018), which was the emphasis in the *Montgomery* judgment. The court in *Montgomery* took the view that it was not necessary for it to consider whether, if the appellant was unable to establish *sine qua non* causation, she could do so on a different basis in light of the decision in *Chester* v *Afshar* (2004).

5.2.3   Remedies

Ordinarily, in delict and the law of negligence, the award of damages should reflect the pursuer's position had the negligence not occurred. Yet in information disclosure cases – and assuming that the pursuer established that had they known of the risk they would not have undergone the treatment – damages should restore the patient to their position had they undergone no treatment. Without the treatment they would have been unwell. Damages awards tend to not reflect that, but rather to reflect the loss occasioned by the invasion of privacy. On that point, consider the award in *Goorkani* v *Tayside Health Board* (1991), discussed above, which reflected this, even though the pursuer failed to prove causation. It is at least arguable that the decision in *Montgomery*, in moving away from the professional standard of care to one based on personal autonomy, means that the law now supports a right of personality in the disclosure of medical risk cases.

Based on the so-called 'nervous shock' cases in English law, damages for psychiatric injury would not be awarded in the absence of physical injury. In Scots law, however, there is authority in *Stevens* v *Yorkhill NHS Trust and South Glasgow University Hospital NHS Trust* (2006) that the action of *solatium* for wounded feelings caused by an affront to the right of personality lies in the *actio iniuriarum*. However, this case dealt with unauthorised removal of organs (see Chapter 7) where, under the *actio iniuriarum*, the defender's conduct requires to be intentional. It is a moot point whether the *actio* can be developed or extended to cover affront caused by negligence, and following the decisions in *Montgomery*. On the other hand, psychiatric harm that arises from the failure to follow a professional practise, as in *McCallum* v *Morrison* (2023), may be a sufficient basis for an action in assault, as discussed above.

5.2.4 The exception of therapeutic privilege

If a defender can prove that the patient would have suffered psychological disadvantage had the material information been given to them, the defence of therapeutic privilege would be established. In *McLaughlin* v *Greater Glasgow Health Board* (1981), the doctor had explained the sterilisation operation to the pursuer, but had – according to the pursuer – not given her sufficient explanation to enable her to reach a decision on undergoing the operation. The defenders admitted that, ordinarily, it would be good medical practice to advise a patient of the risk of failure and that continued use of contraception would be required, but in this case subjecting the patient to potential anxiety was not sound medical practice. The pursuer's case failed on the strength of the test in *Hunter* v *Hanley* (1955). Similarly, in *Moyes* v *Lothian Health Board* (1990), Lord Caplan observed that clinical judgement may be used to determine whether a patient will be sufficiently alarmed as to be put off the treatment, or whether the level of alarm may render the treatment itself ineffective.

That said, the law has moved on since the judgments in *McLaughlin* and *Moyes*, through cases such as *Chester* v *Afshar* (2005) and indeed *Montgomery* (2015), discussed above. This means that paternalism is less and less acceptable and hence that recourse to therapeutic privilege is appropriate only in exceptional cases.

5.3 LAWFUL TREATMENT OF ADULTS WITH INCAPACITY

In respect of those over the age of 16 years, there is in Scots law a rebuttable presumption of capacity under *Lindsay* v *Watson* (1843), enacted in the Adults with Incapacity (Scotland) Act 2000. The *Lindsay* case involved the administration of the property of a ward by his trustees, and the argument that he (Edwin Lindsay) could not appear in his own capacity on the ground that he was 'of week intellect'. In the first footnote to the case Lord Cuninghame had this to say on the issue of presumed capacity:

These defenders have no legal or official charge or control of Mr Lindsay's person. If he is insane, it has not been legally proved. His sanity, therefore, must be presumed. If he is sane, there is no defence against this action. To proceed on the assumption that he is insane, would be very dangerous indeed.

Incapacity requires to be established under the terms of s 1(6) the 2000 Act. Where a person lacks capacity by virtue of their mental incapacity – permanently, by virtue of their mental health, or temporarily, perhaps by virtue of unconsciousness – treatment may be authorised in certain circumstances. These include necessity and authorisation under the 2000 Act. In these circumstances the treatment must be given in the patient's interests. Section 1(4) sets out the factors that require to be taken into account in determining whether, and if so in what form, an intervention is to be made in respect of a person that lacks capacity.

5.3.1   Common law provisions

5.3.1.1 Necessity

Circumstances of emergency or medical necessity justify treatment without consent. The clearest example is the unconscious patient brought into hospital by ambulance, when they may have given consent to one surgical procedure, but during that surgery another procedure is deemed necessary: *Craig v Glasgow Victoria and Leverndale Hospitals Board of Management* (1976). The requirements for treatment to be lawful are that it is required for the patient's survival, rather than being medically convenient, and that there is a reasonable chance that consent will be given by the reasonable patient in that patient's position.

The English law was set out in *Re F (mental patient: sterilisation)* (1990). Treatment is lawful if it is in the patient's best medical interests, being necessary to save their life, improve their condition or prevent deterioration of that condition. According to the Scottish Law Commission in *Mentally Disabled Adults* (Scot Law Com Discussion Paper No 94, 1991), the decision in *Re F* would be followed north of the border. Indeed, the test in *Re F* was used in *L v L's Curator ad Litem* (1997), as discussed below.

Powers granted to doctors under the Adults with Incapacity (Scotland) Act 2000 are without prejudice to any other law, which may be taken to refer *inter alia* to the doctrine of necessity. The statutory provisions exist in addition to rather than as an alternative to existing provisions, unless otherwise specified. It is likely, however, that recourse should be had first to the provisions of the 2000 Act and if no applicable provision can be found there, recourse can be had to the doctrine of necessity, but this has not yet come before the courts in Scotland.

5.3.1.2 Negotiorum gestio

The so-called Institutes of Roman law are books based on *The Institutes of Justinian and Gaius*, a sixth-century BCE codification of the *corpus juris civilis*, or 'body of civilian law'. The institution of *negotiorum gestio* has been defined in Vol 15, para 87, of the *Stair Memorial Encyclopaedia*:

> In both Roman and Scots law, the legal institution of *negotiorum gestio* may be defined as 'the voluntary management by one person (the *negotiorum gestor*) of the affairs of another (the *dominus negotii*) without the consent or even the knowledge of the other'.

It arises *ex lege*, that is, automatically through the operation of the law. In other civilian and mixed legal systems it has been extended to cover consent to medical intervention, albeit in emergency situations and, as considered further in Chapter 8, may be applicable to the discontinuation of life-prolonging treatment. This is so because, according to Bell, the doctrine works on the 'presumption' that the dominus 'would, if aware of the circumstances, have given a mandate for [the gestor's] interference'.

The doctrine has not yet been extended beyond cases of patrimonial interests in Scots law, so as to cover the preservation of health, or rescue where life is endangered. Even so, in a legal system such as Scots law which has received *negotiorum gestio*, the English doctrine of necessity serves little purpose. Most acts in respect of another's affairs could amount to *negotiorum gestio*, including entering into legal relations.

It is at least theoretically possible that the institution might be extended to cover the situation in which one person acts on behalf of another who cannot give consent because they have been incapacitated by illness or injury from so doing on their own behalf. No reference was made to *negotiorum gestio* in *Craig v Glasgow Victoria and Leverndale Hospitals Board of Management* (1976), above, perhaps because policy considerations limit its extension to situations in which life and personal safety are endangered. Those factors include that the rescuer will not have the intention to charge for their expenses in offering their services, and that other delictual liabilities may arise in respect of the person rescued. Overall, we are not concerned here with a duty to rescue, but rather situations in which one party acts on behalf of another in situations in which the second person is unable to give their consent to a medical intervention, and in which the gestor does so on that person's behalf and to their benefit. The effects will likely be little different from invoking 'necessity' as a defence.

5.3.2   Treatment under the Adults with Incapacity (Scotland) Act 2000

5.3.2.1 Legal history

Prior to the 2000 Act, use was made of tutors dative and tutors-at-law, responsible for the personal welfare of patients incapable of giving consent because of their mental incapacity. *L* v *L's Curator ad Litem* (1997) involved a young woman who suffered from autism. The court appointed her mother (the petitioner) as a tutor dative with power to consent to her daughter's surgical sterilisation. The test in *Re F* was used, that is, the treatment had to be in the patient's best interests, that is being necessary to save their life, improve their condition or prevent deterioration of that condition. The power of the court to appoint tutors dative and tutors-at-law was abolished by the Adults with Incapacity (Scotland) Act 2000. As noted below recourse might be had to the Adults with Incapacity (Scotland) Act 2000 in respect of advance statements, as a method for better understanding a patient's wishes.

Under the now-repealed Mental Health (Scotland) Act 1984, mental health guardians could be appointed by a sheriff. These guardians were normally nominees of the local authority, who could require adults to attend for treatment. They could also require access to be given to doctors, mental health officers and others.

5.3.2.2 Medical treatment and research

The Adults with Incapacity (Scotland) Act 2000 provides for a process by which decisions can be made on behalf of adults who lack legal capacity to make them on their own behalf, by virtue of their mental incapacity. The 2000 Act replaced tutors to adults over 16 years of age with a range of Sheriff Court guardianship and intervention orders. Part 5 of the 2000 Act gives authority to medical practitioners to treat or undertake research on incapable adults under certain circumstances; it also applies to dental practitioners, ophthalmic opticians, registered nurses and prescribed individuals who satisfy certain conditions, following amendments to the 2000 Act made by the Smoking, Health and Social Care (Scotland) Act 2005. In this way, both the vulnerable adult and the practitioner are legally protected.

The certificate of capacity must be in a prescribed form and for a specific period of up to three years if, in the opinion of the person, any of the conditions or circumstances in the 2007 Regulations (2007/100, Reg. 30) apply in respect of the adult. The conditions and circumstances are that the adult is suffering from a severe or profound learning disability, dementia or a severe neurological disorder, such that they are incapable in respect of decisions about medical treatment, and the condition is unlikely to improve.

There is also a code of practice under the Act, which does not have statutory authority but may be used as an example of good practice.

'Incapable' and 'incapacity' are defined in s 1(6) as being 'incapable of acting, making, communicating or understanding decisions or retaining the memory of decisions as mentioned in the Act, by reason of mental disorder or inability to communicate because of physical disability'.

The general principles under s 1 of the Act applicable to an intervention are that:

1. it should achieve a benefit not otherwise achievable;

2. it is the least restrictive option;

3. account is taken of past and present expressed wishes and feelings as far as this is practicable and

4. there is consultation with another specified person or persons, as far as is reasonable and practicable. Specified persons include '[a]ny guardian, continuing attorney, welfare attorney or manager of an establishment exercising functions under [the] Act'.

Part 5 of the 2000 Act requires the involvement of a 'proxy' in decision-making. Under the Code of Practice, a proxy means a 'welfare attorney, person authorised under an intervention order or a welfare guardian with powers relating to the medical treatment in question'.

Welfare attorneys appointed under Part 2 of the Act may authorise medical treatment but may not give proxy consent to certain forms of treatment for mental disorder or place the granter in a hospital for mental disorder against their will.

In some circumstances medical practitioners may require the consent of persons authorised by a welfare intervention order issued under Part 6 of the 2000 Act.

5.3.2.3 Authority of the medical practitioner

Under s 47 of the Adults with Incapacity (Scotland) Act 2000, where a medical practitioner primarily responsible for the patient's care certifies that they are of the opinion that a patient is incapable of making a decision on their own behalf in relation to the treatment proposed, the doctor may do what is reasonable in the circumstances. This authority is in relation to medical treatment and must be to safeguard or promote the physical or mental health of the patient. It may be exercised by someone else appointed by the doctor primarily responsible for the patient's care. There is a prescribed form for the certificate of incapacity. It must specify the period during which the authority will exist. This can be for up to one year. It may be revoked if circumstances change.

This authority does not include or authorise the use of force or detention, unless immediately necessary and only for as long as it remains necessary. Neither does it allow actions inconsistent with an existing court decision.

5.3.3   Authorisation of treatment

5.3.3.1 The parens patriae jurisdiction and proxy consent

As *parens patriae*, the Court of Session may act as the legal guardian of children and incapable adults. As such, it may exercise a common law jurisdiction to protect the interests of those people. It was in that capacity that the court appointed tutors dative, until such tutors were abolished by the Adults with Incapacity (Scotland) Act 2000. Before that, in *Law Hospital NHS Trust v Lord Advocate* (1996), the court found that the scope of the jurisdiction was not defined and neither can it be. The jurisdiction remains important with regard to the withdrawal of life support and as a mechanism to cater for unforeseen circumstances not covered by legislation.

Section 50 of the Adults with Incapacity (Scotland) Act 2000, as amended by the Adult Support and Protection (Scotland) Act 2007 (asp 10), s 59(1), makes provision for medical treatment where a guardian or welfare attorney has been appointed. If authorised under an intervention order, that person or body may have powers in relation to medical treatment. In disagreements between the doctor with primary responsibility for the care of the patient, and the proxy, the doctor is to ask the Mental Welfare Commission to nominate a second doctor to give an opinion. Authority to treat will be given if the second doctor agrees with the first, having consulted with the proxy.

Any person with an interest in the patient's personal welfare may appeal the decision to the Court of Session. This applies to the decision of the first doctor and that of the second. Decisions on medical treatment, other than those made under s 50, may be appealed to a Sheriff Court by any person with an interest in the patient's welfare.

5.3.3.2 Research

The only research permissible on adults legally incapable of giving their consent is research into cause, diagnosis, treatment or care of their incapacity or other treatment administered during their incapacity. Further conditions are set out in s 51 of the Adults with Incapacity (Scotland) Act 2000, as amended by a range of clinical trials regulations. They include that the research is likely to produce a real and direct benefit to the adult or – in exceptional circumstances – where it is likely to improve scientific understanding of the adult's incapacity.

5.3.3.3 Treatment

Provisions for consent to medical treatment are made in both the Adults with Incapacity (Scotland) Act 2000 and the Mental Health (Care and Treatment) (Scotland) Act 2003. The latter created a framework for support for adults with a mental health disorder, whether or not their legal capacity causes them to fall within the ambit of the 2000 Act. The 2003 Act provides for both voluntary and compulsory treatment.

While mental disorder is defined in both Acts as including mental illness, personality disorder and/or learning disability, there are some differences between the two provisions. For example, they differ in their definitions of 'adult' and of 'incapacity', with the 2000 Act including those unable to communicate, while the 2003 Act does not contain that inclusion.

Authority to treat an incapable adult requires a certificate of incapacity under the 2000 Act, although the certificate will not authorise the use of force or detention other than in cases of necessity. Neither will it cover specific treatments such as electro-convulsive therapy or hospitalisation against the adult's will, and following amendments by the Human Tissue (Authorisation) (Scotland) Act 2019 has a range of withdrawal and opt-out options available to them.

However, when the adult is formally detained under the 2003 Act, and assessed as requiring treatment, the treatment must be authorised under the 2003 Act rather than the 2000 Act. Even so, under s 36 of the 2003 Act, those detained under the emergency provisions cannot be treated on a compulsory basis. If consent is required, it should be given by the adult himself or through a certificate issued under the 2000 Act.

5.4   MEDICAL TREATMENT OF CHILDREN

5.4.1   Responsibility of parents

Parents have the responsibility of ensuring that their children receive appropriate medical treatment. This is governed by the Children (Scotland) Act 1995. Based on the right to consent to a 'transaction' on the child's behalf, parents also have the right to consent or refuse treatment on their child's behalf, as long as decisions are taken in the interest of safeguarding the child's health and welfare. This right is that of both parents, as long as it has not been removed from one of them as part of a divorce or custody settlement.

Failure to fulfil this responsibility could expose the parent to the scrutiny of and sanction by child protection bodies.

Under the Children (Scotland) Act 1995, the Court of Session or a sheriff may make a specific issue order requiring a parent to consent to treatment on the child's behalf if that treatment is in the child's interests and the parent has withheld their consent. The Court of Session retains its *parens patriae* jurisdiction over the exercise of parental power, and holds no greater power than the parent of a child that has the requisite decision-making capacity. Referral may be made to a children's hearing that a child is likely to be seriously impaired in their health or development due to lack of parental care. A parental failure to consent to necessary medical treatment falls within this ground for referral. Once a ground for referral is established, the hearing may make a supervision requirement for the child to submit to medical examination or treatment. A compulsory supervision order may include a requirement that the local authority arrange a specified medical or other examination of the child or a specified medical or other treatment for the child, within the meaning of s 87 of Children's Hearings (Scotland) Act 2011.

A child subject to a child assessment order, child protection order, compulsory supervision order, interim compulsory supervision order or medical examination order, which orders examination or treatment, retains the same legal capacity to consent as under the 1991 Act.

5.4.2   Capable children below the age of 16

5.4.2.1 Consent

The Age of Legal Capacity (Scotland) Act 1991 abolished pupillarity and stipulates that the child under 16 lacks capacity to enter into transactions. However s 2(4) of that Act also stipulates that a person under the age of 16 years has the capacity to consent on their own behalf to surgical, medical or dental procedures if, in the opinion of a qualified medical practitioner, they are capable of understanding the nature and possible consequences of the proposed treatment. This is about the child's capacity, without reference to their welfare.

It is important to stress that the omission of 'best interests' from the Scottish legislation is a *prima facie* exception. The rationale is that the child has legal capacity to consent irrespective of considerations of welfare. This was a policy decision by the Scottish Law Commission in its 1987 foundation report. That report concluded that the 'welfare' test would be restrictive, unnecessary and logically incoherent with a scheme in which a child had been found sufficiently mature to give their own consent.

Where there is a disagreement between the mature minor and their parent on the matter of consent, a specific issue order under the Children (Scotland) Act 1995 would not be competent, as the parents lose the right of veto under the 1991 Act where the child has been assessed as competent by the medical practitioner. Neither does the 1995 Act permit a person to give consent on behalf of a child to the storage of gametes under the Human Fertilisation and Embryology Act 1990. That follows the 2008 amendment to the Human Fertilisation and Embryology Act 1990.

Courts in England and Wales take a different approach to competent minors than that taken in Scotland. For a start, in Scotland a person is regarded as an adult for medical decision-making purposes at the age of 16. In England, the age of full capacity is 18. The difference is in the age at which constraints are imposed when it comes to refusals of consent: 16 in Scotland and 18 in England and Wales. Even so, both jurisdictions recognise the child's growing autonomy below 16 by applying versions of the so-called 'Gillick' test in England. On the face of it, the difference between the two jurisdictions is that in Scotland the doctor is not required to make an assessment of whether the treatment is in the child's best interests, and while the rule in Scotland is legislatively articulated, it is a jurisprudential matter in England and Wales.

The court in *Gillick* v *West Norfolk and Wisbech Area Health Authority* (1986) found that a child under the age of 16 may consent to treatment in their best interests where they have sufficient maturity and intelligence to understand the nature and implications of the proposed treatment. This is about the child's welfare as well as their capacity.

5.4.2.2 Refusal

Most commentators in Scotland are of the view that the power to consent carries with it the power to refuse treatment. Courts in England and Wales have taken a different view. It remains to be seen whether it will be followed north of the border when such cases come before the courts. The cross-border differences are worth arguing, but the courts in Scotland have not yet ruled on the matter. In any event, the child's legal representative may act only where the child cannot do so. Indeed, in *Houston, Applicant* (1996) the sheriff found it illogical that the capable minor's decision should be overridden by his parent. Further, the power of refusal is implied in s 90 of the Children (Scotland) Act 1995, which provides that a child's consent to a medical examination is required, even in the presence of a court order or a supervision requirement of a children's hearing authorising the medical examination.

5.4.3   Gender-affirming treatment and recognition

Like the law on abortion, this has become an issue which has been the subject of public protest and activity in both the Westminster and Scottish parliaments. A small number of Gender Identity Services operate in Scotland,
though not on a self-referral basis, and not offering a specialist service for
children under the age of 16 (children and adolescents under the age of 18
are catered for). There is however a clear clinical pathway for those suffering
'gender dysphoria' (the feeling that a person's emotional and psychological
identity is at variance with their birth sex), that may begin with the prescription of puberty blockers to delay the onset of puberty. The Scottish
Government has also funded the NHS Gender Identity Services: Strategic
Action Framework 2022–2024.

This has proved to be a controversial issue due to the view that a prepu-
bescent child will not have the capacity to consent to starting what might
be seen as an inexorable journey towards gender reassignment. The counter
argument is that puberty blockers serve to allow a person time to develop
a better understanding of their gender identity, and to further consult with
health care professionals. In Scotland matters of consent and capacity will fall
under the terms of the Age of Legal Capacity (Scotland) Act 1991, whereas
in England and Wales they fall under the rule in *Gillick*, as considered above.

While there is no Scottish case in point, the judgment in *Bell* v *Tavistock*
(2020) will be instructive on issues of capacity and consent, as well as those
of the quality of information and advice given, and a person changing their
mind on the basis of inferior advice. The High Court considered whether or
not a young person aged under 18 will have the capacity to consent to taking puberty blockers. The court found that a *Gillick*-competent minor would
have that capacity as long as they understood both the nature and consequences taking puberty blockers and of the possibility of later embarking on
a clinical route that would have an impact on fertility and sexual functioning. They would also have to understand a range of surgical and medicinal
side-effects, including those associated with experimental treatments such as
puberty blockers.

It is unlikely, though not impossible, that under the Age of Legal Capacity
(Scotland) Act 1991 s 2(4) a qualified medical professional will believe that
a patient under the age of 16 can comprehend this information so as to find
that they have capacity to consent. The strictness of these conditions reflects
the gravity of the decisions that are involved, and the irreversibility of many
of the medical procedures to be undertaken.

Perhaps more importantly, the issue falls under the terms of the Gender
Recognition Act 2004, which applies to the whole of the United Kingdom.

It sets out the terms under which a person may be legally recognised in their chosen gender.

Under the 2004 Act, in order to apply for a Gender Recognition Certificate that will be issued by a Gender Recognition Panel – whether that be following surgery or not – an applicant must be at least 18 years of age and have lived in the other gender, or have changed genders under the law of a country outside of the United Kingdom. The Panel must be satisfied, based on expert medical evidence from someone practising in gender dysphoria, that the applicant has or had gender dysphoria, lived in the acquired gender for two years and intends to continue to do so until their death. This does not apply if the applicant has undergone or is undergoing treatment to modify their sexual characteristics. Further provision was made in 2014 in respect of the meaning of 'living in another gender'. Statutory declarations are required to be made in respect of whether the person is married or in a civil partnership, and in respect of the consent of their spouse or civil partner to their application for a Certificate.

In March 2022 the Scottish Government introduced the Gender Recognition Reform (Scotland) Bill, which was passed by the Scottish Parliament in December of that year. The Bill never received Royal Assent because the United Kingdom Government took the unprecedented step of bringing a judicial review under s 35 of the Scotland Act 1998 to block the Gender Recognition Reform (Scotland) Bill. In Case: P318-23, *Petition of the Scottish Ministers for Judicial Review of the Gender Recognition Reform (Scotland) Bill (Prohibition on Submission for Royal Assent) Order 2023*, the Court of Session agreed with the UK Government petition to block the bill's submission for Royal Assent. This was on the basis that the bill modified the law on a matter reserved to Westminster.

If Royal Assent had been given, the 2004 Act would have been reformed to reduce the minimum age of applicants from 18 to 16, and the time living in the acquired gender from two years to three calendar months. It would also have dispensed with the requirement for a medical diagnosis of gender dysphoria, and replaced the Gender Recognition Panel with the Registrar General for Scotland for this purpose. As well as those amendments, the bill would have required applicants to undergo three months of reflection and for 16 and 17 year olds to take advice or guidance before making their decision and to have lived in their acquired gender for a period of six months.

Following the judicial review judgment the Scottish Government reasserted its commitment to the terms of the bill, and to negotiate with the UK Government to find a mutually acceptable way forward.

Essential facts

Competent adults

- Treatment of a competent adult patient without their broad consent amounts to the delict of assault.
- There is a rebuttable presumption of competence.
- The omission to provide information sufficient on which to base the patient's consent will amount to negligence. Since *Montgomery* v *Lanarkshire Health Board* this has no longer been governed by the normal test of professional negligence in *Hunter* v *Hanley* (1955).
- The standard of care under *Montgomery* is what information the reasonable patient in that patient's position would have required to properly inform their consent.
- It must be established by the pursuer that, but for the omission to provide the information, they would not have consented to the medical procedure and hence not have suffered the injury.
- The exception of therapeutic privilege may apply where provision of otherwise material information would cause the patient undue anxiety and compromise their treatment.

Incompetent adults

- Treatment of adult patients who lack capacity by virtue of their mental health may be authorised if it is in their best medical interests or is justified by necessity. This is governed by the Adults with Incapacity (Scotland) Act 2000 and the Mental Health (Care and Treatment) (Scotland) Act 2003.
- There may be a common-law basis in *negotiorum gestio* to provide treatment on behalf of adults who lack capacity.

Minors

- Treatment of minors under the age of 16 is subject to the consent of those with parental authority. This is governed by the Children (Scotland) Act 1995.
- Minors under the age of 16 who are mature enough to understand the nature and implications of the treatment or research may consent to or refuse treatment on their own behalf. This is governed by the Age of Legal Capacity (Scotland) Act 1991. A capable minor's decision cannot be overridden by his parent.

- Despite statutory provisions, courts retain a residual *parens patriae* jurisdiction over minors; this power is no greater than that of parents.
- Specific provisions apply under the Gender Recognition Act 2004 to recognition of a different gender from a person's gender at birth.

Essential cases

Moyes v Lothian Health Board (1990): the right of a patient to decide about the risks they take is a part of the doctor's duty to take reasonable care.

Law Hospital NHS Trust v Lord Advocate (1996): the patient's consent renders lawful that which would otherwise be unlawful.

Re F (mental patient: sterilisation) (1990): the doctor may treat the mentally incompetent patient where it is in the patient's best medical interests.

Chatterton v Gerson (1981): the tort of battery is appropriate where there has been no consent; failure to disclose an inherent risk should be litigated in negligence.

Thomson v Devon (1899): treatment without consent constitutes an assault.

Kelly v Hazlett (1976): lack of proper information communicated by the medical practitioner can vitiate an apparent consent and constitute grounds for liability in battery. Failure to properly advise can amount to negligence.

Craig v Glasgow Victoria and Leverndale Hospitals Board of Management (1976): 'necessary procedure' includes any operation the surgeon saw as necessary at the time of surgery; permission was not limited to the minor operation discussed before surgery.

Bonthrone v Secretary of State for Scotland (1987): information to be provided to a patient by a doctor is governed by the normal test of professional negligence in *Hunter* v *Hanley* (1955).

Hunter v Hanley (1955): the standard of care expected is that which the reasonable medical practitioner would adopt in a similar situation

Hussain v Houston (1995): the doctor was convicted of indecent assault because the contact with his patients bore no relation to their actual medical complaints.

Winnik v Dick (1984): where there is a duty of care, successfully proving *volenti non fit iniuria* means that the pursuer accepted the risk of the defender's negligence; this will absolve the defender from the consequence.

Sabri-Tabrizi v Lothian Health Board (1998): risks must be assumed before or at the same time as the negligent omission.

Lindsay v Watson (1843): there is a rebuttable presumption of mental capacity in adults.

Sidaway v Bethlem Royal Hospital Board of Governors (1985): the professional standard as set out in the *Bolam* judgment was appropriate to information disclosure cases.

Bolitho v City and Hackney Health Authority (1998): the court required the medical opinion to be logical and coherent, so diluting to an extent the *Bolam* test; that test is applicable to the causation enquiry.

Pearce v United Bristol Healthcare NHS Trust (1998): suggested courts could be becoming more sympathetic to the view that doctors should disclose information to patients about significant risks, where 'significant' means knowledge that could affect the decision of a reasonable person whether or not to give their consent.

Chester v Afshar (2005): the House of Lords began with the presumption that standards of information disclosure had become patient-centred. Causation is to be assessed by reference to the doctor's duty, as it is a duty to inform of a risk, which failure led to the risk materialising.

McLaughlin v Greater Glasgow Health Board (1981): there is nothing in the scope of professional duty that should not be assessed according to *Hunter v Hanley* (1955). On therapeutic privilege: subjecting the patient to potential anxiety may not be sound medical practice.

Montgomery v Lanarkshire Health Board (2015): overturned the decision in *Sidaway* in support of a subjective patient-centric standard of information disclosure.

McCulloch v Forth Valley Health Board (2023): the doctor is not under any obligation to discuss a treatment that they do not consider amounts to a reasonable alternative, distinguishing the patient-centric standard applicable to material risks under *Montgomery*, and the medical professional standard applicable to information on alternative treatments under *Hunter v Hanley*.

Goorkani v Tayside Health Board (1991): even if the pursuer fails to prove causation, having proved negligence, the court may award damages for *solatium*.

Stevens v Yorkhill NHS Trust and South Glasgow University Hospital NHS Trust (2006): the action of *solatium* for wounded feelings caused by an affront to the right of personality lies in the *actio iniuriarum*.

L v L's Curator ad Litem (1997): the test in *Re F* was used. Treatment must be in the patient's best interests, that is necessary to save his life, improve his condition or prevent deterioration of that condition.

Gillick v West Norfolk and Wisbech Area Health Authority (1986): a child under the age of 16 may consent to treatment in their best interests where they have sufficient maturity and intelligence to understand the nature and implications of the proposed treatment.

Houston, Applicant (1996): it is illogical that the capable minor's decision should be overridden by his parent.

Bell v Tavistock (2020): a high level of understanding is required for *Gillick*-competent minors to be prescribed puberty blockers.

6 CONFIDENTIALITY AND PRIVACY

The ethical standard of confidentiality dates back at least as far as the Hippocratic Oath, which specifies that all information gained in professional practice should be kept secret. In this clause lies the context of the doctor–patient relationship, as well as the obligation. The obligation has been part of Scots law for more than 150 years. Its breach entitles the victim to damages for *solatium*, as well as possible pecuniary remedies.

Although in medical law, 'confidentiality' is a term used in a broad sense that includes privacy, strictly speaking in law there is a difference between privacy and confidentiality. Something is confidential once it has been confided in another party in the context of a relationship in which the obligation arises. Breach of the right to privacy comprises an intrusion into a private sphere. In medical law and practice both elements tend to coexist. Indeed, in the English case of *Campbell* v *MGN plc* (2004), Baroness Hale observed that, 'It has always been accepted that information about a person's health and treatment for ill-health is both private and confidential. This stems not only from the confidentiality of the doctor-patient relationship but from the nature of the information itself'.

Codes of practice have been published for the benefit of medical practice, such as the NHS Scotland Code of Practice *Protecting Patients Confidentiality* (2023). Breach of these codes will serve only as evidence in support of the delict of breach of confidence in civil law. There is, however, statutory provision in the Data Protection Act 1998 and Human Rights Act 1998, which enacts the European Convention on Human Rights, that gives further definition to the right to privacy.

However, the duty of confidentiality is not an absolute. As we shall see, it exists subject to several exceptions such as breach justified in the public interest or by virtue of legal processes.

6.1 MEDICAL PROFESSIONAL STANDARDS

The World Medical Association elaborated on the Hippocratic Oath in its Declaration of Geneva in 1947 to provide for respect for patients' secrets, even after their death. The declaration advocates a right of patients to expect this. If confidentiality were not presumed, the risk is that patients may be less forthcoming in consultation, to the detriment of their care. Yet the declaration anticipates that certain exceptions will apply.

In the context of the National Health Service in Scotland, the Caldicott Framework was introduced in 1999 to cater for a system in which it will not be the medical practitioner who handles the confidential information, but clerical and administrative staff.

6.2 THE CALDICOTT FRAMEWORK

In 1999 the NHS in Scotland adopted, through a Management Executive Letter, the Caldicott Framework for England and Wales following the Caldicott Committee Report of 1997. That Framework recognised that the NHS is increasingly sophisticated and requires the transfer of patient data. It recommended the principles to be followed to ensure that patient-identifiable information is passed among government agencies only under certain conditions. It also recommended the introduction of guardians to ensure that an NHS number is used instead of the patient's name, for example. Any flow of patient-identifiable information should be tested against the following principles:

1.   the use or transfer of information should be justified;

2.   patient-identifiable information should not be used unless necessary;

3.   the minimum necessary patient-identifiable information should be used;

4.   access to patient-identifiable information should be on a 'need to know' basis;

5.   everyone on the clinical and non-clinical staff should be aware of their responsibilities and

6.   every use of patient-identifiable information must be lawful.

The Security Advisory Group for Scotland (CSAGS) was set up, and in 2002 published its *Final Report on Protecting Patient Confidentiality*. The report recommended against legislation giving statutory force to the exceptions to the duty of confidentiality as had been enacted in England and Wales. A National Health Service in Scotland (NHSiS) *Code of Practice on Protecting Patient Confidentiality* has however been published. Scottish Ministers have also issued guidance in the form of the publication *Code of Practice on Confidentiality and Disclosure of Information*. The guidance is provided to contractors who provide services under the three NHSiS primary medical services contracts (general practitioners, for the most part).

6.3   DOMESTIC AND EUROPEAN LEGISLATION

Although guidelines do not have statutory force, some provisions exist that give legislative force to the obligation of confidentiality in certain circumstances. This may have to do with the disease condition, as in the National Health Service (Venereal Diseases) Regulations 1974 or the Human Fertilisation and Embryology Act 2008. It may also impose a more general duty of confidentiality on providers of primary medical services, as in the National Health Service (General Medical Services Contracts) (Scotland) Regulations 2018. For the most part, however, the duty is a common law one, albeit a duty considered in terms of the European Convention on Human Rights (ECHR).

Article 8 of the ECHR provides:

1. Everyone has the right to respect for his private and family life, his home and his correspondence.

2. There shall be no interference by a public authority with the exercise of this right except such as is in accordance with the law and is necessary in a democratic society in the interests of national security, public safety or the economic well-being of the country, for the prevention of disorder or crime, for the protection of health or morals, or for the protection of the rights and freedoms of others.

There may be some conflict with Art 10 on freedom of speech as regards privacy, but Art 8 has built into it some of the exceptions to the general rule. The European Court of Human Rights ruled on Art 8 and medical information in *Z* v *Finland* (1997). The court noted that respect for confidentiality is vital for public confidence in the health service and for the privacy of the patient. If there has been an apparent breach of confidence, it is important for the court to examine carefully the reasons for the disclosure. A three-stage test was set out by the court in order for disclosure to be justified. Disclosure must be:

1. in accordance with the law;

2. in pursuance of a legitimate aim (e.g. public interest) and

3. 'necessary to a democratic society', which later case law found supported exchange of information among government agencies.

Domestic judicial interpretation of privacy and confidentiality under the ECHR is the concern of the common law.

6.4 COMMON LAW PROVISIONS

Because Scottish case law on medical confidentiality is sparse, recourse might be had to the English law, which has in turn had recourse to Art 8 of the ECHR. Scotland is in effect a signatory to the ECHR as a component of the United Kingdom. Art 8 asserts the right to privacy.

The 'equitable wrong' of breach of confidence in English law influenced the Scots delict of breach of confidence. Under both systems, the confider imparts information to the confident where unauthorised disclosure will allow a remedy.

This also applies to third parties who received the information knowing its nature to be confidential. In *X* v *British Broadcasting Corp* (2005), the Court of Session found that knowledge of the confidential nature of the information is to be tested subjectively rather than objectively. In addition, unless the disclosure is defamatory, there is no authority beyond *obiter dicta* for whether an action lies against a third-party disclosure that is *bona fide* or accidental.

6.4.1 The delict/tort of breach of confidence

In the English law, the classic formulation on breach of confidence was set out in the trade secrets case of *Coco* v *A N Clark (Engineers) Ltd* (1968). For an action to succeed, the information must be of a confidential character, disclosed in circumstances giving rise to an obligation of confidence and have been used without authorisation to the detriment of the confider. An equivalent obligation in pre-contractual negotiations was found to have a delictual basis in *Levin* v *Caledonian Produce (Holdings) Ltd* (1975), in which the defender used information that had been disclosed in pre-contractual negotiations. The Lord Ordinary found that the relationship of trust and confidence is based in the law of delict.

The test in *Coco* was reformulated by both the *Spycatcher* case and by the ECHR. In the *Spycatcher* case (*Attorney-General* v *Guardian Newspapers Ltd (No 2)* (1990)), the House of Lords developed the equitable wrong of breach of confidence. It found that the duty arises when the information comes to the knowledge of the confider, where the confidant knew or agreed that the information was confidential. The place of this *dictum* in Scots law has been doubted in *Quilty* v *Windsor* (1999), arguably because it turned breach of confidence into a privacy tort.

In the *Spycatcher* case it was also stressed that the relationship between the parties could give rise to a duty of confidence and that the confident was bound (in equity) by conscience. While the relationship between the parties is important in Scots law, the delict of breach of confidence cannot be based on equity, which does not form part of Scots law in its peculiar English sense of finding remedies where the common law is inadequate to the task.

The final requirement in the *Coco* test of harm to the confider is no longer required in English law (see *Cornelius* v *De Taranto* (2001), discussed below) and Scots law does not require harm other than wounded feelings (also discussed below).

In the *Spycatcher* judgment Lord Goff limited the duty of confidentiality. He found that once the information has entered the public domain, it is no longer confidential in nature. Neither does the duty apply to useless or trivial information. His third limiting factor was public interest: the public interest in disclosure may outweigh the general public interest in maintaining confidentiality. It is this balance which was struck between the right to respect for private life and the right to freedom of expression in Arts 8 and 10 respectively of the ECHR.

6.4.2 Article 8 ECHR

The English law was further developed through the ECHR and s 6 of the Human Rights Act 1998, which comprises the transposition into domestic law of Art 8 of the Convention. In *Campbell* v *MGN Ltd* (2004), the House of Lords found that 'the privacy of personal information [is] something worthy of protection in its own right'. Medical information would fall within the definition of personal information in terms of the Data Protection Act 1998, for example. Article 8 and s 6 apply to Scotland.

In *von Hannover* v *Germany* (2005), the European Court of Human Rights found that, under Art 8 of the ECHR, Member States are under an obligation to protect individuals from interference in their private life by public authorities. States must also ensure protection of private life between and among individuals. The domestic interpretation of the dictum in *von Hannover* came in *Douglas* v *Hello! Ltd* (2005) in which it was held that the State is under an obligation to protect individuals from invasion of their privacy by others. That case concerned the publication of photographs of Michael Douglas and his wife Catherine Zeta-Jones by *Hello!* magazine, against their will and their having already sold the rights to the pictures to *OK!* magazine. As regards the factors to be taken into account to determine the extent to which the public interest outweighs the general rule that hearings should be privately held, the Court of Protection in *W* v *M (An Adult Patient)* (2012) listed among other factors whether other convention rights are engaged, in particular Article 10.

There is some debate as to whether the effect of Art 8 should be a direct one in the domestic law or whether it should be an 'indirect horizontal' one – that is, Art 8 should be given expression through the law of delict in Scotland or equitable wrongs in England. While the importance of Art 8 is stressed by the courts, there remains a tendency to resort to breach of confidence as the cause of action rather than using Art 8 directly as the cause of action.

6.4.3 Invasion of privacy and breach of confidence

The 'right to privacy' is understood to be the right to protection of personal information. This is different from confidentiality. Some information is inherently private. Once it is divulged in confidence, it becomes confidential too. This will be the case within the doctor–patient relationship. An action for breach of confidence, therefore, will not necessarily protect all private information. This is because some private information will already be in the public domain and hence not subject to confidentiality, yet still worthy of protection under Art 8. This was the case in *Douglas* v *Hello! Ltd* (2005), in which it was found that non-consensual photography of an individual in a public place could amount to an invasion of privacy. It would not, however, amount to a breach of confidence, although unfortunately in that case, the court had to 'shoe-horn' the invasion of privacy into an action for breach of confidence.

This raises the question of what information is 'confidential' and what information is 'private'. In English law the judgment in *Attorney-General* v *Guardian Newspapers Ltd (No 2)* (1990) was developed in *A* v *B plc* (2002). The latter case found that a duty of confidence arises when a party subject to the duty 'knows or ought to know that the other person can reasonably expect his privacy to be protected'. In *Campbell* v *MGN Ltd* (2004), the court found that this also applies to the balancing of Arts 8 and 10 (privacy balanced against free speech). The duty of confidentiality arises when the publisher knows or ought to know that there is a reasonable expectation of confidence. The reasonable expectation of privacy discussed in *Douglas v Hello Ltd* (2005) demonstrated the two-stage process that asks first whether the claimant had a reasonable objective expectation of privacy, and if so, whether that expectation is outweighed by other considerations such as the public interest. This two-stage test was endorsed by the Supreme Court in *Bloomberg LP* v *ZXC* (2022).

Significantly, there is no requirement for there to have been a prior confidential relationship. In *Douglas* v *Hello! Ltd* (2005), it was found that the nature and form of the information may be sufficient for the obligation to arise.

Certain types of information are recognised as confidential, such as medical information within the doctor–patient relationship. There are limits to considering medical information inherently confidential, however. According to the Court of Appeal in *Campbell* v *MGN Ltd* (2004), information on medical treatment is not the same as information regarding attendance at Narcotics Anonymous in the case of Naomi Campbell. The House of Lords, however, found that for there to have been a breach of confidence, the information disclosed must be private in nature and be information the claimant wants to protect. Because Naomi Campbell's treatment for drug addiction was about her physical and mental health, and her treatment, information about those matters was similar in nature to private and confidential information. It was therefore worthy of protection, as the assurance of confidentiality was essential to effective treatment.

6.4.4 Striking a balance between privacy and freedom of expression

In *Campbell*, the court said that once information is deemed private, a balance should be struck between the individual's right to privacy and the public interest in publicity. These rights are reflected in Arts 8 and 10 of the ECHR, respectively. It is important to consider various facets of this balancing act and the provisions that will allow or prevent disclosure of otherwise private information.

6.4.4.1 Freedom of expression

In *Reynolds* v *Times Newspapers* (2001), Lord Steyn considered freedom of expression to be the rule rather than the exception, with interference requiring justification. However, in balancing Arts 8 and 10, freedom of expression is not given any prior weighting. This is despite the fact that Art 10 includes the freedom to 'receive and impart information and ideas without interference by public authority and regardless of frontiers'. Article 10 does, however, specify that the right carries with it responsibilities and duties, with Art 10(2) providing for 'preventing the disclosure of information received in confidence'.

6.4.4.2 Risk to third parties and detriment

Breach of confidence may be justified where there is a risk of harm to third parties or in the public interest. This is reflected in the General Medical Council guidelines on patient confidentiality, as well as in the case law. The scenario envisaged by this exception is one in which a crime may be prevented by disclosure. The GMC argues that patient consent to disclosure should ideally be sought.

In the English case of *W* v *Egdell* (1990), a psychiatric patient (W) who had been convicted of five manslaughter charges sought a transfer to a less secure facility. This required a medical report, which was produced by Dr Egdell. The report was unfavourable, contending that W remained dangerous and psychopathic. For this reason, the report was withdrawn by W's solicitor. Dr Egdell, however, passed his report on to W's hospital and W sued for breach of confidence. The court held that two public interests should be balanced against one another: the interest in confidentiality against the public interest in public safety.

In this case the interest in public safety prevailed, but the court found that disclosure has limitations. For example, it cannot be to the press or widely disseminated, but channelled to the correct public authority. It is also important that the risk is a real one.

The case of *Coco*, discussed above, required the element of harm to the party whose information is disclosed, in order for their claim in breach of confidence to be successful. It is difficult to envisage what harm might have been suffered by W had the court found the disclosure unjustified. Whether detriment to the complainant was required in medical confidentiality cases was settled in *Cornelius* v *De Taranto* (2001). In that case the disclosure itself was considered detrimental to the claimant even although the use of the disclosed report did not cause the claimant any other detriment.

This is not dissimilar to the position in Scots law in which an action would lie in *solatium* for wounded feelings arising from disclosure of private information. This would not require proof of patrimonial loss, as was the case in *AB* v *CD* (1904); *sub nom Watson* v *McEwan* (1905).

6.4.4.3 HIV-positive health care workers

The issue of HIV-positive health care workers challenges the balance between the public interest in confidentiality against public interest in disclosure. In *X* v *Y* (1988) the court had to consider whether a newspaper was entitled to publish the names of two doctors with AIDS. Although, under the National Health Service (Venereal Diseases) Regulations 1974 the health authority must take steps to ensure confidentiality, the newspaper argued that disclosure was justified in the public interest. On the grounds that AIDS patients should feel uninhibited in attending for treatment and that the risk of transmission was negligible, an injunction preventing publication was granted.

6.4.4.4 Unauthorised disclosure

There is some debate as regards the proper place for the cause of action in English law, where a confidence is breached. Traditionally regarded as an equitable wrong, there has been argument that the action should be in tort or in unjust enrichment (in the case of invasions of privacy through commercial publication, for example). What is clear in both English and Scots law is that courts are required to give effect to both Art 8 and Art 10 of the ECHR. This was made clear in *Douglas* v *Hello! Ltd* (2005). The court also found that it was unsatisfactory to 'shoe-horn' privacy actions into breach of confidence even although it is arguable that Art 8 acts to separate the two actions.

6.4.4.5 The actio iniuriarum and disclosure of medical records

In Scots law, breach of confidence, and the misuse of private information, is a delict, and courts are required to give effect to Art 8 on privacy. This was recognised in *Lord Advocate* v *Scotsman Publications* (1989). Yet it is unclear what direction the law is likely to take in this area. It is possible that Scots law could develop along similar lines to English law, using existing delictual categories or developing new categories. There is also authority for arguing that an action may lie in *solatium* for hurt feelings or affront under the *actio iniuriarum*. This would be a comfortable fit, given the ruling in *Stevens* v *Yorkhill NHS Trust and South Glasgow University Hospital NHS Trust* (2006) and other case law. *Stevens* was discussed in Chapter 5. The court found that the action of *solatium* for wounded feelings caused by an affront to the right of personality lies in the *actio iniuriarum*. However, this case dealt with unauthorised removal of organs rather than a breach of medical confidence or invasion of privacy.

Yet the *actio iniuriarum* sets out to protect rights of personality or *dignitas*, and includes protection of autonomy, privacy and confidentiality. It is also able to co-exist with the nominate delicts, including breach of confidence. For these reasons, it is arguable that Scots law will, when the time comes to rule on the matter, find little difficulty in accommodating Art 8 of the ECHR within the civilian tradition, because the *actio* is a rights-based action that requires to balance competing rights, such as may be required between Arts 8 and 10. Courts would, however, still be required to apply the European Convention on Human Rights.

6.4.4.6 Action against third parties

While *Lord Advocate* v *Scotsman Publications Ltd* (1989) did not determine when the obligation of confidence arises, it is a *prima facie* obligation. In that case Lord Keith of Kinkel found that 'Scots law in this field was the same as that of England'. Confidentiality is also an implied term of a contract, where there is one, or a consequence of the legal relationship between doctor and patient, where there is not (see *AB* v *CD* (1904), discussed above). The question arises as to when the obligation can be imposed on third parties outwith the doctor–patient relationship.

Where confidential information is passed to a third party in breach of confidence, this does not mean that the information is in the public domain and hence that the duty of confidence falls away. There is still an obligation on the third party to keep the information confidential. In *Lord Advocate* v *Scotsman Publications Ltd* the court found this to be the case where the information was known by the third party to be confidential in nature and was received from a source other than the confider.

It was an open question as to whether the obligation applied to third parties who received the information without knowing it to be confidential. In its 1984 Report on *Breach of Confidence*, the Scottish Law Commission pointed out that one of the situations in which an obligation of confidence arises in respect of a third party is where a reasonable person in the circumstances would have realised that the information was confidential in nature. This may be due to the circumstances of disclosure of the nature of the information, such as medical records. In *Quilty* v *Windsor* (1999), the court found the action against a third party to be irrelevant in the absence of evidence that the documents in question had been transmitted in confidence by the hospital authorities, or were obtained by the defender in the knowledge that they had been communicated to him in breach of an obligation of confidence. There is support for this position in *Osborne* v *British Broadcasting Corp* (2000). As for cause of action, once again, the *actio iniuriarum* may be appropriate as it arises from an affront following unauthorised disclosure of private information.

In *X* v *British Broadcasting Corp* (2005), the 17-year-old pursuer had agreed to be filmed in a television documentary about criminal court proceedings. She then withdrew her consent, seeking reduction of the 'contributor's agreement' she had signed and an interdict against broadcast of the film. The defender argued that the information was in the public domain, as the actions that were filmed had taken place in a public place and material in a social services report read out in an open court. The court, however, found that the balance of Arts 8 and 10 fell in the pursuer's favour, as the personally important information was not readily available or in the public domain. This may appear odd, as the interdict was granted for breach of confidence, yet Art 8 is about a right to privacy.

The *actio iniuriarum* was invoked following unauthorised disclosure of medical records by a third party in *Russo* v *Hardey* (1997), which further underlines that the *actio* has a role to play in the protection of privacy. The pursuer in this case was a party litigant and disclosure arose during litigation.

The general practice had sent records of both mother and son to the solicitor acting for the mother. On realising the error, the records were demanded back. They were sent back but the copies made were retained and used. The son alleged that the solicitors had wrongly used their records, albeit having obtained them by mistake. Proof before answer was allowed. It was found that the law recognises a duty of confidentiality on third parties and that the duty was a delictual one which could found an action for *solatium* alone.

6.5   EXCEPTIONS TO THE GENERAL RULE

It was pointed out earlier in this chapter that, as well as a balance having to be struck between privacy and freedom of expression, the duty of confidentiality is not without exceptions. These are discussed below and range from express consent of the patient to justification in the public interest.

6.5.1   The health care team

Although clinical data should not be processed without the consent of the patient, their consent may be explicit or implicit. On confidentiality, the General Medical Council acknowledges the role that implied consent plays in what would otherwise be a breach of confidence, through the sharing of personal data among members of the health care team. This is necessary in the interests of the patient's care but, according to the GMC booklet on confidentiality, the doctor is required to ensure that the patient is aware that his information will be shared with other health care professionals engaged in that patient's care. This may involve professionals in the organisation primarily involved in the patient's care or information shared among various organisations, as may be the case if the patient is referred to a specialist unit. If the patient objects, this should be respected except if that will pose a risk to others and to the general public. In any event, it is important that where information is passed to other health care professionals, this is done on the understanding that it is confidential in nature.

6.5.2   Clinical audit and express consent

The same principles applying to the health care team also apply to clinical audit, which is necessary in the provision of health services. Again, it is important that the patient is made aware that his personal information will be used in clinical audit and that he consents to that use. The information should be anonymised where possible and practicable but, where this is not possible or practicable, express consent should be given to the use of that data in clinical audit.

Express consent is also required for the disclosure of personally identifiable data used in research and administration. But once data is anonymised, it is no longer considered confidential, according to *R* v *Department of Health, ex parte Source Informatics Ltd* (2000).

6.5.3 Legal processes requiring disclosure

In some instances the law will require disclosure of personal medical information. For example, some statutes expressly require notification of certain diseases and an action brought following personal injury would almost necessarily require disclosure of the nature of that personal injury.

6.5.3.1 Legislation

The most obvious examples of statute not just allowing but compelling disclosure of medical information are the Infectious Diseases (Notification) Act 1889 and the Public Health (Scotland) Act 1897, which were repealed by the Public Health etc (Scotland) Act 2008, but the 1897 Act continues to have effect for the purposes of section 101 of the National Health (Scotland) Act 1978 (protection of health boards and common services agency). Sections 13–16 of the 2008 Act place a duty on medical practitioners to notify health boards of any suspicion of the presence of a range of diseases and pathogens. The list includes certain 'notifiable' diseases such as cholera, plague, relapsing fever, smallpox and typhus, and other diseases in 'epidemic proportions', now including COVID-19. The name, age, sex, address and occupation of the patient are to be notified. Similar provisions apply under the Misuse of Drugs (Supply to Addicts) Regulations 1997, and the Abortion (Scotland) Regulations 1991.

In addition, there are statutes that require the provision of certain information to government bodies. For example, under regulations subordinate to the Medical Act 1983 and the National Health Service (General Medical Services Contracts) (Scotland) Regulations 2018, medical practitioners are required to maintain records pertaining to patient care and to provide certain information to health boards when required to do so. This exception may therefore be seen in the light of that concerning information passed among members of the health care team.

Some statutes require a doctor to supply regulatory, investigative or governmental bodies or the NHSiS with information relating to patients, for example Fitness to Practise investigations, or that may assist the registrar in carrying out their functions.

Under the Scottish Public Services Ombudsman Act 2002, where the Ombudsman is investigating a health service body – as one of the 'listed authorities' falling within its purview – it may require listed authorities to supply information or produce documents relevant to the investigation, including patient records. Patient consent should first be sought for disclosure of identifiable information, although the GMC recognises that in some circumstances disclosure without consent may be justified, such as under the public interest exception.

6.5.3.2 Litigation

Under both the common law and the Administration of Justice (Scotland) Act 1972, disclosure of personal data is justified for the purpose of enabling litigants to prove their averments in civil proceedings. This may be necessary in both criminal (assault) and personal injury litigation. Even so, objections may be raised on the ground of confidentiality or indeed public interest immunity. For example, in *P* v *Tayside Regional Council* (1989), a foster mother contended that she had contracted hepatitis B from a child placed in her care by a local authority. She applied for disclosure of the child's hospital records. The court rejected the defender's claim to public interest immunity on the ground that the public interest in justice outweighed that in confidentiality and that it would require a weighty public interest to prevent a party from litigating in favour of confidentiality.

Although the information exchanged between doctor and patient is privileged, this does not exempt the medical practitioner from being required to give evidence in litigation. This is settled practice in the law of evidence, and applies to both criminal and civil hearings, and is required to be considered in light of Art 10 of the ECHR. In addition, Part 2 of the Data Protection Act 2018 permits the processing of personal data to assist in the detection and prosecution of crime, among the listed public interest exceptions.

6.5.4 The *incapax*

Discussion of breach of confidence and the patient's consent raises questions surrounding the position of incapable adults and capable minors. In general, similar principles apply to these persons that apply in consent generally, as discussed in Chapter 5.

6.5.4.1 Minors under the age of 16

As a general principle, both children and adults have a right to confidentiality, which includes information on medical matters as well as information held by carers and social workers. This takes on particular importance when it comes to competent minors and information kept confidential to the exclusion of their parents. While there are some similarities, the test for whether the competent minor is entitled to confidentiality is not the same as that applied to consent of competent minors.

A minor may wish that information on contraception or abortion be kept confidential. The court would not find this problematic where that minor has attained sufficient capacity under the Age of Legal Capacity (Scotland) Act 1991. Where, on the other hand, the minor has not met the test of competence under the 1991 Act, they would not have had the capacity to enter into that confidential relationship in the first place. In this instance the obligation of confidentiality would be in place only in exceptional circumstances and disclosure should be only to an appropriate third party, such as an advocate or carer.

6.5.4.2 Incapable adults

Although the GMC advice is the same for incapable adults and minors, the Adults with Incapacity (Scotland) Act 2000 allows the medical practitioner primarily responsible for the patient's care some specific authority. This includes an authority to do what is reasonable in the treatment of the incapable adult, where 'treatment' is broadly defined as 'any procedure or treatment designed to safeguard or promote physical or mental health'. The prescribed conditions which other health care professionals must satisfy are set out in the Adults with Incapacity (Requirements for Signing Medical Treatment Certificates) (Scotland) Regulations 2007. Disclosure is therefore justified if it is in the patient's medical interests. Refusal may require an appropriate certificate of incapacity, although consent may, under the 2000 Act, be given by the patient's proxy. It should be borne in mind that during the passage of the 2000 Act, the Scottish Parliament specifically rejected the language of 'best interests' in favour of terminology such as interventions that will benefit the adult, or authorisation of the least restrictive treatment option available.

6.5.5 Specific categories

Particular provisions as to disclosure of otherwise confidential information apply to specific categories of person. These categories include possible victims of abuse or neglect, the deceased patient and genetic information that may also apply to parties other than the patient. These are often around questions of confidentiality within the family.

(The right of confidentiality between spouses exists even in the instance of an abortion, because there is no right of veto under the Abortion Act 1967.)

6.5.5.1 Victims of neglect or abuse

Where a doctor is aware of or suspects abuse or neglect by a family member, the GMC advises that the doctor must pass on this information to an appropriate authority or responsible person. This is done in the patient's best interests, but where it is felt disclosure would not be in the patient's best interests this should be discussed with an experienced colleague. This right to report is not a duty to do so, although the GMC advises that the police or social workers should be contacted.

6.5.5.2 The deceased patient

Confidentiality should be maintained even after the patient's death. However, the obligation is flexible and depends on circumstances, including any directions from the patient before their death. Under the Access to Health Records Act 1990, their personal representative is allowed access to the health records of the deceased made after 1991, as is anyone who may have a claim arising out of their death. Relatives and successors may fall within this category.

6.5.5.3 Genetic information

Because genetic information may apply to a patient's relatives too, the issue is a complex one. Several genetic conditions, such as cystic fibrosis, fall into the category of information which may be of interest to the patient's family, as disclosure may affect their decisions as to raising a family themselves or to have embryos screened before implantation. In such situations, a balance should be struck between the patient's interest in confidentiality and the public interest in limited disclosure, where family members are also members of the public.

6.5.5.4 Disclosure of medical information about parents of adopted children

Under the Adoption and Children (Scotland) Act 2007 the Scottish Ministers may make regulations that provide for the disclosure of information about the health of the natural parents of a child who is, may be or has been adopted. The person to whom the information is disclosed must have a duty of confidentiality in relation to the information. Regulations were passed in 2009 in this regard, under which neither the child nor the adoptive parents of that child have an automatic right to access information about the health of the child's natural parents. Yet where the adoption agency has been unable to find information on genetic or transmissible disease in the adopted child's natural parents, a medical practitioner holding such information must disclose it to the agency upon request. The information must be added to the child's medical record and treated by the agency as confidential.

6.5.5.5 Anonymised data

In *R* v *Department of Health, ex parte Source Informatics Ltd* (2000), the applicant was a company which collected data on prescribing habits of general practitioners and sold this on to pharmaceutical companies. The data was anonymised first, by removing patient-identifiable data such as name, address and postcode. The Department of Health issued guidance to the effect that disclosure amounted to a breach of confidence. The company sought a declaration that the policy was wrong. The court held that disclosure was not a breach of confidence provided that the patients were not identifiable. As long as patients' autonomy was not compromised and their privacy not put at risk, and they had no property in the information or right to control its use.

6.5.6 A duty to breach confidence

It has been considered whether, on the basis of some American jurisprudence, a situation could arise in which there is a duty to breach confidence in some circumstances. The American jurisprudence arose from the case of *Tarasoff* v *Regents of University of California* (1976). In that case, a university medical centre was found liable for not warning a woman that her former boyfriend had expressed violent feelings towards her during therapy. He went on to kill her and he was convicted of first-degree murder in *People* v *Poddar* (1973).

According to what became known as the '*Tarasoff* doctrine', there is a duty on a third party to breach confidentiality where the patient poses a threat to the third party who is the foreseeable victim of violence. The doctrine has been developed subsequently to apply to damage to property in *Hedlund* v *Orange County* (1983); to general unspecific victims in *Lipari* v *Sears* (1980); and to arson in *Peck* v *Counselling Service of Addison County* (1985). In 1985 the California legislature codified the doctrine to prevent a slippery slope.

It is considered that such a slippery slope would not be permitted in Scots or English jurisprudence because the doctrine, through its development, dispensed with the requirement of foreseeability, which is a strict requirement in tort and delict. For the wrong of a party to be actionable, a duty of care must first exist. In the scenarios of the American jurisprudence, foreseeability and proximity were insufficient to give rise to a duty of care in Scots law. This is clear from the line of nervous shock cases such as *Alcock* v *Chief Constable of South Yorkshire Police* (1992). *Tarasoff* was considered by the

Bench in *Palmer* v *Tees Health Authority* (1999). It was found that in cases of harm to third parties, for liability to arise in negligence, an identifiable class of victim should exist, yet the question was left open regarding the position where the victim themself was in fact identifiable or identified.

This kind of situation arose in *ABC* v *St George's Healthcare NHS Foundation Trust* (2020), which involved the duty to disclose genetic information to a third party, that is, a non-patient of the doctor in question. The doctor knew of their patient's diagnosis with Huntington's disease, and that there is a 50 per cent risk that any child would inherit that gene. The claimant in this case was the patient's pregnant daughter. He refused permission for medical staff to disclose his diagnosis to his daughter even though the two had both attended family sessions and he knew of her then pregnancy.

Her argument was that had she been informed she would have been tested and terminated the pregnancy had the gene been passed to her foetus. It was not known whether her child had inherited the gene or the disorder due to the practice of not testing for late onset diseases. The claimant brought an action in negligence and under Art 8 ECHR.

Significantly the court found that she was owed a public interest duty of care to breach confidentiality, which is a duty already laid out in professional guidelines. There was however found to be no breach of that duty.

6.6 REMEDIES

Disciplinary action by the General Medical Council should not be underestimated, as the consequences to the medical practitioner's career may be serious. Yet that cannot be considered a remedy open to the patient whose confidence has been breached. Although there are several options open to the patient, none will be able to undo the wrong, as is the case in medical negligence more generally. Nonetheless, the basis for a remedy in Scots law lies in delict.

6.6.1 Interdict

A patient may apply for an interdict where they are aware of imminent disclosure. This is a commonly sought remedy, but is of little or no use after disclosure. In allowing an interim injunction, courts must have due regard to the human right to freedom of expression, as discussed above. Scots law has no equivalent of the English 'super injunction' preventing defenders from publishing any information other than giving information about the nature of the content.

6.6.2 Delivery or destruction

Because medical records are owned by the NHSiS, they cannot be vindicated by the patient or their delivery demanded. They may be destroyed where they are incorrect or false, however.

6.6.3 Financial damages

This remedy may be available where, for example, the patient suffered nervous shock that was foreseeable as a consequence of the breach of confidence. However, according to *Levin* v *Caledonian Produce Holdings Ltd* (1975) (a non-medical case), the measure of damages is the market value, which would not be high in the case of ordinary patients, but may be high in the case of celebrities.

6.6.4 Damages for *solatium* and patrimonial loss

There may be grounds for an award of *solatium* for wounded feelings following unauthorised disclosure, and to patrimonial loss that may be attributed to the wrongful use of the confidential information, according to *Pine Energy Consultants Ltd* v *Talisman Energy (UK) Ltd* (2008). There is justification for the *solatium* claim in the judgment in *AB* v *CD* (1904), discussed above, as the Scottish Law Commission found that case to be authority for disclosure causing wounded feelings to be a justifiable head of damages. In *Hardey* v *Russel and Aitken* (2003) the *actio iniuriarum* was invoked as a remedy for wounded feelings arising from the unauthorised disclosure of NHSiS medical records relating to the pursuer.

6.6.5 Recompense

Where the defender has been unjustifiably enriched through the disclosure of confidential information, a remedy for recompense may be open to the pursuer. There is a justification for this in *Levin* v *Caledonian Produce Holdings Ltd* (1975).

6.6.6 Statutory protection of trade secrets

Trade secrets are protected by UK statute in the form of the Trade Secrets (Enforcement, etc) Regulations 2018, which provides for a number of remedies, including delivery or destruction, and payment of recompense. The information is required to be defined as a secret under the regulations, and is unlikely to apply to the doctor–patient relationship by virtue of the requirement to have a commercial value due to its secrecy.

6.7   ACCESS TO MEDICAL RECORDS

Medical practitioners are required by regulations to maintain records of patient examinations and to ensure that those records are accurate and accessible. Patients, on the other hand, have certain rights of access to those medical records. These rights exist by virtue of several directives and conventions, such as the European Convention on Human Rights and Biomedicine. They also exist by virtue of domestic statute, from the Data Protection Act 1984 to the Access to Medical Reports Act 1988, the Access to Health Records Act 1990 and latterly the Data Protection Act 2018, and the United Kingdom General Data Protection Regulation 2016. On this basis a data subject has a right to information on the purposes for which their data are being processed, and those persons who will have access to their data. The data may be withheld if in the opinion of the relevant health professional providing access, that provision is likely to cause them or another person serious harm. This covers data held on living and deceased persons. That access is an Article 8 ECHR entitlement was confirmed by the European Court of Human Rights in *MG* v *United Kingdom* (2002), although the right can be circumscribed by the interests of third parties. The ECtHR in *KH and Others* v *Slovakia* (2009) found that the right must be given practicable effect.

Rights of access may also be allowed by virtue of the common law. While the records themselves are owned by the NHS or the general practice, the patient retains the right of access to the information in the records and may obtain a copy upon payment of a fee.

6.7.1   The common law

Common law access may be justified by virtue of the litigation process discussed above as a reason for breach of confidence. It appears, however, that there is a rebuttable presumption against a right of access. *Boyle* v *Glasgow Royal Infirmary and Associated Hospitals* (1969) involved an action in damages raised by a couple following the death of their daughter. Their argument was that the mother had a right of access by virtue of having been a patient at the hospital. This argument was rejected, as the value of the records was in advancing medical science as well as in the interests of the patient's care. It was not in the patient's best interest to allow access as of right. It is certainly arguable that the position has moved on since that case, particularly by virtue of statute.

6.7.2   The Data Protection Act 2018

The passing of the European General Data Protection Regulation (GDPR) 2016/679 meant that the Data Protection Act 1998 was repealed by the Data

Protection Act 2018, which provides a new legal framework for data protection, in conjunction with the United Kingdom General Data Protection Regulation (UK GDPR). Its subject-matter is reserved to Westminster under Sch 5 to the Scotland Act 1998. It has the aim of protecting privacy. Before the 1998 Act, access was governed by the statutes mentioned above. The Data Protection Act 2018 came into force on 25 May 2018.

6.7.2.1 The six data protection principles

There were eight data protection principles and several data protection terms that were introduced by the 1998 Act. These were carried over into the General Data Protection Regulation (GDPR) and hence Chapter 2, s 34 of the Data Protection Act 2018 on the UK GDPR. Medical records are covered by the provisions of the definition of Sensitive Personal Data in s 8 on medical care. Terms used in the 2018 Act have the same meaning as those in Art 4 of the GDPR. As such 'personal data' is information relating to a directly or indirectly identified or identifiable natural person, who will be the 'data subject'; 'processing' applies to any operation(s) performed on personal data, be it 'collection, recording, organisation, structuring, storage, adaptation or alteration, retrieval, consultation, use, disclosure by transmission, dissemination or otherwise making available, alignment or combination, restriction, erasure or destruction'. A 'controller' is the natural or legal person, authority or agency the determines the purposes and means of data processing, and a 'processor' is a 'natural or legal person, public authority, agency or other body which processes personal data on behalf of the controller'.

Albeit heard before the passage of the 2018 Act, according to the English case of *Durant* v *Financial Services Authority* (2003), to fit within the definition of 'personal data', the data must not simply be capable of identifying the individual, but must impact on the data subject's privacy or have the subject as the focus of the data. In addition, the 'filing system' in question must be of a high standard (using a system of cataloguing and indexing, for example). If the persons or the data involved do not fall within the definitions in the Act, the Act will not apply.

Data controllers (the practice or health authority) must, in the processing of sensitive personal data, adhere to the following principles set out in Art 5 GDPR, carried over from the 1998 Act, insofar as personal data shall be:

1. processed lawfully, fairly and transparently in relation to the data subject;

2. collected for specified, explicit and legitimate purposes and not further processed in a manner that is incompatible with those

purposes, apart from archiving in the public interest, or for scientific or historical research or statistical purposes;

3. adequate, relevant and limited to what is necessary in relation to the purposes for which they are processed;

4. accurate and, where necessary, kept up to date, having regard to the purposes for which they are processed;

5. kept in a form which permits identification of data subjects for no longer than is necessary for the purposes for which they are processed; and stored for longer periods insofar as the personal data will be processed, and stored solely for archiving purposes in the public interest, or for scientific or historical research purposes and

6. processed in a manner that ensures appropriate security of the personal data, including protection against unauthorised or unlawful processing and against accidental loss, destruction or damage.

6.7.2.2 Access rights and exemptions

Section 7 of the 1998 Act gave patients rights of access to obtain copies of their personal data. The 1998 Act was repealed and replaced by the Data Protection Act 2018, which assimilated the United Kingdom General Data Protection Regulation (UKGDPR) in the European Parliament and Council (EU) Regulation 2016/679. Rights of access are contained in Ch III (arts 12–23), as amended by the Data Protection, Privacy and Electronic Communications (Amendments etc) (EU Exit) Regulations 2019. These provisions were carried over into Ch 3 of the 2018 Act. The data subject has the right of confirmation of whether their personal data is being processed, and to have access to that data, including information as to other recipients of that data. These applications are referred to as subject access requests (SARs).

SARs may be made in writing, verbally or electronically, or by a third party on behalf of the data subject. There should be no fee for this provision and the data should be supplied within one month, in an intelligible and accessible format, which includes an explanation of terms and abbreviations and interpretation of slides and X-ray films.

The data subject has a right to request rectification and erasure, and the controller has an obligation to inform them whether the request has been granted or refused, and the reasoning for the latter if that is the case. The controller may restrict the right of access, wholly or partly, where this is necessary and proportionate in the interest of public safety, national security or to protect third parties, and must record the reasons for any restrictions.

The right of access is subject to certain exemptions, including if the request is manifestly unfounded or excessive, or where the request is malicious.

The Secretary of State may create such exemptions and has done so under the Data Protection Act 1998 in the case of the Data Protection (Subjects Access Modification) (Health) Order 2000, which allowed an exemption where access to the sensitive personal data would be likely to cause serious harm to the physical or mental health of the data subject or a third party. A further example applied to the Human Fertilisation and Embryology Act 1990. Access may be refused where another individual may be identified through that access, unless that individual has given their consent. This will not preclude provision of that data in an anonymised form which does not identify that individual. A court may be required to determine the reasonableness of this course of action. Account should be taken of the duty of confidentiality, steps taken to obtain consent and the person's capacity to give it, and whether there was an express refusal by that person. The possibility that disclosure may cause harm to the individual should also be taken into account.

6.7.2.3 Third party rights

According to s 55 of the 1998 Act, third parties must not knowingly or recklessly obtain or attempt to obtain access to another person's personal data without the data controller's consent. This protected both the patient as data subject and the doctor as data controller. The exemption of necessity applied where, for example, disclosure is necessary for the prevention of a crime. Similarly, a public interest exemption applies. A person who reasonably presumed entitlement to access was also exempt from the prohibition. Contravention is an offence, as is selling the data or offering it for sale. This was repealed by the 2018 Act.

Offences relating to personal data are now set out in s 170 of the 2018 Act, and include a third party obtaining, disclosing or retaining personal data without the controller's consent, procuring that data from another person or offering to sell that data. It is a defence to show that the person acted in the reasonable belief that they had the right to do as they did, or had the consent of the controller. As if respecting ECHR Art 10 rights, it is also a defence to act with a view to publishing the material 'by a person of any journalistic, academic, artistic or literary material, and … in the reasonable belief that in the particular circumstances the obtaining, disclosing, procuring or retaining was justified as being in the public interest'.

6.7.2.4 Remedies

Certain remedies for improper processing of data exist. These map on to those for breach of confidence discussed above. Under s 13 of the Data Protection Act 1998, a person whose data is processed by the data controller contrary to the Act is entitled to compensation if they suffer damage or distress thereby. This may occur where processing of sensitive personal data is done that is not done in the interest of the data subject. Breaches envisaged in the Act were where processing is done for 'journalistic, artistic or literary' purposes. With this in mind, damages could have been on a compensation basis for the value of the data or on a *solatium* basis following distress caused by improper processing. These provisions were carried over into sections 167–169 of the 2018 Act under the UK GDPR. Following a successful application by the data subject, a court may order compensation on much the same basis, paid by the processor or controller, unless the latter can show they were not responsible for the event that gave rise to the damage.

A Sheriff Court or the Court of Session may also make an order that requires steps to be taken to secure compliance with the legislation, including doing so within a particular time frame.

In addition, if the data are inaccurate, the subject may under sections 46–48 apply for an order for their rectification or erasure, in keeping with the six principles set out above. The court would order rectification or replacement and destruction of the inaccurate record, or simply the addition to the record of a statement correcting the data.

6.8   FREEDOM OF INFORMATION

Confidentiality and freedom of information are two sides of the same coin. The Freedom of Information (Scotland) Act 2002 grants a right of access to all types of information held by Scottish public authorities. This right is subject to exemptions, such as the information being confidential in nature, or disclosure falling within the public interest exception. The Act also imposes certain compliance obligations on public authorities, which includes all health bodies under the NHSiS umbrella.

Access is allowed to information that public authorities are under an obligation to disclose, unless it was obtained by the public authority under an obligation of confidentiality. Being two sides of the same coin, there is no obligation to divulge information that is the subject of the Data Protection Act 2018, although difficulties may arise as to which data falls within which category. These may need to be resolved by the Information Commissioner and may in turn be appealed to the Court of Session.

Essential facts

Medical professional standards

- The duty of confidentiality dates from the Hippocratic Oath and the Declaration of Geneva and has been given effect in the common law.
- The standards of the medical profession have been set out in guidance published by the General Medical Council.
- Scottish Ministers have also published guidance on confidentiality in the medical profession.
- Guidelines do not have statutory force.
- The duty of confidentiality is a common law one, but must be considered in terms of the European Convention on Human Rights.

Domestic legislation and the ECHR

- Article 8 of the Convention provides that everyone has the right to respect for their private and family life, home and correspondence. This may not be interfered with by a public authority other than in accordance with the law.
- Article 10 may be in tension with Art 8 as it concerns freedom of expression.
- For disclosure of confidential information to be justified, it must be in accordance with the law, in pursuance of a legitimate aim and 'necessary to a democratic society'.

Common law provisions

- Scotland is in effect a signatory to the ECHR as a component of the United Kingdom, in which the Human Rights Act 1998 enacts the Convention. It is for the Scottish courts to determine matters relative to the Convention.
- Under English law, breach of confidence is an equitable wrong.
- Under Scots law, breach of confidence is a nominate delict.
- The tort of breach of confidence was set out in a line of cases leading to *Attorney-General* v *Guardian Newspapers Ltd (No 2)*, which found that the duty of confidence arises when the information comes to the knowledge of the confider, where the confidant knew or agreed that the information was confidential. The relationship between the parties could give rise to a duty of confidence. The confident was bound (in equity) by conscience.
- The requirement of harm to the confider is no longer required.

- The English law was further developed through the ECHR and s 6 of the Human Rights Act 1998, which comprises the transposition into domestic law of Art 8 of the Convention. In *Campbell* v *MGN Ltd* (2004) the House of Lords found that 'the privacy of personal information [is] something worthy of protection in its own right'.
- While the relationship between the parties is important in Scots law, the delict of breach of confidence cannot be based on equity, which does not form part of Scots law.
- Pursuers in Scotland may have a remedy through the *action iniuriarum*, which protects personality rights (*dignitas*) against invasion through the action of *solatium* for wounded feelings caused by the affront of invasion of privacy.
- *Douglas* v *Hello! Ltd* (2005) held that the State is under an obligation to protect individuals from invasion of their privacy by others under Art 8.
- The Data Protection Acts offer a statutory level of protection of confidential information where medical records are classed as 'sensitive personal data'.
- The 'right to privacy' is different from confidentiality. A balance requires to be struck between privacy and freedom of expression. Some information is inherently private. Once it is divulged in confidence, the recipient is bound by an obligation of confidentiality. Certain types of information are recognised as confidential, such as medical information within the doctor–patient relationship.

Exceptions to the general rule

- Breach of confidence may be justified by freedom of information, risk to third parties, the public interest and public safety, disclosure among members of the health care team, the data having been anonymised, clinical audit and express consent, and legal processes requiring disclosure (legislation and litigation).
- Similar principles that apply to the *incapax* and the capable minor, in the law on capacity and consent, apply to those persons in relation to confidentiality.
- Provisions as to disclosure of otherwise confidential information apply to specific categories of person including possible victims of abuse or neglect, the deceased patient and genetic information that may also apply to parties other than the patient.

- The American *Tarasoff* doctrine (requiring breaches of confidence in certain circumstances) does not directly apply in Scots law, but may do following *ABC v St George's Healthcare NHS Foundation Trust* (2020), where duty of care to a non-patient was based on proximity and foreseeability, and Art 8 ECHR.

Remedies

- Disciplinary action by the General Medical Council should not be underestimated, as the consequences to the medical practitioner's career may be serious.
- Further remedies include interdict, delivery or destruction, financial damages, damages for *solatium* and recompense.

Access to medical records

- Medical practitioners are required by regulations to maintain records of patient examinations and to ensure that those records are accurate and accessible.
- Patients have certain rights as regards access to their medical records by virtue of the principles of the Data Protection Act 1998, that were carried over into the European General Data Protection Regulation, which was in turn carried over into the Data Protection Act 2018. These provisions give patients the right to access and obtain copies of their personal data, which must be communicated in an intelligible and permanent form, except where supply in a permanent form is impossible, would involve 'disproportionate effort' or where the subject agrees, or has sought the information digitally.
- The right of access is subject to certain exemptions such as the public interest.
- Third party rights of access may be permitted only if the request is made on behalf of the data subject.
- Certain remedies for improper processing of data exist. These map onto those for breach of confidence.

Freedom of information

- The Freedom of Information (Scotland) Act 2002 grants a right of access to all types of information held by Scottish public authorities, subject to exemptions such as the information being confidential in nature.
- There is no obligation to divulge information that is the subject of the Data Protection Act 2018.

Essential cases

Z v Finland (1997): breach of confidence is justified if disclosure is in accordance with the law, in pursuance of a legitimate aim and necessary to a democratic society.

X v British Broadcasting Corp (2005): third-party knowledge of the confidential nature of the information is to be tested subjectively rather than objectively.

Campbell v MGN Ltd (2004): 'the privacy of personal information [is] something worthy of protection in its own right'. Medical information would fall within the definition of personal information; this can include information on treatment for drug addiction as it relates to physical and mental health. The duty of confidentiality arises when the publisher knows or ought to know that there is a reasonable expectation of confidence. This test can be used to balance Arts 8 and 10 (privacy against free speech) of the ECHR.

Douglas v Hello! Ltd (2005): the State is under an obligation to protect individuals from invasion of their privacy by others. There is no need for a prior relationship of confidence for the obligation to arise; the nature and form of the information may be sufficient.

W v M (An Adult Patient) (2012): listed factors to be taken into account to determine the extent to which the public interest outweighs the general rule that hearings should be privately held.

Reynolds v Times Newspapers (2001): freedom of expression is the rule rather than the exception; interference requires justification.

W v Egdell (1990): public interest in confidentiality must be balanced against public interest in safety to justify disclosure of otherwise confidential information.

Cornelius v De Taranto (2001): disclosure itself was considered detrimental to the claimant, even although the use of the disclosed report did not cause the claimant any detriment.

AB v CD (1904), *sub nom* **Watson v McEwan (1905)**: an action would lie in *solatium* for wounded feelings arising from disclosure of private information. This would not require proof of patrimonial loss.

X v Y (1988): on the grounds that AIDS patients should feel uninhibited in attending for treatment and that the risk of transmission was negligible, an injunction preventing publication of the names of two doctors with AIDS was granted.

Stevens v Yorkhill NHS Trust and South Glasgow University Hospital NHS Trust (2006): there is support in the case for the use of the *actio iniuriarum* to justify damages for *solatium* for wounded feelings flowing from a breach of confidence.

Levin v Caledonian Produce (Holdings) Ltd (1975): the relationship of trust and confidence is based in the law of delict.

Lord Advocate v Scotsman Publications Ltd (1989): in Scots law, breach of confidence, and the misuse of private information, are delicts. A duty of confidence applies to third parties where the information was known by the third party to be confidential in nature and was received from a source other than the confider.

Quilty v Windsor (1999): the action against a third party for breach of confidence must contain evidence that the information was transmitted in confidence or was obtained by the defender in the knowledge that it had been communicated in breach of an obligation of confidence.

R v Department of Health, ex parte Source Informatics Ltd (2000): anonymised data is no longer considered confidential, as long as the patient's autonomy was not compromised and their privacy not put at risk, they had no property in the information, or the right to control its use.

Durant v Financial Services Authority (2003): to fit within the definition of 'personal data', the data must impact the data subject's privacy or have the subject as the focus of the data. The 'filing system' in question must be of a high standard.

MG v United Kingdom (2002): confirmed Art 8 entitlement to access to one's personal data, circumscribed by the interests of third parties.

KH and Others v Slovakia (2009): the right of access to personal data must be given practicable effect.

Pine Energy Consultants Ltd v Talisman Energy (UK) Ltd (2008): following unauthorised disclosure of confidential information there may be a claim for patrimonial loss, but this must be attributable to the wrongful use of the confidential information.

7 THE HUMAN BODY AND TRANSPLANTATION

This chapter is concerned with the ownership and control of the human body and human tissue, including issues of property law, organ donation and transplantation, post-mortems and xenotransplantation. It is concerned with both the living human body and the body after death but before cremation or burial, in respect of both the entire human body and parts of the human body. This chapter will also deal with the controversies around the issue of organ retention and unauthorised post-mortem examinations. The various causes of action and remedies will be considered where applicable.

7.1 TRANSPLANTATION

Transplantation of human organs is regulated by a recently reformed statutory regime that significantly changed the mechanism of consent to organ donation. This was done by amending the Human Tissue (Scotland) Act 2006 (the 2006 Act). As this is an area devolved to the Scottish and Welsh legislatures, there are slight differences between the Human Tissue (Authorisation) (Scotland) Act 2019 (the '2019 Act') and the Organ Donation (Deemed Consent) Act 2019 that applies to England and the Human Transplantation (Wales) Act 2013 that applies in Wales. These differences will be pointed out where relevant, but the focus will be on the system as it applies in Scotland.

Under s 1 of the 2006 Act, Scottish Ministers are under a duty to support and develop transplantation programmes and to ensure that measures are in place regarding the supply, storage and use of donated body parts. What is new in the 2006 regime (s 2) is that there are powers for Ministers to provide financial and other support to those providing transplant services or services related to transplantation. Further provisions allow for co-operation with authorities in England and Wales in the provision of services.

The 2006 Act makes provision for transplantation, research, authorisation (by the deceased) and offences in connection with human organ transplantation. These provisions in the 2006 Act on the *use* of body parts for those purposes do not, however, apply in the following circumstances, which will be discussed further below:

(1) activities conducted under procurator fiscal authority;

(2) removal of body parts during a post-mortem;

(3) retention of tissue samples or organs in certain circumstances set out in the 2006 Act; and

(4) removal, retention or use of body parts of persons who died more
     than 100 years before the coming into force of s 3 of the 2006 Act.

The surgeon removing the body part must be satisfied, on physical examination, that the patient is dead. The 2006 Act does not specify how this is to be
established, but does stipulate that it may be established only by a registered
medical practitioner or someone authorised by regulations to do so. (The
definition of death is discussed further in Chapter 8.) It is also necessary to
obtain consent from the procurator fiscal for the donation to proceed, in
order to ensure that the body is no longer required for the procurator fiscal's
purposes. The appropriate authorisation must have been given for the donation. There is no longer any role under the terms of the 2006 Act for the
person in lawful possession of the body.

7.1.1   Dead bodies

The use of parts of a dead body for transplantation or research is governed
by the terms of the 2006 Act as amended. Until the passage of the 2019 Act,
the transplantation of human organs and tissue was governed by a so-called
opt-in system. The opt-in system required parties donating organs to actively
and voluntarily opt in to the organ donation system. The new opt-out system, in contrast, is based on presumed consent to post-mortem use of organs
and tissue.

Opt-out systems operative in different countries may be 'hard' or 'soft',
where 'soft' denotes a presumed consent but still considers the wishes of
relatives, as is the option favoured by most European countries that use a presumed consent system. It was the option favoured by the Scottish Parliament
in the 2019 Act. Subject to exceptions discussed below, including the absence
of an opt-out declaration, adults are deemed to have authorised the removal
of body parts after their death and the use of those organs for transplantation.
A registered medical practitioner needs first to establish that life is extinct
(the legal definition of death is discussed in Chapter 8 of this book). If the
person removing the organ is not a registered medical practitioner, that person must be satisfied that a registered medical practitioner has examined the
body to confirm that life is extinct. A registered medical practitioner may
authorise any suitably qualified and trained person to remove body parts for
the purposes of transplantation or research.

Due to the need to account for technological advances, the term 'body
parts' is preferred to 'organs'. Those organs are subject to 2012 regulations
based on European legislation on quality and safety, and there are also 2019
provisions that allow removal from, and use of, body parts from the deceased
for the purposes of quality assurance.

Deemed consent will not apply if information is provided by a person in a 'qualifying relationship' with the deceased, that would lead a reasonable person to conclude that the donor would not have consented.

7.1.2   Adults

7.1.2.1   Deemed authorisation for transplantation

The Human Tissue (Authorisation) (Scotland) Act 2019 amended the Human Tissue (Scotland) Act 2006 to provide for a so-called soft 'opt-out' system of organ and tissue donation for the purposes of transplantation. Under a soft opt-out system an adult is deemed to have authorised the removal and use of parts of their body after their death, for transplantation purposes, where at the 'relevant time' there is no express authorisation for removal of body parts and no opt-out declaration in that respect. 'Relevant time' for these purposes is set out in s 17K(2) of the 2006 Act, added as s 27(4) of the 2019 Act. In relation to a living person, it means when, in the view of a health care worker primarily responsible for the person's medical treatment:

i.   the person is likely to die imminently (including as a result of the withdrawal of life-sustaining treatment);

ii. the person is receiving life-sustaining treatment, and the decision to withdraw that treatment has been taken by that health worker; *and*

iii. in the case of a person who is 12 years of age or over, that health worker is of the view that the person is incapable by reason of ill health of making a decision about the removal and use of a part of the person's body for a purpose of transplantation, research, etc.

In relation to a deceased person, 'relevant time' means immediately before the person's death.

These provisions do not apply to those not ordinarily resident in Scotland for at least 12 months before the relevant time. Those persons are called 'non-resident adults', and are discussed below. Neither do they apply to adults incapable of understanding the nature and consequences of deemed authorisation, or to certain excepted body parts. These are listed in 2020 regulations and include the brain, reproductive organs, spinal cord, parts of limbs and muscle and nervous tissue.

Deemed authorisation provisions also do not apply to particular parts of the adult's body if a person has given evidence to a health worker that would lead a reasonable person to conclude that the adult's most recent view was that they were unwilling for that body part to be used for transplantation.

7.1.2.2 Express authorisation and withdrawal

S 3 of the 2006 Act was amended by s 5(2)(a) of the 2019 Act to allow for express authorisation to remove and use one's body parts for transplantation, research, education and training, or for audit or quality assurance. This must be in writing if it is for transplantation, or orally if given to the register organisation. The same rule applies to its withdrawal, which will also take place if the adult makes an opt-out declaration, or if a person gives evidence to a health care worker that would lead a reasonable person to conclude that the adult's most recent view is an unwillingness to have their organs removed for one of the purposes mentioned above. An express authorisation in force at the relevant time takes precedence over any authorisation for a post-mortem examination.

7.1.2.3 Opt-out declaration and withdrawal

Similarly, by virtue of the 2019 Act, adults may declare that they do not authorise removal and use of a part of their body after their death for transplantation or any of the other purposes such as search and audit. This 'opt-out declaration' must be in writing or expressed orally if it concerns transplantation, and in writing for any other purpose. It remains in force until it is expressly withdrawn. As is the case with express authorisation, an opt-out declaration may be regarded as withdrawn if a person provides evidence to a health care worker that would lead a reasonable person to believe that it is not in line with the adult's most recent view on removal and use of the body part for the purpose specified.

7.1.3 Nearest relative

The introduction of deemed authorisation provisions and the amendments to the 2006 Act had the effect of allowing authorisation to be given by the potential donor's nearest relative, before or immediately after their death.

7.1.3.1 Definition

The definition of 'nearest relative' is an established hierarchy, which means that recourse should be had initially to the person at the top of the hierarchy and, if they are unavailable, to the persons progressively lower down the hierarchy. The definition is the same as the 2006 Act, which was not amended by the 2019 Act; it is similar to that in the Mental Health (Care and Treatment) (Scotland) Act 2003, but differs from the provisions in the Human Tissue Act 2004 for England and Wales, which gives equal weight to pairs of people (such as parent or child; stepfather or stepmother). The hierarchy in Scotland with respect to the deceased adult is as follows:

1. spouse or civil partner;

2. cohabitee;

3. child;

4. parent;

5. brother or sister;

6. grandparent;

7. grandchild;

8. uncle or aunt;

9. cousin;

10. niece or nephew;

11. friend of long standing (undefined in the 2006 Act).

Half-blood relationships can be treated as whole-blood relationships and step-relationships as natural relationships, although, where there is more than one person in a given category, preference will be given to whole-blood and natural relationships over half-blood and step-relationships respectively.

7.1.3.2 Authorisation by the deceased or by their 'nearest relative'

It is an offence to remove a body part for use for transplantation, research, etc., without authorisation, but defensible if the accused shows a reasonable belief that authorisation had been given. The offence carries a penalty of up to 12 months' imprisonment or a fine of up to level 5 of the standard scale (£5,000) or both, on summary conviction. Conviction on indictment is subject to up to three years' imprisonment or a level 5 fine or both.

In recognition of the fact that many people express wishes to friends and family during their lifetime – be it verbally or in writing – the 2006 Act set up a system of authorisation. If a person wants to authorise organ donation after their death, they may register their name on the NHS Organ Donation Register, although even this step will not guarantee that their intentions are clear. Authorisation may be given by an adult prior to their death and may be given verbally. If desired, it may be in writing. If there is an authorisation in force immediately before the adult's death, it will take precedence over a post-mortem examination authorised by that adult or by another person.

Problems emerge where a person has not communicated their wishes as regards organ donation after their death. The 2006 Act provides for a system of authorisation by the deceased's 'nearest relative' as defined in the Act. This is allowed under s 7 under certain circumstances such as there being no prior authorisation already in place.

The nearest relative may also give authorisation for a non-resident adult or adult incapable of understanding deemed authorisation. This applies where there is at the relevant time no express authorisation in force by the adult and no opt-out declaration, and the relative has no actual knowledge that the adult was unwilling for the body part to be removed and used for transplantation or was incapable of making a decision about that process. The relative must be satisfied that the adult was not unwilling for the body part to be removed and used for transplantation.

The same requirements apply where a provision is made in respect of an adult incapable of understanding the nature and consequences of the deemed authorisation, along with the additional requirement to have regard to the adult's past wishes and feelings in as much as they are reasonably ascertainable. This also applies to excepted body parts as discussed above and is subject to the same conditions.

Deemed authorisation applies only to the removal and use of body parts for transplantation. Yet the adult's nearest relative may after their death authorise the removal and use of body parts for the purposes of research, education and training, subject to the same conditions.

The authorisation given by the deceased's nearest relative must be in writing and signed, or given orally to a health worker; the authorisation may not be withdrawn. Authorisation cannot be given where the nearest relative is aware that the deceased was unwilling for their organs to be donated for transplantation. It is not competent to draw an inference of unwillingness from an absence of a positive declaration.

For authorisation by a nearest relative to be valid, the medical practitioner must be satisfied that the views expressed verbally do in fact apply to the deceased and that they authorise the removal of their organs for transplantation. The practitioner must keep a record of the proceedings.

7.1.3 Children

The same principles apply to the consent to organ donation of children between the ages of 12 and 16 as apply to consent and confidentiality. They may authorise organ removal after their death for transplantation, research or audit, but this must be done in writing and may be withdrawn by the child but only in writing. Authorisation given to a register organisation may be given orally or in writing; if authorisation is given in this way it may be withdrawn orally or in writing. If authorisation is for one of the purposes other than transplantation it must be in writing. Under the 2019 Act, the child may make an opt-out declaration which will render the original declaration to have been withdrawn. That opt-out declaration may itself be withdrawn by the child.

The same provisions that apply to adults also apply to the child in respect of their most recent wishes. Authorisation is treated as withdrawn if a person provides information to a health worker that would convince a reasonable person that the child's most recent view was an unwillingness to donate.

As with adults, that authorisation takes precedence over authorisation for a post-mortem examination.

Unless aware of the child's unwillingness for their organs to be so used – and in the absence of written authorisation by the child – the person with parental responsibilities may give authorisation. That person may also make the same decisions as may be made by a person in the position of nearest relative. Authorisation by the person with parental responsibilities or the child's nearest relative must be in writing and signed, or given to a health worker and, except for the purposes of transplantation, may be withdrawn. It must be in respect of that child and made when the child is older than 12. It is subject to the same conditions as apply to nearest relatives: that there is no opt-out declaration in force and there is no actual knowledge that the child's most recent view was of unwillingness for their organs to be removed for transplantation or other purposes under the 2006 Act.

Authorisation on behalf of children under 12 years of age for use of part of the child's body for transplantation, training/education, research or audit or quality assurance may be given by the person with parental responsibilities for that child at the relevant time. It must be in writing and signed. The same conditions apply to children under 12 as apply to those over 12 in respect of knowledge of the child's most recent view and that they would be not unwilling for their organs to be so used after their death. Where there is no one with parental rights and responsibilities to authorise removal and use of the child's body parts after their death, or if that person is incapacitated, the legislation sets out a list of persons able to give authorisation in such circumstances. The list includes a person who had been recently involved in that child's upbringing, a grandparent or a sibling; such persons are ranked in the same sequence as nearest relatives.

Section 13 of the 2006 Act provides for the preservation of organs after removal and for maintaining the body in a condition that will allow transplantation. Preservation of this sort must take place in a National Health Service facility and permits only the least invasive techniques. This provision does not apply to research, audit and training, although tissue samples may be removed for the purpose of determining the organ's viability (tissue typing).

7.1.4   Pre-death procedures relating to transplantation

7.1.4.1   Procedures and the duty to inquire

Because part of the rationale for the 2019 reforms was to increase organ transplant rates, provisions have been put in place to further support this policy initiative. They take the form of pre-death procedures and a duty on health carers to make specific inquiries into those procedures. Those inquiries deal with the authorisation procedures as set out above in respect of authorisation for transplantation, but this time in respect of the pre-death procedures.

The procedures themselves are medical and ethical. A procedure may be carried out only if it falls into one of two types A and B, and only if the health worker carrying it out considers that certain requirements are met, and has no knowledge that the person was unwilling for it to be so carried out. Types A (routine medical, e.g. taking blood samples or X-rays) and B (more invasive, e.g. biopsies) procedures are set out in the 2020 and 2021 Regulations respectively. They were added to s 16 of the 2006 Act.

Authorisation for those procedures may be given by the person themselves or the nearest relative or indeed a person with parental rights and responsibilities; these follow the same requirements as set out above. Again, regard is to be had to constructive knowledge of the person's most recent views and any retraction made. As these are pre-death procedures the requirements as set out in the amended s 16 of the 2006 Act are:

1.   the person is likely to die imminently (including as a result of the withdrawal of life-sustaining treatment);

2.   where the person is receiving life-sustaining treatment, the decision to withdraw that treatment has been taken by that health worker;

3.   the carrying out of the procedure is necessary to ascertain the suitability of the part of the person's body for transplantation or to increase the likelihood of successful transplantation;

4.   the carrying out of the procedure is not likely to cause more than minimal discomfort to the person and

5.   the carrying out of the procedure is not likely to harm the person.

7.1.4.2   Standards of quality and safety of human organs intended for transplantation

The 2012 Regulations require certain activities to be carried out around the procurement process to ensure the quality and safety of the organs to be used. The Human Tissue Authority (HTA) may not grant a licence for transplantation unless it is satisfied the applicant has met the required licencing conditions as regards quality and safety. Further duties have been placed on the HTA with respect to record keeping and a traceability system, and to follow up on living donors in certain situations.

7.1.5 Establishment and maintenance of register: duties of Scottish Ministers

The 2019 Act amended the 2006 Act to require the Scottish Ministers both to promote information and awareness about how transplantation may now be authorised and deemed to have been given, including the nature and timing of pre-death procedures, as well as to annually review this information.

Ministers are required to establish and maintain a register for this purpose. The Register is to include information that relates to persons who authorise post-mortem removal and use of the deceased's body parts for transplantation, and persons who do not give such authorisation. Ministers may delegate that function to an external organisation.

The Register is not open to the public. Information on that Register may be disclosed about a person on it, to a medical practitioner, those authorised by regulations or health workers carrying out enquiries as part of pre-death procedures. Those procedures include enquiries into the views of the potential donor for the purpose of establishing their views on use of their organs for transplantation. This may involve disclosure to others, including the nearest relative or someone consulted on the donor's last known view. It may also involve disclosure to a person with parental rights and responsibilities, or any other person with relevant knowledge, where the potential donor is a child.

7.1.6 Donation under the Anatomy Act 1984

The 2006 Act amended the 1984 Act as applied to Scotland. The subject-matter of the 1984 Act falls within the legislative competence of the Scottish Parliament, as does that of the Human Tissue Act 1961, the Corneal Tissue Act 1986 and the Human Organ Transplants Act 1989.

The 1984 Act governs the use of the cadaver for (macroscopic) anatomical examination for teaching and study purposes. It applies only to those who died after 1988, when the Act came into force. The activities governed under the 1984 Act include acts on the 'anatomical specimen', that is, the whole body, and on parts of the body, such as dissection, removal of parts, prosthesis, etc.

Under s 4 of the 1984 Act, bodies originating outside of Scotland are subject to further provisions aimed at ensuring that the law of the country of origin has been complied with. There should have been no previous examination undertaken on imported bodies other than removal of body parts for research, education and training and that examination must be completed within three years of the donor's death. Lawful possession is possible thereafter, but only for the purpose of disposal.

Premises carrying out such anatomical examinations are required to be licensed under the 1984 Act. The activities may not take place without a death certificate and licence to carry out the examination. Licences are issued by the Scottish Ministers.

Examinations are lawful if a person has given their consent prior to their death. That consent is valid only if the deceased was aged over 12 years when giving it and the consent was given in writing, signed and witnessed by one person.

Following the much-publicised *Bodyworks* exhibition in 2004, the public display of anatomical specimens is prohibited under s 6A of the 1984 Act, as added by s 53(9) of the 2006 Act. This prohibition does not include the display of visual images or display for the purpose of paying last respects to the deceased. Under s 11 of the 1984 Act, if an offence is committed, the offender cannot be guilty of any common law offence relating to unlawful anatomical examination.

7.1.7   The living donor

Not all organ donations are received from deceased donors, but different restrictions have been placed on donations made by living donors under the 2006 Act. The situation in which donors are related to recipients is the same as that in which donor and recipient are unrelated. The same scrutiny applies to all donations.

Unlike its predecessor (the Human Organ Transplants Act 1989), the 2006 Act makes provision for donation of parts of organs such as the liver, regenerative tissue such as bone marrow and for whole organs such as kidneys. While regenerative tissue may be removed from a child, it is an offence under s 17 to remove non-regenerative tissue from a child. It is also an offence under s 17 to remove any organ or tissue from an adult with incapacity, and to use the organs illegally removed. Scottish Ministers may define exceptions to the offence, but have not yet done so. These offences carry a penalty following summary conviction of up to 12 months' imprisonment or a fine of up to level 5 on the standard scale (£5,000) or both.

7.1.8   Trafficking

Under s 20 of the 2006 Act it is an offence to traffic in human organs, subject to any exemptions Scottish Ministers may enact. This offence comprises giving or receiving reward for the supply or offer to supply any part of the human body for transplantation. This includes seeking another person to commit the offence, negotiation or offer of supply for reward that contemplates trafficking. Advertising these services is also an offence. Under the Health and Care Act 2022, if a person who is ordinarily resident in Scotland does an act outside the United Kingdom that would be an offence if committed in Scotland under the 2006 Act, the person is guilty in Scotland of that offence. These offences also carry a penalty following summary conviction of up to 12 months' imprisonment or a fine of up to level 5 on the standard scale (£5,000) or both.

7.1.9 Xenotransplantation

Cross-species organ grafting is known as xenotransplantation. The technique involves growing body parts using an animal as the host. The best-known example is the growing of a human ear on the back of a mouse. This subject-matter is reserved to Westminster under Head J2 of Sch 5 to the Scotland Act 1998. Any developments once regulated by an advisory body to the Department of Health called the Xenotransplantation Interim Regulatory Authority are now regulated by research ethics committees. The same rules that apply to consent, negligence and confidentiality will apply to xenotransplantation procedures.

7.1.10 Licensing of activities relating to the use of tissue

A licence is required to store tissues or cells intended for human application; the same applies to import from or export to a third country. The Human Tissue or Authority (HTA) may authorise the distribution, procurement or transfer of human tissue or cells. The HTA is also responsible for regulation of the premises in which activities are carried out, and the qualifications and identity of individuals designated in the licence. A person authorised by the HTA may require the production of documentation for inspection and arrange for access to premises for their inspection, if need be, by force. Anything on the premises may be seized upon reasonable grounds that is required for the HTA to fulfil its functions. It is an offence to fail to produce documents upon request.

The HTA is required to keep a register of all licences applied for, granted, suspended or revoked, and must put in place procedures for communicating information on any serious adverse events or reactions that required action to be taken. Certain general functions of the HTA have been extended to Scotland by the 2007 regulations.

The HTA is also required to published codes of practise that give practical guidance and lay down expected standards in relation to the activities carried out under the terms of a licence. One or more appeal committees must be maintained with the function to reconsider variation or revocation of licences. A person aggrieved by a decision of such a committee may appeal to the Court of Session.

Information collected in pursuance of a licence or third party agreement must be kept up to date, available for tracing purposes and securely held. Disclosure of information collected from a donor, whether living or deceased, is permissible only where it has been anonymised so that neither donor nor recipient is identifiable. It is an offence to disclose information in breach of this provision that may lead to a fine up to the statutory maximum or a three-year prison term, or both.

7.2   POST-MORTEMS

Post-mortem examinations take place under the authority of the procurator fiscal in certain circumstances. They are also conducted by hospitals to determine morbidity and cause of death. The practice of taking and retaining tissue samples and organs of children following post-mortem examination, and doing so without informing the parents or gaining their consent, led to calls for tighter regulation. This led to some of the provisions in the 2006 Act, following recommendations of the Independent Review Group on Retention of Organs at Post Mortem and related matters. It also led to a consideration by the courts of the cause of action available to those parents and to appropriate heads of damages.

7.2.1   Civil liability in Scots law for affront under the *actio iniuriarum*

Three Scottish post-mortem cases from the early twentieth century suggested the possibility of an action in damages for *solatium* brought by relatives of those on whom an unauthorised post-mortem examination or organ removal and retention was carried out. These cases were *Pollock* v *Workman* (1900), *Conway* v *Dalziel* (1901) and *Hughes* v *Robertson* (1912). The action is based on affront. This is a distinct form of action to that for psychiatric injury, which is based on 'nervous shock' at learning of the wrong perpetrated. It constitutes a form of personal injury.

The interpretation of the three post-mortem cases determined the outcome of the organ retention cases of the twenty-first century. All three cases involved post-mortem examinations instructed by a solicitor with a view to establishing cause of death, but *Conway* v *Dalziel* also involved the retention of organs. In that case, two medical practitioners retained the organs of a deceased workman. His widow sued his former employer for wounded feelings. The case failed on a technicality, but there was indication in the

THE HUMAN BODY AND TRANSPLANTATION

judgment that without the technical error, the case for *solatium* may have had more merit. There is also some authority in these cases for the proposition that a claim lies in *solatium* rather than in nervous shock following negligence. This is supported by the judgment in *AB* v *Leeds Teaching Hospital NHS Trust* (2005), discussed below, in which the court did not consider the Scottish post-mortem cases to have been founded on negligence. The difference between the two actions is that the former requires an affront, while the latter requires a personal injury.

The action for affront under the *actio iniuriarum* is brought by the surviving relatives and is based on the unauthorised interference with the body of the deceased, causing an affront to the *dignitas* of the pursuer.

Stevens v *Yorkhill NHS Trust Hospital and South Glasgow University Hospital NHS Trust* (2006) involved a claim for *solatium* following the alleged affront to the feelings of parents of a child whose organs were removed and retained at post-mortem. The court found that Scots law recognises the claim for *solatium* as based on the *actio iniuriarum*, that is, where there is no *damnum*, but an affront was inflicted either intentionally or recklessly. It was also found that the defender owed the pursuer a duty of care, despite the pursuer not having made averments in support of the existence of a doctor–patient relationship. The duty was owed at the time when consent was sought to the carrying out of a post-mortem. It was based on proximity between the doctor and the pursuer. The duty of care included disclosure that removal and retention of organs may take place. The duty was breached, leading to liability in damages. More recent judicial consideration of the relationship between the psychiatric harm, the duty of care, assault and the *actio iniuriarum* came in Sheriff Court case of *McCallum* v *Morrison* (2023), as discussed in Chapter 5.

7.2.2   Civil liability in English law in negligence for psychiatric harm

The English case of *AB* v *Leeds Teaching Hospital NHS Trust* (2005) was the lead case among several which involved the unauthorised retention of organs of deceased children at post-mortem examination. The case was litigated according to established principles and tests applied to nervous shock cases. It was based on the allegation that psychiatric harm was a foreseeable consequence of a failure to counsel the plaintiffs that the post-mortem examination may involve removal and retention of organs. As a nervous shock case, a close tie of love and affection between the claimant and the primary victim is required, as well as a short space of time between the event and the psychiatric injury.

In *AB* v *Leeds*, the court found that the parents of the deceased child were primary victims, unlike the secondary victims envisaged in nervous shock cases such as *Alcock* v *Chief Constable of South Yorkshire Police* (1992). The child could not have been a victim, as no duty of care is owed after death. It was therefore important to determine whether a duty of care was owed to the parents. The court found that there was a doctor–patient relationship between the parents and the hospital and that the provision of information was not merely an administrative matter. It was considered fair, just and reasonable to find that there was a duty of care in the circumstances.

On the provision of information, the court found both the *Bolam* and *Bolitho* judgments (discussed in Chapters 4 and 5 of this book) to be relevant in determining whether the hospital's omission was reasonable. It found that the duty of care included provision of information on what the post-mortem examination would involve and that it was a breach of duty to fail to inform the parents that organs may be retained. Even so, not all of the claims were successful; success depended on the degree of foreseeability of harm and on proof of causation.

On the basis of this case and considering the nervous shock case law, the following requirements are essential:

- the resulting psychiatric illness must be a foreseeable result of the specific act or omission relied upon by the claimant;

- there must be a sufficient likelihood that the psychiatric illness will occur;

- it must be foreseeable that psychiatric illness would have been suffered by that particular claimant and

- the standard of care is judged by the standard of the consultant paediatrician rather than the consultant psychiatrist, as the defender is in the former occupation.

7.2.3 Post-mortems under the Human Tissue (Scotland) Act 2006

Part 2 of the 2006 Act provides a framework for the authorisation of hospital post-mortems. These are distinguished from anatomical examinations performed under the 1984 Act. Neither does the 2006 Act apply to the bodies of those who have been dead for 100 years or more.

Section 23 defines a post-mortem examination as the 'examination of the body of a deceased person involving its dissection and the removal of organs, tissue sample, blood (or any material derived from blood) or other body fluid'.

7.2.3.1 Authorisation

Similar principles that apply elsewhere in the 2006 Act apply to authorisation for post-mortem examinations. As such, adults may before death give authorisation for removal and retention of organs for transplantation, research and audit after their death. Separate and similar provisions apply to mature minors and children as apply to organ donation, etc. These have been set out above.

The authorisation may be either written or verbal, although verbal authorisation requires to be given in the presence of two witnesses and written authorisations may be only withdrawn in writing. Verbal authorisations may be withdrawn verbally, in the presence of two witnesses.

Adults may nominate a person or persons to give authorisation on their behalf. Nominees must be appointed in writing, with the appointment signed and witnessed by one person who is not the nominee. The witness must certify that the adult (or the child if that is the case) in their opinion understands the effect of the nomination.

The same hierarchy of 'nearest relative' is applicable to this part of the 2006 Act. In the absence of an authorisation by the adult or the appointment of a nominee, the deceased's 'nearest relative' may give authorisation. This must be in writing and can be withdrawn, but only in writing in the presence of a witness.

The mature minor may also give such authorisation. It must be in writing, signed and witnessed by two people. The same nomination provisions apply to mature minors as apply to adults. What is different is the use of the 'nearest relative' hierarchy, which in the case of the mature minor means that authority rests with the minor's parents. Such authorisation made on behalf of the minor must be in writing, be in respect of that particular minor, authorise the activity in question and be signed on behalf of the child. It must also be witnessed by one witness. A statement is required to be added to the effect that in the opinion of the person with parental rights and responsibilities, the child understood the nature and effect of the authorisation.

Authorisation may be given in respect of minors under the age of 12 for removal and retention of organs. This may be given by the person with parental rights and responsibilities immediately before the child's death. It must be written, signed and witnessed by two people. The same applies to its withdrawal.

Under the 2006 Act, organs removed and retained are different to tissue samples removed and retained. Any part of the body removed and retained following proper authorisation will form part of the deceased's medical records. They may be removed and retained for the purposes of audit, education, training and research following proper authorisation. It is an offence to perform a post-mortem examination without authorisation, although it will be a defence to show reasonable belief that authorisation had been given. Conviction on summary procedure carries a penalty of up to 12 months' imprisonment or a fine of up to level 5 on the standard scale (£5,000) or both. On indictment, the penalty is a fine of up to level 5 or up to three years' imprisonment or both.

7.2.3.2 Interface with procurator fiscal purposes

As the 2006 Act relates to hospital post-mortems only, it does not apply to post-mortem examinations conducted for the procurator fiscal's purposes. The procurator fiscal is required to examine the body of a person suspected to have been involved in criminal activity and must inquire into all sudden, suspicious or unexplained deaths.

That said, s 26 of the 2006 Act requires that if there is reason to believe that the body of the deceased is required for procurator fiscal purposes, a hospital post-mortem may proceed only following permission from the fiscal. This may be verbal, but must later be confirmed in writing. Organ and tissue samples no longer required by the procurator fiscal become part of the deceased's medical records. Samples removed and retained for procurator fiscal purposes may be subsequently used for the purposes of education, training and research. This does not require authorisation.

7.3   PROPERTY RIGHTS

The ownership and control of the whole or parts of the human body are regulated by the common law. As such Scots property law as it applies to corporeal movables is applicable.

7.3.1   The whole body

Property law is concerned with things rather than natural persons. This means that people can be the subject rather than the object of real rights. While one may donate parts or the whole of the body after death or parts of the body while alive, one is prohibited from selling one's body or body parts.

The question arises whether it is possible in law to own a corpse before its burial. There is some civil law authority in *McGruer, Petr* (1898), *per* Sheriff-Substitute Scott-Moncrieff, to the effect that the answer to that question is no. The dead body, therefore, is *ex commercium*. It is for this reason that it is not possible to steal a corpse once buried, as theft can be committed only on owned objects. The crime in question is the violation of sepulchres, but that applies only to buried corpses.

While there is no obligation to dispose of a dead body in Scots law (unlike English law), there is an entitlement of next-of-kin, relatives or executors to arrange for the burial. If they do not make arrangements, the local authority has a duty to do so under the National Assistance Act 1948.

While there are no rights of ownership, there is a right of possession. According to *Evans* v *McIntyre* (1980), and *Rees* v *Hughes* (1946), this right is held by the deceased's executor, as it is that person who would decide on arrangements for the burial. Problems arise where no executor has been appointed. In that case, the nearest relative may enjoy that right. Although there is no authority on the point, it is the nearest relative who would have an action in *solatium* for unauthorised interference with the corpse, so it is arguably they who would have rights of possession in the corpse.

7.3.2 Body parts

7.3.2.1 Parts taken from a living person

It is worth noting at the outset that under Art 21 of the European Convention on Human Rights and Biomedicine, 'the human body and its parts shall not, as such, give rise to financial gain'.

However, because body parts are capable of transfer through donation, property law is applicable (although certain transactions, such as trade, are prohibited, as discussed above). There is authority to the effect that a part removed from the body is capable of ownership by the person from whose body it was removed and an abandoned thing becomes Crown property if it was capable of ownership. There is also a statutory duty of reasonable care on the possessor of lost or abandoned property, under the Civic Government (Scotland) Act 1982. There is a duty to report the fact of having taken possession of the thing. There is certainly an untested argument that the property law rules of occupation should confer original title on the first occupier of the thing.

The American case of *Moore* v *Regents of the University of California* (1990) dealt with the ownership of a cell line developed from a sample of cells taken from a patient. A patent was sought. This application was opposed by Moore. The court was reluctant to find that there was property in living human cells, but did find for the patient on the basis of breach of a fiduciary duty and lack of informed consent.

In the Scots law of *specificatio*, a person who in good faith makes a new thing out of other things, through skill, acquires ownership of the new thing. That person has a duty to compensate the source or the person who had ownership before the *specificatio*, to the tune of the value of that part prior to incorporation. There is, however, no authority on this point in respect of human organs and body parts for a remedy, sought by the original possessor. Neither is the doctor–patient relationship a fiduciary one, as it was in *Moore*.

In the recent jurisprudence there is evidence of an emergent relationship between property law and the law of contract, with that of negligence. In the Scottish case of *Holdich* v *Lothian Health Board* (2013) the pursuer, whose sperm samples had been damaged while in storage, argued that the sperm was his property and that accordingly he could seek reparation for damage to moveable property on the ground of breach of contract between gamete provider and cryostorer, with consequential mental injury.

The pursuer's delictual mental injury case in *Holdich* was based primarily as a claim that was consequential on property damage in breach of contract *et separatism*. Their case was that the sperm samples amounted to corporeal movable property, and were therefore capable of possession, due to the reception of the Roman law of *occupatio*. They also averred that the contract was a real contract of deposit. The defence argument was the 'no property' rule that pre-dated *Yearworth*, apart from the 'work and skill' exception, and the body of legislative jurisprudential authority that prohibits trade in human material. The court found that the property theory was dependent on the production of the samples as an essential legal fact, which ought to have been in the pleadings, but was not.

In any event, Lord Stewart was not persuaded by the mode-of-production argument as affecting *occupatio*, but did go on to point out that the sources of law had 'merged and *solatium* came to be recognised as the head of damages for pain and suffering arising from bodily injury as well as for hurt feelings and other non-patrimonial losses'. This indicated the relevance of the *actio iniuriarum* to the position in Scots law.

Lord Stewart's view on the property-contract case was that it might have been better expressed, as the sperm in a container as the 'thing' in question is capable of being the subject of a contract for safekeeping, but that this renders the *res* not as property, but as an object.

The Outer House of the Court of Session allowed the claim to proceed to a full hearing on the basis that, according to Lord Stewart, 'the claim in delict for "pure" mental injury caused by negligent out-of-body damage to sperm is apt for proof and certainly cannot be rejected out of hand', and that 'if the delictual case is to go to proof I think the property-contract case should be remitted for probation too'. It was recognised that this was an emergent area of law. It was also one which was able to draw on an existing jurisprudence, such as the loss of chance doctrine, in this case in respect of the loss of the opportunity to have a family.

There is considerable support in this judgment for 'loss of autonomy' as standalone head of damages. The 'pure mental injury' case was seen as analogical to 'pure economic loss', where the central question is whether the pursuer's mental injury was reasonably foreseeable by the defenders, which Lord Stewart indicated would require evidence around the so-called 'third-stage tests' of 'assumption of responsibility', 'fair, just and reasonable', and the principle of 'distributive justice'. He allowed proof before answer.

The decision in *Holdich* followed, and can be contrasted with, the English case of *Yearworth v North Bristol NHS Trust* (2009), where Lord Stewart had said in *Holdich* that to 'put a Kilt on *Yearworth*' cannot be done, principally because of the peculiarities of English property law that allow for a claim for bailment, or an automatic presumption of a right of return of property following its transfer for the purpose of possession and storage. This concept is unknown to Scots law.

Yearworth was also concerned with the common law treatment of the issue of ownership of parts or products of a living human body. In that case the sperm of six men was stored due to their incumbent infertility following cancer treatment. The sperm was destroyed due to a technical failure in the storage facility. The negligence cases that followed included for mental distress and loss of chance of paternity. There it was held that, for the purposes of claims in negligence, the men had a property interest in the sperm which they had ejaculated so that it could be stored for future use, and wrongful interference in property was actionable *per se* in contract *et separatism*.

A further point of distinction between the decisions in *Holdich* and *Yearworth* can be seen through the lens of the German law theory of the 'functional unity' [*eine funktionale einheit*] that stored gametes have with the living body (BGHZ 124, 52 (VI ZR 62/93), 09.11.1993). This appealed to Lord Stewart as 'plausible' in *Holdich*, but not to Lord Judge in *Yearworth*. The theory of 'functional unity' would see stored gametes as part of the body from which they came, given that storage is ancillary to their use under the Human Fertilisation and Embryology Act. Whereas the Court of Appeal saw the liability as essentially tortious, Lord Stewart in the Court of Session wondered whether the German decision had been given statutory effect, by enacting a new section 253 of the German Civil Code, on 'intangible damage'. This allows for financial damages for bodily injury that leads to a non-pecuniary loss. This was appealing to Lord Stewart, but the pursuers did not base their claim on bodily injury. It does however suggest an avenue that might be pursued in future cases, many of which Lord Stewart saw as 'waiting in the wings', albeit based financial loss consequent on mental injury.

7.3.2.2 Parts taken from a dead person

The organ retention cases are in point here. In these cases, tissue samples and organs of deceased children were retained by hospitals without authorisation. In England, *AB* v *Leeds Teaching Hospital NHS Trust* (2005) was heard under the tort of wrongful interference with the parents' right of possession, which was to depend on whether the parents had a right of possession in the first place.

Under Scots law, the child's surviving relatives have an action in delict under the *action iniuriarum* for *solatium* for affront. This was discussed above, in relation to post-mortems.

The difference from English law is that in Scots law the relationship with the deceased is important, while in English law the body parts acquire characteristics of property through skilful dissection and the production of tissue slides.

Intellectual property in body parts requires that the product be novel for a patent to be awarded, yet under the European Patent Convention this would not be possible in the case of biological material. However, the Patent Convention applies to 'life', which does not cover human cell lines and DNA. For these, the applicable European Directive is that on biotechnological inventions. Article 6 requires substantial benefit to humans or animals. It also prohibits patents that involve human cloning, modifying human genetic identity and industrial or commercial use of human embryos.

Essential facts

Transplantation

- Regulation of transplantation is devolved to the Scottish Parliament and regulated under the Human Tissue (Scotland) Act 2006, as significantly amended by the Human Tissue (Authorisation)(Scotland) Act 2019.
- Organs may be removed from the deceased and used for transplantation, research, education, training and audit, as long as the patient is dead and the removal and use are authorised.
- It is an offence to act without authorisation.
- Express authorisation may be given by the deceased before their death or by the deceased's nearest relative.
- A hierarchy of 'nearest relatives' is set out in the 2006 Act for the purpose of authorisation.

- The same principles apply to the consent to organ donation of children between the ages of 12 and 16 as apply to consent and confidentiality. Express authorisation is competent if the mature minor understands the nature and consequences of what they are authorising.
- The person with parental responsibility for the child under 12 may give or withdraw authorisation on behalf of the child.
- A child aged between 12 and 16 may make an authorisation or opt-out declaration but this must be in writing.
- These principles are drawn from the Age of Legal Capacity (Scotland) Act 1991.
- The 2019 Act changed the system from an opt-in to an opt-out system, though without displacing the express authorisation provisions.
- In the absence of an opt-out declaration or withdrawal of express authorisation, a person is deemed to have given consent to the removal and use of their organs for transplantation, training/education, research or audit or quality assurance.
- An authorisation may be overwritten if a person provides evidence to a health worker, that would lead a reasonable person to conclude that the adult's most recent view is that they were unwilling for that body part to be used for transplantation.
- Consent and withdrawal are required to be in writing, signed and witnessed.
- The new system in the 2019 Act includes pre-death procedures such as a duty to inquire into various matters of medical procedure, and a ministerial duty to promote awareness of the system, and to establish and maintain a register of transplants under the new system.
- The Anatomy Act 1984, as amended by the 2006 Act, governs the use of the cadaver for macroscopic anatomical examination for teaching and study purposes.
- The 1984 Act makes provision for the premises licensed to carry out research and teaching using cadavers, including those not originating in Scotland.
- Under the 1984 Act, consent to the use of a person's body after their death is valid only if made after the deceased was 12 years of age and had knowledge and understanding of the implications of their consent. Consent must be in writing, signed and witnessed.
- Different restrictions are placed on donations by living donors, under the 2006 Act.

- Under the 2006 Act, live donations are provided for in respect of regenerating tissue and parts of organs, although it is an offence to remove regenerative tissue from a child under 16 years of age or to remove organs from an adult with incapacity.
- It is an offence to give, receive, offer, advertise or act as an agent for reward in respect of human organs. This is defined as trafficking in human organs.
- A licence is required to store tissues or cells intended for human application; the same applies to import from or export to a third country.

Post-mortem examinations

- Post-mortem examinations take place under the authority of the procurator fiscal where the person is suspected to have been involved in criminal activity; the fiscal must inquire into all sudden, suspicious or unexplained deaths.
- They also take place within hospitals to ascertain cause of death, etc. These are regulated under the 2006 Act.
- The same principles of authorisation apply to hospital post-mortem examinations as apply to organ donation for transplantation, research, audit and teaching. As such, authorisation may be given by the deceased before their death, by his nominee or, in the absence of authorisation by either, by the deceased's 'nearest relative' in the hierarchy set out in the 2006 Act.
- Different provisions apply to whether authorisation and withdrawal of authorisation may be verbal or is required to be in writing, signed and witnessed.
- Authorisation may be given by the mature minor, in the absence of which it may be given by the person with parental rights and responsibilities, as is the case with children.
- Body parts and tissue samples properly removed and retained from part of the deceased's medical records.
- It is an offence to perform a post-mortem examination without proper authorisation.
- In English law, removal and retention of tissue and samples of the deceased give rise to an action in negligence based on nervous shock suffered by the parents as primary victims.
- In Scots law, the unauthorised removal and retention of tissue and organs gives rise to an action in damages for *solatium* for affront under the *actio iniuriarum*.

- As a result of the circumstances that gave rise to the case law, Part 2 of the 2006 Act provides a framework for the authorisation of hospital post-mortems.
- Authorisation for post-mortem examination follows similar rules to those set out in respect of organ donation. These rules apply to authorisation, nominees, 'nearest relative' and the rules applicable to minors and mature minors.
- Further rules apply to whether the authorisation and its withdrawal must be in writing, signed and witnessed.

Property rights
- The ownership and control of the whole or parts of the human body are regulated by the common law.
- The whole dead body is outside of commerce and hence not capable of ownership or theft.
- The deceased's next-of-kin, relatives or executors are entitled to arrange for the burial.
- While there are no rights of ownership, there is a right of possession of the whole human body, and hence that person would have an action in *solatium* for unauthorised interference with the corpse.
- Because body parts are capable of transfer through donation, property law is applicable to them.
- There is an untested argument that the property law rules of occupation should confer original title on the first occupier of a thing.
- In the Scots law of *specificatio*, a person who in good faith makes a new thing out of other things, through skill, acquires ownership of the new thing, but there is no authority on this point in respect of human organs and body parts, for a remedy sought by the original possessor.
- Article 21 of the European Convention on Human Rights and Biomedicine reads: 'the human body and its parts shall not, as such, give rise to financial gain'.
- The organ retention cases are applicable to body parts taken from the deceased.
- There is judicial authority to suggest that there is a claim in delict for pure mental injury caused by negligent damage to sperm samples, loss of the opportunity to have a family and loss of autonomy as a standalone head of damages. Those claims have their basis as consequential upon property damage in breach of contract.

Essential cases

McGruer, Petr (1898): it is not possible in law to own a corpse before its burial.

Evans v McIntyre (1980), citing **Rees v Hughes (1946)**: possession rights are held by the deceased's executor as it is that person who would decide on arrangements for the burial.

Moore v Regents of the University of California (1990): the court was reluctant to find that there was property in living human cells.

AB v Leeds Teaching Hospital NHS Trust (2005): tissue samples and organs of deceased children were retained by hospitals without authorisation. The case was heard under the tort of wrongful interference with the parents' right of possession. It was the lead case among several which alleged that psychiatric injury had been suffered as a result of the negligent failure to inform of the possibility that tissue and organs may be retained at post-mortem. The court found that there was a doctor–patient relationship between the parents and the hospital. Both the *Bolam* and *Bolitho* judgments were relevant in determining whether the hospital's omission was reasonable. The duty of care included provision of information on what the post-mortem examination would involve and failure to inform the parents that organs may be retained was a breach of that duty.

Stevens v Yorkhill NHS Trust Hospital and South Glasgow University Hospital NHS Trust (2006): in the Scottish organ retention case it was found that the true juridical basis of the claim was in an action in damages for *solatium* based on the *actio iniuriarum*. The duty of care was based on proximity between pursuer and doctor. That duty included disclosure that removal and retention of organs might take place. The duty was breached, leading to liability in damages.

Yearworth v North Bristol NHS Trust (2009): a property interest is recognised where there was negligent damage to sperm samples.

Holdich v Lothian Health Board (2013): the delictual claim for 'pure mental injury' was based on damage to sperm samples as moveable property.

8 MEDICAL FUTILITY, EUTHANASIA AND ASSISTED SUICIDE

Several medico–legal issues are raised at the end of life. Many relate to the improved ability of technology to prolong life, but others relate to the expectation that technology might be used to hasten death. These questions lead to others surrounding medical futility and the prospect of treatment continuing to provide a benefit. Other questions are raised surrounding assisted suicide, the value and authority of advance statements, and euthanasia, all of which raise further questions as to the values attributed to human life.

8.1 DEATH IN LAW

It was clear from parts of Chapter 7 that death is essential for certain activities, such as some organ donations, to take place legally. Yet death is not defined in statute in Scotland. Because natural death is a process rather than an event in the medical sense, it is at times important in law to establish a point after which a person is said to have died. Several possibilities exist, based on the functioning of the heart, lungs and brain. While the first two can be maintained artificially, the third can not.

Even if the brain stem is irreparably damaged and the patient is in a permanent vegetative state (PVS), medico–legal questions may be raised as to whether the patient can be 'allowed to die'. It is for this reason that the PVS cases are instructive when considering the definition of death.

In *Law Hospital NHS Trust* v *Lord Advocate* (1996), Janet Johnson had been in a PVS for three years without prospect of recovery or awareness of her surroundings. She remained medically alive by artificial means. In *Finlayson* v *HM Advocate* (1979), the patient was in a PVS following an injection of controlled drugs. The accused had been charged with culpable homicide. Both cases involved the maintenance of life by artificial means, raising the question of the timing and justification for ending that life. In *Finlayson*, it was considered that switching off the life-support machinery did not break the chain of causation between the actions of the accused and the death of the victim, yet it was also assumed that the victim was legally dead, as far as the criminal law was concerned, only once life-support was discontinued. From this, it is reasonable to assume that death occurs when the whole brain or the brain stem is dead. Indeed, this was confirmed by the Supreme Court in *Barts Health NHS Trust* v *Dance & Battersbee* (2022), which examined the circumstances in which a declaration of legal death can be made on the basis of brain stem testing.

8.2   FUTILITY AND INCAPACITY

'Futility' refers to demands by or on behalf of the patient for treatments that will not serve the desired medical ends or not be in the patient's best medical interests. It is not exclusive to end-of-life decisions, as it may also be invoked, for example, in connection with the non-treatment of new-born infants. What is important is that 'futility' refers to the medical prognosis rather than any question of resources. It follows that the patient's wishes, autonomy, interests and quality of life are central to decisions on futility.

Those decisions, in turn, may be those made by the courts, and following the more recent jurisprudence discussed below, by the medical practitioner. Despite recommendations by the Scottish Law Commission that the law should state that treatment can be withdrawn when it is unlikely to be of benefit to a patient, this is not an issue that is specifically dealt with in the Adults with Incapacity (Scotland) Act 2000. The 2000 Act does not impose a duty on a medical practitioner to administer futile treatment, but does specify under s 1(2) that no medical intervention should take place unless it will be to the adult's benefit. The Code of Practice to the Act indicates that there is no duty to provide futile treatment.

While he was not comfortable with its use, Lord Mustill in *Law Hospital* did accept that in the circumstances of that case a 'best interests' test could be applied. He also used the language of 'futility', if the issue is viewed in the negative. Treatment may be withdrawn where it is not in a patient's best interests to be kept alive artificially, where there is a clear diagnosis and where the prognosis is 'so futile that the ward truly has no interest in being kept alive'. The court found that there would be no breach of the duty of care if a doctor withdraws treatment that serves no purpose other than pro-longing life. In reaching such a decision the doctor should take the views of the patient's family and carers into account. That is because rather than asking whether treatment withdrawal is in a patient's best interests, a more important question is what the patient's preference would be if they were capable of expressing one.

Although it predated the 2000 Act, which does not apply a 'best inter-ests' standard for incapacious adults, the decision in *Law Hospital* remains the leading Scottish case on futility. The decision aligns with that in *Aintree University Hospitals NHS Foundation Trust* v *James* (2013), where the Supreme Court considered the correct approach to judging the 'futility' of medical treatment, in the context of considering whether life-sustaining treatment should be withheld from a legally incapable adult patient. There the court was concerned with the meaning of 'futility' and 'no prospect of recovery' in the Mental Capacity Act 2005, in this context. The court found that it is not about whether it is lawful to withhold treatment, but whether it is in the patient's best interests to provide it. If it is not in their best interests, then withholding treatment will be lawful.

8.2.1 Selective non-treatment of children

Children are not legally capable of making treatment decisions. It follows that a 'substituted judgement' test cannot apply because the patient was never capable of making a decision on their own behalf and hence the question of what they would have decided cannot be asked. The same applies to legally incapable adults, as discussed below. Different legal regimes operate in England and in Scotland, with the English law governed largely by the common law and Scots law set out in the Children (Scotland) Act 1995.

8.2.1.1 The Children (Scotland) Act 1995

Although no analogous decisions have been reported in Scotland, there have been a number of fatal accident inquiries of interest. These have indicated that where a decision to not resuscitate a child was made in the child's interests and constituted a reasonable clinical decision, the determination of the inquiry has supported the non-treatment decision. Similar decisions have been reached in respect of the decision against giving a liver transplant to a teenage girl.

Where there is a conflict of views between the parents and the medical practitioners involved with the child's care, the decision should be referred to the courts. This should be done through a specific issue order under the Children (Scotland) Act 1995. Both the person with parental rights and responsibilities and the medical practitioner may apply in their capacity as persons having an interest under s 11. Orders made under the 1995 Act will take precedence over common law orders of the court. A 'best interests' test would be brought to bear on a decision to withdraw life-prolonging treatment from a child younger than 16.

8.2.1.2 English common law and human rights

In the absence of Scottish authority, English decisions on children born with severe disabilities will be persuasive, particularly because a 'best interests' test is appropriate in Scots law for incapacious infants. The case law indicates that a 'best interests' test has been used in balancing the quality of a disabled or shortened life against ending that life. Consent to surgery was refused by the parents of a child born with Down's syndrome and an intestinal complaint in *Re B (a minor) (wardship: medical treatment)* (1992). The surgery may have given the child a life expectancy of 20–30 years. The court found that the operation should be performed, as the expected quality of life outweighed life's destruction.

These cases often deal with the distinction between actively hastening death and passively allowing the patient to die. A case dealing with this active/passive distinction was *Re C (a minor) (wardship: medical treatment)* (1989). In that case the child was brain damaged and terminally ill. The decision in *Re B* was distinguished in finding that the child's welfare was paramount. An operation to treat the child in order to allow a peaceful death was permitted.

Similarly, in the leading decision of *Re J (a minor) (wardship: medical treatment)* (1992), the child was not dying, but was disabled. Placed on a ventilator following premature birth, the child was expected to live no longer than his teens and to do so in a state of limited intellectual ability. The court had to decide the permissible course of action should J collapse again. The question before the court was whether to approve the withholding of life-prolonging treatment. The court would not allow active steps to be taken to hasten death. It used a 'substituted judgement' test to ask what J might have decided and found that it was not in his best interests to ventilate him if he was to stop breathing, unless it was considered medically appropriate to do so.

This first *Re J* was approved in another case of that name: *Re J (a minor) (wardship: medical treatment)* (1992). The latter case used the 'best interests' test to assess future quality of life and sanctioned medical decision-making in such cases. That courts will not tell members of the medical profession how to perform their role was emphasised in *Re C (a baby)* (1996). The case involved a baby who became brain damaged from meningitis. The court approved of the medical expert agreement that it was not in her best interests to be ventilated artificially. As such, courts will not *require* doctors to treat children in such circumstances.

These decisions pre-dated the enactment of the Human Rights Act 1998, by which point the 'best interests' test had become accepted as appropriate in these circumstances. Certain Articles of the European Convention on Human Rights, as enacted by the 1998 Act, became important too. These are Art 2 on the right to life, Art 3 prohibiting inhuman and degrading treatment and Art 8 on respect for private life. In *A National Health Service Trust* v *D* (2000), a hospital sought declaration that non-resuscitation of a 19-month-old child with irreversible lung disease would be consistent with Arts 2 and 3. The court found that Art 2 would not be infringed if non-treatment was in the child's best interests. In addition, the non-treatment decision by its nature protected the child from inhuman and degrading treatment, being in her best medical interests. It was found in *Glass* v *United Kingdom* (2004) that treatment contrary to parental wishes and without court authority violated Art 8.

The case of *Re A (children) (conjoined twins: surgical separation)* (2000) dealt with both selective non-treatment and treatment in the child's best interests. It involved the separation of conjoined twins that would allow one to live at the expense of the death of the other. The separation was opposed by the parents, who relied on Art 2 of the ECHR that disallows intentional deprivation of life. Because surgery on Mary would end her life, the court could not authorise it. The two children were considered separate persons even though Mary's life depended on her sister Jodie. It was found that the benefits to Jodie outweighed Mary's inevitable death. It was, however, considered impossible to invoke the best interests test in respect of both girls; the court considered its decision in terms of the lesser of two evils. It was found that 'best interests' should include emotional and welfare interests.

There have been several cases that have post-dated the Human Rights Act 1998 and which also received a great deal of media attention. Chief among these was the case of Charlie Gard in *Great Ormond Street Hospital for Children NHS Foundation Trust* v *Yates and others* (2017). Charlie was born with infantile onset mitochondrial DNA depletion syndrome (MDDS), due to genetic mutations in his DNA. His condition deteriorated to the point that his parents sought experimental treatment in the United States of America, which the medical team at Great Ormond Street Hospital did not think was in his best interests. The Court of Appeal agreed with this view as there was no chance of the experimental treatment succeeding. The Supreme Court and the European Court of Human Rights declined Charlie's parents' appeal.

A similar finding followed in the case of Alfie Evans in *Evans & Anor* v *Alder Hey Children's NHS Foundation Trust & Anor* (2018). Alfie also suffered from a neuro-degenerative condition. The medical team took review that further treatment would be both inhumane and futile, but his parents wanted to take him to Italy for experimental treatment. The court found that it was in Alfie's best interests for treatment to be withdrawn particularly given that his parents had not shown that the proposed experimental treatment could have been of medical benefit to Alfie. Importantly the Supreme Court found that the parents did not enjoy unlimited rights over Charlie's care.

Finally, the opposite conclusion was reached by the Supreme Court in the case of Tafida Raqeeb in *Raqeeb and Barts Health NHS Trust* (2019) in which Tafida's best interests favoured her transfer to Italy for continued life-sustaining treatment, despite her being unaware of her surroundings. The case was heard under s 8 of the Children Act 1989 and the declaration made as part of the court's inherent jurisdiction.

This line of case law is important as far as English jurisprudence is concerned, but it is important to remember that the position in Scotland remains that as described below in the discussion of *Law Hospital NHS Trust* v *Lord Advocate* (1996) and under the *parens patriae* jurisdiction. There have to date been no similar cases in Scotland.

The English jurisprudence supports the following propositions, which are persuasive authority in Scotland:

1. According to *Re C (a minor) (wardship: medical treatment)* (1990) and *A National Health Service Trust* v *D* (2000), parental views on treatment will be accorded great respect by doctors and the courts, but are not conclusive as to the court's determination of the baby's best interests. Conversely, according to *Glass* v *United Kingdom* (2004), apart from life-threatening emergencies, a doctor is not entitled to impose medical treatment over the protests of the parents.

2. Courts evaluate the child's best interests by weighing the likely benefits and burdens of treatment from the child's standpoint; it approaches the issues as if it were a reasonable and responsible parent. This was evident in *Re T (a minor) (wardship: medical treatment)* (1997) and *Portsmouth NHS Trust* v *Wyatt (a child) (medical treatment; parents' consent)* (2004).

3. It is for the courts to resolve disputes between parents and doctors, or among members of the medical team, as regard's a child's medical treatment.

4. Courts will for the most part accept medical recommendations on prognosis and best interests. If the medical view is that treatment will provide no benefit, or only a short term benefit, which is outweighed by pain and suffering, the court will not require the treatment to be given. The converse is also true, despite parental objections, according to *Re B (a minor) (wardship: medical treatment)* (1992).

5. 'Best interests' are not confined to 'best medical interests', but include emotional and other welfare interests, as in *Re A* (2000), and courts have been known to reject medical advice, as happened in *Re T (a minor) (wardship: medical treatment)* (1997).

6. Perhaps most importantly, there is a strong presumption in favour of life, as in *Re J (a minor) (wardship: medical treatment)* (1990). This is not irrebuttable and in exceptional circumstances may be outweighed

by the child's best interests in favour of a peaceful death, as was the case in *A National Health Service Trust v D* (2000), *Portsmouth NHS Trust v Wyatt (a child) (medical treatment; parents' consent)* (2004) and *Re Winston-Jones (a child) (medical treatment; parents' consent)* (2004).

8.2.2 Withdrawing or withholding treatment from adults

As mentioned above, it is appropriate to use a 'substituted judgement' test in making a non-treatment decision on behalf of the adult *incapax*, whereas this is not appropriate in the case of children. This is because adults will have been legally capable prior to entering the permanent vegetative state, for example, which will render such an assessment possible, whereas children will not have been capable in the legal sense. This is more an evidential and practical difference, rather than a legal one, because futility cases still require recourse to a 'best interests' test regardless of the age of the incapacious patient.

8.2.2.1 The permanent vegetative state

A person is in a PVS if they do not have, and are never going to recover, awareness of their surroundings or who show no response to tactile, visual, auditory or noxious stimuli, or have no awareness of language or ability to communicate. As accurate diagnosis is crucial, *Practice Note (persistent vegetative state: withdrawal of treatment)* (1996) requires evidence from two independent medical practitioners that the patient is, in fact, in a permanent vegetative state. In PVS situations the 'substituted judgement' test is important, as is the doctrine of 'double effect' which considers it acceptable to administer a palliative treatment even although its effect will be to hasten death (e.g. morphine in high doses).

The English case of *Airedale NHS Trust v Bland* (1993) followed the Hillsborough football stadium disaster in which many died or were injured. Anthony Bland suffered brain damage caused by lack of oxygen and had no hope of recovery. Although he could breathe on his own, he was insensate and was fed through a gastric tube. He did not feel pain. The health authority was supported by his parents in its application to discontinue feeding and hydration. The court considered this to amount to medical treatment and therefore to fall within the category of decisions surrounding withdrawal of life-sustaining treatment.

The distinction between acts and omissions was important to the decision of the court. It held that treatment could lawfully be withdrawn in the patient's best medical interests where it was futile to prolong life. The House of Lords, however, found that Bland did not have any interests in a PVS. Neither would withdrawal of treatment be a criminal act where there was no positive duty to maintain life. For this reason, there would be no violation of Art 2 ECHR. Withdrawal of treatment, on the other hand, would mean that he would be allowed to die of his existing injuries.

In Scotland, the Court of Session may authorise a medical practitioner to withdraw life-prolonging treatment from a patient in a PVS if continuing with that treatment is not in the patient's interests. In *Law Hospital NHS Trust v Lord Advocate* (1996), Janet Johnstone was in a PVS following a failed suicide attempt four years prior to the case. The question before the court was whether to authorise the withdrawal of life-sustaining treatment. The court had the benefit of the decision in the *Bland* case. As in *Bland*, Janet Johnstone was fed artificially, was unaware of her surroundings and had no prospect of recovery. Continuing with hydration and feeding would be of no benefit to her and hence was futile.

As was the case in the *Bland* judgment, it was found that Janet had no best interests that could be served by any treatment decision and that the declaration sought was lawful and treatment could be withdrawn. The court set out a clear statement of the appropriate procedure to be followed in such cases in obtaining authority from the Court of Session, under its *parens patriae* jurisdiction, for withdrawal of futile life-sustaining treatment. Aside from rules of procedure, the judgment specified that the following should be lodged with the petition:

- at least two medical reports on the patient's condition, describing the proposed course of action and the steps that will be taken to allow death to occur with dignity;
- a statement of the first diagnosis of PVS (British Medical Association Guidelines advise that treatment should continue for at least the first 12 months of the patient's insentience);
- a statement of any views on treatment decisions that the patient may have expressed prior to going into a PVS.

The court should be asked to appoint a *curator ad litem* to act on behalf of the patient (as the petition will be brought by the hospital or family of the patient).

This statement of practice is set out at the end of reports of the First Division's decision in *Law Hospital NHS Trust v Lord Advocate* (1996). The judgment also set out the following common law principles to be followed in making negative treatment decisions on behalf of patients in a PVS:

1. it is not competent for the Court of Session to issue a declarator in respect of the criminal or otherwise nature of the withdrawal of treatment. A declarator should be confined to the civil law

consequences. Any decision to prosecute on the same set of facts remains with the Lord Advocate. Following the *Law Hospital* decision, the Lord Advocate in a statement said he would not authorise prosecution of a medical practitioner who acts in good faith and with the authority of the Court of Session to cause life-sustaining treatment to be withdrawn from a patient in a PVS, leading to the death of that patient;

2. although a declarator was competent, it was also possible to petition the court to invoke its inherent *parens patriae* jurisdiction. Authorising discontinuing treatment through this route and using the 'best interests' test will resolve any questions of delictual liability arising from the acts or omissions of medical practitioners;

3. however, neither procedure is strictly necessary where the discontinuance of treatment is in the patient's best interests. That said, without the court's approval, there is no guarantee that prosecution will not follow.

8.2.2.2 A note on best interests and negotiorum gestio

It will have been noted that there appears to be a paradox in operation in applying the 'best interests' test while at the same time holding that the patient in a PVS has no best interests. Yet the courts in both *Bland* and *Law Hospital* approved of its use – even if the Lord Ordinary in *Law Hospital* felt the issue was more a matter of determining whether, in terms of a choice between 'life and a sort of death', it is 'just and proper to grant the authorisation in the circumstances as viewed from the position of the patient'. It is not about best interests as much as it is about whether continuing with life-prolonging treatment will serve any interest at all, where treatment is futile. Neither is it about whether the patient's interests will be served by allowing them to die. Rather, it is about whether it is in their interest to be kept alive.

If treatment will serve no interest, there will be no balance to be struck. Seen this way, the 'best interests' test is applied in the negative sense. What is critical is that the wishes of the patient's family and the issue of resources should not obscure a decision that should be taken from the point of view of the patient in a PVS. What is important is the question to be asked and answered by the court. The courts in *Bland* found that rather than asking whether the action should be taken that will kill the patient, the question should be whether the medical practitioner should continue to provide treatment that will prolong the patient's life. A problem with this approach is that arguably the two questions are inseparable and to try to separate them is an act of semantics.

This kind of reasoning around actions taken on behalf of another re-invites a reflection on the utility of *negotiorum gestio*, where artificial nutrition and hydration might be likened to aliment in the Roman law *actio negotiorum gestorum contraria* which lay in respect of aliment furnished to children. Scots law deriving more from the Roman law than it does from the otherwise otiose English doctrine of agency of necessity, an action based on *negotiorum gestio* was recognised, albeit *obiter* in the Sheriff Court in *Gilbert* v *Hannah* (1924). The Roman law required the absence of the *dominus*, but *ignorantia* amounted to the equivalence of absence. This requisite element was carried forward in the modern Scots law which places *negotiorum gestio* as a common law basis for intervening on behalf of a person incapable of managing their own affairs due to a mental or physical disability or incapacity, including a compromised level of consciousness in *Parker's Executors* v *Esso Petroleum Co Ltd* (1971) or non-age in *Fulton* v *Fulton* (1864). Invoking *negotiorum gestio* would mean that an unauthorised action by a medical practitioner is rendered lawful if the practitioner acted in the belief that the patient would have approved of the action taken on their behalf. (It also technically creates an obligation of remuneration on behalf of the patient.)

This test has more than a passing similarity to a 'substituted judgement' test, which would run somewhat contrary to the position in the English jurisprudence as indicated above. It nonetheless carries the endorsement of authoritative texts such as Gloag and Henderson, and the Scottish Law Commission report of 2014 on *Adults with Incapacity*. Under the authorship of Laura Dunlop KC, that report considered circumstances in which a person does not have capacity and where 'informal arrangements are made by relatives or friends, the principle of *negotiorum gestio* could supply the basis in legal principle for authorisation of [the accommodation decision that has been made]'.

8.2.2.3 Best interests and the minimally conscious state

Among the Principles set out in s 1 of the Mental Capacity Act 2005 is that 'An act done, or decision made, under this Act for or on behalf of a person who lacks capacity must be done, or made, in his best interests'. It is note-worthy that 'best interests' does not form part of the Adults with Incapacity (Scotland) Act 2000, so it is at least arguable that the English case law considered below is not directly applicable in Scotland and will at best be persuasive. S 1 of the 2000 Act sets out the principles according to which interventions will be permitted. These include that the intervention will be of benefit, the least restrictive option and will take account of a range of views as to the likely wishes of the incapacious adult. There is a sense in which fulfilling these requirements will amount to a body of evidence in support of a *negatorium gestio* justification for intervention on the patient's behalf.

As if continuing the semantic debate on 'best interests', questions have arisen in English jurisprudence in respect of patients in the so-called 'minimally conscious state'. A good example is *W* v *M* (2011) in which M had suffered a brain injury that left her in what was initially diagnosed as a PVS. Upon further investigation it transpired that she was in a minimally conscious state, as she did not meet the criteria for PVS. Her awareness of her environment was intermittent at best and she was entirely dependent on others, with a ten-year life expectancy. Her partner and sister took the view that she would not want to be kept alive in that state and the family sought a declaration under the Mental Capacity Act 2005 that it was in M's best interests for artificial nutrition and hydration (ANH) to be withdrawn. The court employed a 'balance sheet' approach in declining that authorisation as M's life was not unduly burdensome.

On the other hand, in the English case of *M* v *N* *(By her litigation friend, the Official Solicitor)* (2015), the Court of Protection held that doctors could lawfully withdraw clinically assisted ANH from a patient in a minimally conscious state. Mrs N suffered from the progressive degenerative impact of multiple sclerosis. Her daughter sought the declaration that continued ANH was contrary to Mrs N's best interests. The best interests assessment was done on the basis of the framework of the Mental Capacity Act 2005 and its Code of Practice, which placed great emphasis on the importance of personal autonomy and the obligation to be alert to direct or indirect discrimination against those who lacked capacity. 'Best interests' decisions of an incapacious individual had to factor in their past and present (where relevant) wishes and identifiable codes and beliefs by which they had lived. In this case the court found that Mrs N would have considered continued treatment to have been 'grotesque'.

8.2.2.4 The diminished role of the court

The then-Lord Advocate said in April 1996 that he would not authorise the prosecution of a qualified medical practitioner (or any person acting on the instructions of such a practitioner) who, acting in good faith and with the authority of the Court of Session, withdraws or otherwise causes to be discontinued life sustaining treatment or other medical treatment from a patient in a persistent, or permanent, vegetative state, with the result that the patient dies.

Like a declarator, an authorisation order will give guidance and reassurance of the lawfulness of discontinuance.

In the *Law Hospital* (1996) case mentioned above (at the end of which is the Lord Advocate's statement), however, the court made it clear that the appropriate form of process for obtaining the authority of the Court of Session was a petition to that court to exercise its *parens patriae* jurisdiction. The authorisation that follows would order discontinuance of treatment to render lawful that which would otherwise be unlawful in the absence of the patient's consent to discontinuance. Yet the requisite petition to the Court of Session was not the theory followed in *Law Hospital*, in which Lord President Hope observed that a petition was not necessary in every case where it is intended to withdraw treatment. The overall position appears to be that, where discontinuance would be in the patient's best interests, the hospital is entitled to discontinue treatment without patient consent or judicial authorisation.

A similar position has been taken by courts in England. For example, *M (by her litigation friend B)* v *A Hospital* (2017) indicated that the court was not the source of the lawfulness. The role of the court was to identify whether treatment was lawful or not, and not to render unlawful treatment lawful, or lawful treatment unlawful. That case involved a woman suffering from Huntington's disease, who had little awareness of her surroundings. The Court of Protection found that as long as relatives and doctors agreed and medical guidelines were followed, then there was no legal requirement for the decision to be taken by the court.

The Supreme Court has now held that a court order is not always required before withdrawal of the ANH that is keeping a person with a prolonged disorder of consciousness alive. *An NHS Trust* v *Y (Intensive Care Society intervening)* (2018) involved a person in a prolonged disorder of consciousness following a cardiac arrest and cerebral hypoxia from which he had not recovered. In the event Y had died before the Supreme Court appeal was heard, and the family withdrew their petition. Nonetheless, the Supreme Court found that it had not been established that the common law or the European Convention on Human Rights gave rise to the mandatory requirement to involve the court to decide upon the best interest of every patient in such a state before ANH could be withdrawn. However, an exception may exist where there is a difference of medical opinion on prognosis that renders the available options finely balanced, or where there is a lack of agreement from those with an interest in the patient's welfare.

The significance of a movement away from requiring judicial support for withdrawal of ANH should not be underestimated.

8.2.2.5 Acts and omissions

The distinction between acts and omissions is an important policy device of the courts, though it, too, may be a matter of semantics. In *Bland* the court found that removal of nutrition and hydration was an omission rather than an act. Whereas the *mens rea* was present, the *actus reus* giving rise to a murder conviction was absent in the case of an omission where there is no duty to act. The same distinction is important in understanding the active ending of a patient's life through medication (euthanasia or physician-assisted suicide) and withdrawal of the means supporting life, even although the consequence is the same, as the death of the patient will result. However, it may be that the two are therefore morally indistinguishable.

8.2.3 The Adults with Incapacity (Scotland) Act 2000

Under the Adults with Incapacity (Scotland) Act 2000 (the '2000 Act') 'medical treatment' includes any medical procedure designed to safeguard or promote physical or mental health. There is authority under Part 5 of the 2000 Act for the medical practitioner primarily responsible for the care of a patient to do what is reasonable in the circumstances in relation to medical treatment in order to safeguard the patient's physical and mental health. What is excluded from Part 5 is 'negative' treatment.

Section 47 of the 2000 Act, being without prejudice to any common law provision, works to maintain the authority of the decision in *Law Hospital* in respect of patients in a PVS. That said, the 2000 Act allows 'proxy decision-makers' to intervene in the affairs of the incapable adult where that intervention will confer some benefit on the patient that cannot be achieved by another method and having taken into account any previously expressed wishes of the patient. It may be possible, then, to apply for an intervention order under s 53 of the 2000 Act, directing a specific action, and to do so in matters addressed by the court in the *Law Hospital* case. It is considered that a sheriff would be unlikely to grant such an application because of (1) the act/omission dichotomy and (2) the fact that the Scottish Law Commission deliberately excluded from the legislation the withholding or withdrawing of treatment from adult patients in a PVS.

It is perhaps significant that the 2000 Act does not employ the concept of 'best interests'. This is because the 'best interest' test was considered by the Scottish Law Commission to be more appropriate to children, whereas the adults falling within the scope of the 2000 Act will have possessed full capacity prior to the incapacity that caused them to fall within the terms of the legislation. This rationale was accepted by the then-Scottish Executive in its drafting of the legislation.

8.3   ADVANCE STATEMENTS

It will be remembered that the judgment in *Law Hospital NHS Trust* v *Lord Advocate* (1996) specified that in future one of documents to be lodged with a petition to the court seeking authorisation of withdrawal of treatment should be a statement of any views on treatment decisions that the patient may have expressed prior to going into a PVS. This may be considered a form of advance statement, also known as an advance directive or living will. It amounts to a decision on treatment before the medical need arises.

Such a statement must be made when the patient is competent to do so and acted upon when the patient is no longer competent.

Although the Scottish Law Commission recommended legislative reform, the then-Scottish Executive left the matter out of what became the Adults with Incapacity (Scotland) Act 2000.

The issue of advance statements does however form part of the Mental Health (Care and Treatment) (Scotland) Act 2003 (the 2003 Act). Under s 275 such a written and signed statement made by a person with capacity may specify how that person wishes to be treated in the event of their incapacity. A Mental Health Tribunal or medical practitioner must 'have regard' to such a statement and if not followed the medical practitioner must inform the Mental Welfare Commission (and others) by way of a written record that also gives reasons for not having followed the person's advance statement.

The 2003 Act deals with advanced directives only in respect of compulsory treatment. It sets out procedures to be followed in order to express treatment preferences that will be acted upon in the patient's incapacity. The statement must be signed and witnessed and the witness must attest that the patient was capable of making the statement that they made. It may also be withdrawn while the patient is capable of so doing. 'Capacity' under the 2003 Act has the same meaning as that defined under s 1(6) of the 2000 Act, that is, the capacity to make, communicate or understand decisions or retain memory of decisions made in respect of the patient's care.

Although the statement will not be legally binding, the Mental Health Tribunal for Scotland is charged with 'giving effect' to the advance statement. When considering a treatment order, the Tribunal must 'have regard to' any advance statement made. The person treating the adult with incapacity must also have regard to any advance statement made by the patient. Where treatment is given that runs contrary to the terms of an advance statement, a statement of the treatment given must be recorded and added to the patient's medical records. A statement of reasons for acting contrary to the terms of the advance statement must also be added. Under s 276 of the 2003 Act, copies must be sent to the service user (patient), their named person (if any), welfare attorney or guardian and to the Mental Welfare Commission for Scotland.

Additions to the 2003 Act were made by the Mental Health (Scotland) Act 2015. They provide that where a health board receives a copy of an advance statement, or a document withdrawing an advance statement, from a person who made the statement, or someone acting with their authority, the heath board must place a copy of the statement or document with the person's medical records and inform the Mental Welfare Commission for Scotland. The Commission must enter the information in a register of advance statements maintained by it.

The requirement to 'have regard' to an advance statement does not indicate any level of legal protection for the medical practitioner. This lack of protection was pointed out by the Law Society of Scotland in its 2022 report *Advance Choices, and Medical Decision-Making in Intensive Care Situations*. The Law Society of Scotland observed what has been noted elsewhere in this book, that English law relies on a 'best interests' assessment, which is somewhat anathema to Scots law concerning adults with incapacity. It did however apply to treatment withdrawal in *Law Hospital NHS Trust* v *Lord Advocate* (1996).

The law in England and Wales also offers protection to medical practitioners under s 5 of the Mental Capacity Act 2005, when acting in the patient's best interests in the withdrawal of medical treatment. Part 5 of the Adults with Incapacity (Scotland) Act 2000 does not allow withdrawal of treatment in the same way. Because such protections are not offered in Scots law – apart from in matters of futility as discussed above – the Law Society of Scotland offered a legal framework to address the issue. That framework is based on *negotiorum gestio*. In the situation envisaged, the 'absence' of the patient that is required under *negotiorum gestio* for the *gestor* to act on the patient's behalf is a notional one and refers to their incapacity. This was considered in detail in Chapter 5, on lawful treatment of adults with incapacity. For the sake of completion, under *negotiorum gestio* the albeit unnecessary consent would be considered to have been given by the court on the patient's behalf. In terms of advance statements, and in the absence of a statutory 'best interests' test for incapable adults, it remains unclear how to determine what the patient would have wanted. Applying the established Scots law principle of *negotiorum gestio* would see the medical practitioner acting in the reasonable belief that their patient would have allowed them the mandate to act on their behalf in 'benevolent intervention'. It offers a formulation by which a medical practitioner can arrive at a defensible interpretation of an adult's 'will and preferences', that aligns with Principle 3 in the Adults with Incapacity Scotland Act 2000, establishing the adult's prior 'wishes and feelings'.

An example of advance decision-making from the English jurisprudence may be found in *Re C (adult: refusal of medical treatment)* (1994), in which an adult patient with schizophrenia refused an amputation even although he might have died of gangrene as a result. Because his refusal was made during a lucid interval, it was held to be competent when he lacked capacity. Conversely, on the authority of *Re J (a minor) (wardship: medical treatment)* (1990), a patient's request to act contrary to the medical practitioner's clinical judgement or to the patient's best interests will not be legally binding.

R (Tracey) v *Cambridge University Hospitals NHS Foundation Trust (Equality and Human Rights Commission intervening)* (2014) is an English case that discussed the obligation of clinicians to involve a patient in a decision to impose a Do Not Attempt Cardio-Pulmonary Resuscitation ('DNACPR') notice. A key element of the case was whether the failure to do so breached the patient's rights under Art 8 of the European Convention on Human Rights. It was held that while the court should be wary of giving general guidance on circumstances in which it was not appropriate to consult the patient, because a DNAPCR decision could deprive a patient of life-saving treatment, there should be a presumption in favour of patient involvement. This was confirmed in *Winspear* v *City Hospitals Sunderland NHS Foundation Trust* (2015) where the court found that the principle of prior consultation applied also where patient lacked capacity.

As noted above, in England and Wales advance statements have been given statutory authority by the Mental Capacity Act 2005. The effect is that recourse needs to be had to the common law and the persuasive recognition in the English decision in the *Bland* case that advance refusals of treatment will be competent if made by a legally capable person who was properly informed of the consequences of the decision they were making, and not subject to undue influence. It should also be a statement made in respect of the actual treatment being refused.

8.4   ASSISTED SUICIDE

Because suicide and attempted suicide are not criminal offences in Scotland, a person cannot be guilty art and part of either. Yet, killing a person at their request will amount to murder, in terms of *HM Advocate* v *Rutherford* (1947).

Although there is no primary authority specifically on whether it is criminal to help another end his life, criminal liability may follow assisting another to do so, as indicated in *Ross* v *Lord Advocate* (2016), discussed below. This may be on the grounds of recklessly endangering human life or of culpable homicide. It may amount to murder if the intention of committing an act was to end the life of the victim. This would, however, raise the question of whether the action of the victim in ending his life amounted to a *novus actus interveniens* breaking the chain of causation between the act of the accused and the victim's death.

Assisted suicide may happen through a positive act, by providing the means to commit suicide, giving information or advice to do so or through an omission to prevent the person from ending their life. Assistance may be given by another person such as a family member or indeed by a medical practitioner (physician-assisted suicide).

8.4.1 Challenge under the European Convention on Human Rights

In *Ross v Lord Advocate* (2016) the petitioner, Gordon Ross, unsuccessfully sought a declarator that the Lord Advocate's failure to provide guidance constituted an interference with Art 8. The case involved the failure to publish a policy that identified the facts and circumstances that would be taken into account in deciding whether to prosecute a person who had assisted someone to commit suicide. The claimant was a mentally competent man with health impairments, including Parkinson's disease. Those impairments would require assistance in committing suicide, and he anticipated not wanting to continue living. He argued that the failure to publish a prosecution policy was an unjustified interference with the Art 8 rights of the person wishing assistance in committing suicide. The court held that no evidence supported the contention that the law was being applied by the Lord Advocate in an arbitrary way, and he, the Lord Advocate, would continue to prosecute cases that amounted to homicide.

What is important for present purposes is that the court found the Scots law on assisted suicide to be clear: it is not a crime *per se* to assist another to commit suicide, but criminality will depend on a combination of *mens rea* and causation. If a person did something with the knowledge that the action would cause the death of another person, they would be guilty of homicide, if the act was the immediate and direct cause of the person's death. Where to draw the line of causation will be a matter of fact and circumstance in each individual case. The court did not consider that this produces any uncertainty in the law.

The voluntary ingestion of a drug supplied by a third party to end one's life breaks the chain of causation between the assistance and the resulting death. Similarly, according to Lord Carloway in *Ross*, assistance with travel to a place where a person may commit suicide does not constitute a crime in Scots law. It must however be borne in mind that those were comments on the criminal law delivered in a civil court, so would be no more than persuasive in a subsequent criminal trial.

Just as Gordon Ross did in Scotland, Dianne Pretty had done in the English case of *R (on the application of Pretty)* v *Director of Public Prosecutions* (2002). That case involved a woman with motor neurone disease who sought the court's assurance that her husband could help her to die at the time of her choosing, without facing prosecution under the Suicide Act 1961. Dianne Pretty challenged the decision of the Director of Public Prosecutions that he did not have the power to decline to prosecute an offence in advance of the commission of that offence.

Dianne Pretty's claim failed. It had been based on the European Convention on Human Rights. The court found that Art 2 (on the right to life) was intended to *prevent* another person depriving one of life. Article 3 protects dignity in life, but does not grant a right to die with dignity. While Art 8 protects the right to private and family life, interference with that right must be in accordance with the law and she was prevented in law from her proposed course of action. Article 9 protects a freedom of belief; it was held that this does not extend to a belief in assisted suicide. As such, the European Court of Human Rights found that there was no infringement of the Convention.

A key distinction between the two cases is that the Suicide Act 1961 has never been applicable in Scotland. While Dianne Pretty was concerned with prosecution under the 1961 Act, and the possibility of a 14-year jail term imposed on a third party assisting her suicide, Gordon Ross was concerned with a third party being prosecuted under the common law offence of murder or culpable homicide, for assisted him in ending his life.

Although it is technically possible to prosecute for the offence of wicked endangerment of life, someone who provides advice on the means to take their life would not fit the scenario envisaged by Dianne Pretty or Gordon Ross who, because of their medical conditions, would need help to fulfil those wishes.

8.4.2 Physician-assisted suicide

The term 'physician-assisted suicide' is applied where, at the patient's request, a medical practitioner helps end the life of a patient who is incapable of doing so themself. This should be distinguished from a competent refusal of treatment, which is lawful even if it results in the patient's death. In the English case of *Re B (adult: refusal of medical treatment)* (2002), an artificially ventilated tetraplegic woman sought a declaration that artificially keeping her alive amounted to a trespass. The court found in her favour because the adult patient of full capacity may validly refuse treatment and artificial ventilation constitutes medical treatment. This is the case in both England and Scotland. The case is not, strictly speaking, one of physician-assisted suicide as it applies the same principles of consent and refusal considered in Chapter 5.

In physician-assisted suicide, on the other hand, the medical practitioner effectively assisting a suicide may have recourse to the defence of double effect, as discussed above, in which a drug was administered as a palliative that also had the effect of hastening death (e.g. morphine). While the *Pretty* judgment may arguably apply to the medical practitioner, the more recent Supreme Court decision in *R (Nicklinson)* v *Ministry of Justice* (*Nicklinson*) is directly applicable in England.

Tony Nicklinson sought the assistance of a medical practitioner to end his life. Following a stroke nine years prior, he was paralysed and could move only his head and eyes. He could spell out words by blinking, which was interpreted by computer. He did not want to take the option in the *Re B* route and refuse feeding and hydration, as death would be protracted and painful. He wanted to be injected with a lethal drug by someone else or by means of a machine that he could activate. Like Dianne Pretty he sought a declaration either that the former would be lawful if performed by a doctor or, failing that, that section 2(1) of the Suicide Act 1961 was incompatible with his rights under Article 8 ECHR. The Supreme Court also considered whether the code published by the Director of Public Prosecutions (the 'DPP') relating to prosecution of those who were alleged to have assisted suicide was lawful.

The court unanimously held that the issue lay within the UK's margin of appreciation, that the court held the constitutional authority to make a declaration that the general prohibition on assisted suicide was incompatible with article 8 and that this is an issue that Parliament is better qualified to assess. On the matter of compatibility with Art 8, the court found that while the Article was engaged, there had been no infringement. The decision was not unanimous: of the five sitting judges, Lords Neuberger, Mance and Wilson declined to grant a declaration of incompatibility, but Lady Hale and Lord Kerr would have done so. This may be suggestive of a direction of travel in the Supreme Court on this issue, although a further challenge before the European Court of Human Rights also failed, primarily on the basis of the margin of appreciation. As regards the DPP policy, the court unanimously held that the exercise of judgement by the DPP and the variety and relative weight of relevant factors according to the circumstances of each individual case were constitutionally necessary features of the system of public interest-based prosecution.

Following *Nicklinson*, the Divisional Court in *R (Conway)* v *Secretary of State for Justice* (2020) held that it was not bound by existing domestic authority – including *Pretty* and *Nicklinson* – to hold that the blanket ban on assisted suicide in s 2 of the Suicide Act 1961 was compatible with Art 8. The case involved a claimant suffering from a form of motor neurone disease applying for a declaration of incompatibility, which the Court of Appeal refused, also taking the view that there could be no doubt that Parliament was better placed to determine the difficult policy issue of assisted suicide. It took this stance in view of the highly divisive moral and ethical views in society at large.

It is vitally important to bear in mind that these cases will not be directly applicable in Scotland, where the Suicide Act 1961 was never in effect. A Scottish decision will not be a balance between the legislative proscription of assisted suicide and Art 8 ECHR, but more likely determined on the basis of causation and *mens rea* under *Ross* v *Lord Advocate*.

States are generally at liberty to decide which of the three branches of government should be responsible for taking policy and legislative decisions which fall within their margin of appreciation. In the United Kingdom, the assessment as to the risk and likely incidence of abuse if the prohibition on assisted suicide were to be relaxed was made by Parliament in enacting section 2(1) of the Suicide Act 1961. This is a provision that has been reconsidered several times by the UK Parliament. The Scottish Parliament, on the other hand, would not be in a position to repeal the terms of the 1961 Act, but has on several occasions been in a position to consider legalising assisted suicide, in this case by eliding the possibility of a murder or homicide charge.

8.4.3 Bills

A range of bills has been brought before the United Kingdom Parliaments over the last three or four decades. Most recently, in 2024, Lord Falconer introduced the Assisted Dying Bill to the House of Lords. Kim Leadbeater MP brought the Terminally Ill Adults (End of Life) Bill to the House of Commons in November 2024. These bills did not apply to Scotland as the matter is devolved under Sch 5 of the Scotland Act 1998. For a capacious person aged over 18 to be able to avail themselves of assisted dying, they would need to have fewer than six months to live and be ordinarily resident in England or Wales for at least a year. With the approval of two doctors and a High Court judge the applicant could have been prescribed a lethal dose of drugs, which they would have to be able to take themselves. There is a conscientious objection clause allowing medical practitioners to not participate in the activities envisaged in the Bill, and no criminal offence would be committed under the Suicide Act 1961 if following the terms of the Bill.

Similar bills have been brought before the Scottish Parliament in recent years, including those brought by Margo Macdonald MSP in the form of the Right to Die for the Terminally Ill Bill in 2006 and the Assisted Suicide (Scotland) Bill in 2013. Both Bills failed, as did that of Patrick Harvey MSP in 2015, which did not get further than Stage 1.

Voting on bills is not whipped as it is a matter of conscience, and does not fall along party lines. Bills have tended to fail for various reasons, such as insufficient safeguards to protect the vulnerable, the slippery slope (towards euthanasia), the preference for improved palliative care services and the argued resultant negative effects on trust in members of the medical profession.

Most recently in Scotland, Liam McArthur MSP consulted on his Proposed Assisted Dying for Terminally Ill Adults (Scotland) Bill, which was introduced in the Scottish Parliament on 27 March 2024. Some of the terms are significantly different from those that apply in England. They are set out here because although not law, they give an indication of the kinds of so-called 'safeguards' that are embedded in legislation of this nature. Eligibility requires the person to have a terminal illness, which is defined in Cl 2 as 'an advanced and progressive disease, illness or condition from which they are unable to recover and that can reasonably be expected to cause their premature death'. This must have been confirmed in an assessment by a coordinating registered medical practitioner using the forms set out in Schedules 2 and 4. Unlike in England, they must be aged 16 or over, but like England they must have been resident in the jurisdiction for at least 12 months and have sufficient capacity to make and understand the decision. Capacity means not suffering from a mental disorder that may affect their request for assistance to end their life, and being capable of understanding the information and advice about that request, capable of making a decision to make that request and being capable of communicating, understanding and retaining the memory of that decision.

Other cross-border alignments include two doctors having assessed the person's capacity and eligibility, and the person administering the approved substance themselves, while the substance that will end their life will have been approved and provided by a health care professional.

The suicide aspirant will be required to make a signed and witnessed 'first declaration' using the form in Schedule 1, undergo a ten-day 'period of reflection' and then make a signed and witnessed 'second declaration' using the form in Schedule 3. Both declarations must be recorded in the person's medical records, and there is provision for their cancellation. It will be an

offence to coerce or pressurise any terminally ill adult into making any of
the declarations. Summary conviction carries a custodial penalty of up to
two years or a fine up to level 5 on the standard scale (£10,000), or both.
Conviction on indictment will carry a custodial penalty of up to 14 years or
an unspecified fine, or both.

The cause of death on the death certificate is to be recorded as 'the disease or condition directly leading to their death (rather than the approved
substance provided to them by virtue of clause 15 [on the "provision of assistance"]', and broad provision is made for conscientious objection of any person under a duty to participate in anything authorised under the legislation.

Further provision applies to duties on Scottish Ministers to prepare
annual reports and keep the operation of the legislation under review.

8.5   EUTHANASIA

Euthanasia may be defined as putting someone to death in a compassionate manner following their suffering. It may be used interchangeably with
'assisted dying', although this has already been discussed separately. A distinction should be drawn, from the point of view of the person performing the
act of compassion, between active euthanasia (killing) and passive euthanasia
(allowing death). A further distinction is possible from the patient's point of
view: euthanasia may be voluntary, involuntary or non-voluntary, depending on whether the patient can and has expressed an opinion on the issue
of their death.

The subject is not specifically regulated in Scotland. It does not fall within
the terms of either the Adults with Incapacity (Scotland) Act 2000 or the
Mental Health (Care and Treatment) (Scotland) Act 2003. Neither is there
specific mention of the question of euthanasia being reserved to Westminster
under the Scotland Act 1998. This may seem odd, considering that there is
specific mention of human fertilisation and embryology and of abortion
being reserved to Westminster, but because euthanasia falls with the criminal
law, it is in fact a devolved matter (as draft legislation on assisted suicide indicates, and as abortion became through the passage of the Scotland Act 2016).
It will fall within the ambit of those with ministerial responsibility for the
criminal law and hence the decriminalisation of homicide on compassionate
grounds is a devolved matter. It is difficult to imagine a situation in which
different laws are allowed to operate north and south of the border.

8.5.1 Active euthanasia

Although there are no reported Scottish cases in point, three crimes are relevant to active euthanasia: murder, culpable homicide and reckless endangerment of life. While euthanasia will amount to murder, because of the sympathy the facts may invoke, cases may be prosecuted as culpable homicide. Because the law distinguishes between intent and motive, a murder case may be established. While the intent will be consistent with murder, the motive may be altruistic. Such altruism would not affect the legal interpretation of the intent of the accused (*mens rea*), i.e. to bring about the death of another.

The letter of the law does not always accord with its application. It is possible to find a body of largely unreported case law in which the elements of murder were present, but the charge was culpable homicide, and the sentence was lenient following a guilty plea. This is because the mores of society may demand a certain level of flexibility in the common law. For example, in *HM Advocate* v *Brady* (1996), a man fed tranquilisers and alcohol to his brother who was suffering from end-stage Huntington's disease. It was found that this was done at the brother's earnest request. The court found Brady guilty of culpable homicide and admonished him.

As these cases often relate to terminal illnesses, the question arises of whether it makes any difference that the victim would have died anyway. The answer is that in law this makes no difference, as hastening the victim's death has no effect on the criminal nature of the act.

This is in contrast to the doctrine of 'double effect' that applies to and admonishes medical practitioners, in which a palliative is administered even although it will hasten their death. It is perhaps for this reason that there has yet to be a prosecution of a medical practitioner in Scotland for murder by euthanasia. That said, where there is no therapeutic purpose to the treatment, a prosecution will follow. This is what happened in *R* v *Cox* (1992), where a lethal dose of potassium chloride was administered to a patient with a terminal illness who had expressed a wish to end her life. It was administered by her doctor, Dr Cox. His charge of murder was reduced to one of attempted murder, as the victim had been cremated and proof of the cause of death had become impossible to establish. He was convicted of the attempted murder.

8.5.2 Passive euthanasia

An omission to treat leading to the death of the patient may amount to passive euthanasia. This will cover situations in which treatment is withdrawn from the patient in their best interests, as in the *Bland* and *Law Hospital* cases. These selective non-treatment cases should, however, be distinguished from those in which the patient elects non-treatment through a 'do not resuscitate' order. Such orders were recognised as valid in *Re AK (Medical treatment: consent)* (2000) as long as steps have been taken to ensure that they reflect the true wishes of the patient. If it is possible to collapse the distinction between active and passive where the outcome is the same, this would mean that situations such as that in *Re AK* amount to physician-assisted suicide.

Essential facts

Death in law

- There is no statutory definition of death. It is generally and judicially accepted that brain stem death is the definitive medical usage.

Futility and incapacity: children

- 'Futility' refers to demands by or on behalf of the patient for treatments that will not serve the desired medical ends or not be in the patient's best medical interests.
- English case law holds that respect is given by doctors and the courts for the views of parents for or against treatment, but the court's determination of the child's best interests is paramount. A doctor may not impose medical treatment in the face of parental objections.
- Courts weigh likely benefits of treatment from the child's point of view as if the court were the responsible parent.
- English courts have had the role of resolving any conflict between medical professional opinion and parental wishes and will accept medical recommendations on prognosis and whether treatment is in the child's best interests.
- A court will not order that treatment be given where medical opinion holds it to be of no – or only short-term – benefit to the child, but will authorise treatment where there is not much pain or risk. It may do this in the face of parental objection, as indicated in cases such as those of Charlie Gard and Alfie Evans.
- 'Best interests' should include emotional and welfare interests as well as medical interests.
- Scottish courts retain a *parens patriae* jurisdiction over medical decision-making on the child's behalf.
- There is a strong presumption in favour of life, which is rebuttable on the ground of best interests.

- The European Convention on Human Rights has become the mechanism through which these scenarios are adjudicated, particularly Art 2 on the right to life, Art 3 prohibiting inhuman and degrading treatment and Art 8 on respect for private life.

Futility and incapacity: adults

- The appropriate test is one of 'substituted judgement' in deciding whether to withhold or withdraw life-prolonging treatment from an adult in a permanent vegetative state (PVS).
- Before substituted judgement decisions are made, evidence is required from two independent medical practitioners that the patient is, in fact, in a PVS.
- Treatment may lawfully be withdrawn from a patient in a PVS if it is in the patient's best medical interests where it is futile to prolong life, yet, according to the *Bland* and *Law Hospital* judgments, patients in a PVS do not have any best interests to protect.
- Withdrawal of treatment from a patient in a PVS will not be a criminal offence in the absence of a duty to act.
- Following the *Law Hospital* decision, the petitioner in future cases should lodge with the petition at least two medical reports on the patient's condition that describe the proposed course of action and the steps that will be taken to allow death to occur with dignity, a statement of the first diagnosis of PVS and a statement of any views on treatment decisions that the patient may have expressed prior to going into a PVS.
- The principles that apply to a patient in a PVS apply also to a patient in a minimally conscious state.
- As a civil court, it is not competent for the Court of Session to issue a declarator in respect of the criminal or otherwise nature of the withdrawal of medical treatment.
- The distinction between acts and omissions is an important policy device of the courts: omissions are permissible, and acts may be culpable.
- There is authority under Part 5 of the Adults with Incapacity (Scotland) Act 2000 for the medical practitioner primarily responsible for the care of a patient to do what is reasonable in the circumstances in relation to medical treatment in order to safeguard the patient's physical and mental health. What is excluded from Part 5 is 'negative' treatment.

- As is the case in respect of consent and the *incapax*, the principle of *negotiorum gestio* could supply the basis in legal principle for authorisation of treatment withdrawal on behalf of the *incapax*.
- Following the *Law Hospital* decision in Scotland and *An NHS Trust v Y* in England, where there is agreement between the medical team and the family of the incapable person, it is not necessary to seek the approval of the court for treatment to be withdrawn where its continuance is futile.

Advance statements

- An advance statement on treatment decisions must be made when the patient is competent to do so and acted upon when the patient is no longer competent.
- There is judicial authority that advance statements are competent in some situations, but not legally binding if they run contrary to the patient's best interests or to the doctor's clinical judgement.
- The Mental Health (Care and Treatment) (Scotland) Act 2003 deals with advance directives only in respect of compulsory treatment. It sets out the form and procedure to be followed and the authority the statement will have. It was amended by the Mental Health (Scotland) Act 2015 to place duties on health boards to place such statements on a person's medical records.

Assisted suicide

- Killing a person at their request amounts to murder.
- Criminal liability may also be on the basis of culpable homicide or recklessly endangering life.
- The European Convention on Human Rights does not form the basis of assuring an applicant to the court that another person would not be prosecuted for helping them to die at the time of their choosing (her husband, in the case of Dianne Pretty, who suffered from motor neurone disease).
- Unlike England and Wales where assisting a suicide is a crime under the Suicide Act 1961, it is not a crime in Scotland, but prosecution will depend on *mens rea* and causation.
- Physician-assisted suicide is applied where, at the patient's request, a medical practitioner helps end the life of a patient who is incapable of doing so themselves. The doctor may have recourse to the doctrine of double effect.

- Physician-assisted suicide is not lawful in either Scotland or England but there have been several bills that have attempted to change this position. Lawfulness will be subject to a number of so-called safeguards such as capacity, consent and residency in the jurisdiction, as well as diagnostic criteria such as a terminal condition as approved by medical practitioners.

Euthanasia

- Euthanasia may be defined as putting someone to death in a compassionate manner following their suffering.
- As it falls within the criminal law, it is technically devolved to the Scottish Parliament.
- Three crimes are relevant to active euthanasia: murder, culpable homicide and reckless endangerment of life.
- Prosecutions and sentences tend to be lenient, based on culpable homicide rather than murder and not resulting in custodial sentences.
- Hastening the victim's death has no effect on the criminal nature of the act.
- Where there is no therapeutic purpose to the treatment, the doctrine of double effect will be unavailable to the accused and a prosecution will follow.
- Passive euthanasia is arguably no different to the position in the *Bland* and *Law Hospital* judgments.
- 'Do not resuscitate' orders have been judicially recognised as valid if steps have been taken to ensure that they reflect the true wishes of the patient.

Essential cases

Aintree University Hospitals NHS Foundation Trust v James (2013): on 'futility' and treatment withdrawal, it is not about whether it is lawful to withhold treatment, but whether it is in the patient's best interests to provide it. If it is not in their best interests, then withholding treatment will be lawful.

Barts Health NHS Trust v Dance & Battersbee (2022): circumstances in which a declaration of legal death can be made on the basis of brain stem testing.

Re B (a minor) (wardship: medical treatment) (1992): an operation on a child with Down's syndrome to correct an intestinal condition could be performed, as the expected quality of life outweighed the destruction of life.

Re J (a minor) (wardship: medical treatment) (1992): where a child was not dying but severely disabled, the court had to decide whether J should be revived should he collapse again. It was found that in the child's best interests, active steps to hasten death would not be authorised but it was not in the child's best interests to ventilate him if he was to stop breathing, unless it was considered medically appropriate to do so.

Re C (a baby) (1996): where a baby became brain damaged from meningitis, the court approved of the medical expert agreement that it was not in her best interests to be ventilated artificially.

A National Health Service Trust v D (2000): Art 2 of the ECHR on the right to life would not be infringed if non-treatment was in the child's best interests. Non-treatment protected the child from inhuman and degrading treatment under Art 3 of the ECHR as it was by its nature in her best medical interests.

Re C (a minor) (wardship: medical treatment) (1990) and **A National Health Service Trust v D (2000)**: parental views on treatment will be accorded great respect by doctors and the courts, but are not conclusive as to the court's determination of the baby's best interests.

Re B (a minor) (wardship: medical treatment) (1992): 'best interests' are not confined to 'best medical interests', but include emotional and other welfare interests.

Re J (a minor) (wardship: medical treatment) (1990): the presumption in favour of life is not irrebuttable and in exceptional circumstances may be outweighed by the child's best interests in favour of a peaceful death.

Glass v United Kingdom (2004): apart from life-threatening emergencies, treatment contrary to parental wishes and without court authority to treat violates Art 8 of the ECHR on respect for private life.

Re T (a minor) (wardship: medical treatment) (1997) and **Portsmouth NHS Trust v Wyatt (a child) (medical treatment; parents' consent) (2004)**: the court evaluates the child's best interests by weighing the likely benefits and burdens of treatment from the child's standpoint; it approaches the issues as if it were a reasonable and responsible parent.

Re A (children) (conjoined twins: surgical separation) (2000): two girls, conjoined twins, were considered separate persons. The benefits of separating them, giving the stronger twin continued life, outweighed the other's inevitable death. It was impossible to invoke the 'best interests' test in respect of both girls; the court considered its decision in terms of the lesser of two evils. 'Best interests' should include emotional and welfare interests as well as medical interests.

Great Ormond Street Hospital for Children NHS Foundation Trust v Yates and others (2017): futile medical treatment and transport to America for experimental treatment outweighed by child's best interests.

Evans & Anor v Alder Hey Children's NHS Foundation Trust & Anor (2018): futile medical treatment and transport to Italy for experimental treatment outweighed by child's best interests.

Barts Health NHS Trust v Raqeeb (2019): travel to Italy allowed on the basis of best interests.

Airedale NHS Trust v Bland (1993): a patient in a PVS has no interests and withdrawal of feeding and hydration, defined as medical treatment, would be authorised where it was futile to prolong life. Withdrawal of treatment would not be a criminal act where there was no positive duty to maintain life. The patient was allowed to die of his existing injuries.

Practice Note (persistent vegetative state: withdrawal of treatment) (1996): evidence is required from two independent medical practitioners that the patient is in a PVS.

W v M (2011): patient with a ten-year life expectancy in a minimally conscious state justifying withdrawal of artificial nutrition and hydration in the patient's best interests.

M v N (by her litigation friend, the Official Solicitor) (2015): patient with multiple sclerosis in a minimally conscious state justifying withdrawal of artificial nutrition and hydration in the patient's best interests.

M (by her litigation friend B) v A Hospital (2017): the court is not the source of the lawfulness. The role of the court is to identify whether treatment is lawful or not, and not to render unlawful treatment lawful, or lawful treatment unlawful.

Law Hospital NHS Trust v Lord Advocate (1996): the question was whether a patient in a PVS should continue to be fed and hydrated artificially where this treatment was futile. She had no interests that could be served by any treatment decision and it was agreed that the declaration sought was lawful and treatment could be withdrawn. The court set out a clear statement of the appropriate procedure to be followed in such cases in obtaining authority from the Court of Session, under its *parens patriae* jurisdiction, for withdrawal of futile life-sustaining treatment. Certain documents should be added to the petition, such as medical practitioners' reports and a statement of any views on treatment decisions that the patient may have expressed prior to going into a PVS. The court should be asked to appoint a *curator ad litem* to act on behalf of the patient.

Re C (adult: refusal of medical treatment) (1994): a treatment decision made when competent was valid for the patient lacked legal capacity to act.

R (Tracey) v Cambridge University Hospitals NHS Foundation Trust (Equality and Human Rights Commission intervening) (2014): because a DNAPCR decision could deprive a patient of life-saving treatment, there should be a presumption in favour of patient involvement.

An NHS Trust v Y (Intensive Care Society intervening) (2019): it is not necessary to approach the court if doctors and family members agree it is in the patient's best interests for life-sustaining treatment to be withdrawn.

HM Advocate v Rutherford (1947): killing a person at their request will amount to murder.

R (on the application of Pretty) v Director of Public Prosecutions (2002): Dianne Pretty challenged the decision of the DPP that he did not have the power to decline to prosecute an offence under the Suicide Act 1961 in advance of the commission of that offence. Her claim failed, as there had been no violation of the ECHR.

R (Nicklinson) v Ministry of Justice (2015): Parliament is the best place to determine the law on assisted suicide, and s 2(1) of the Suicide Act does not violate Art 8 ECHR.

R (Conway) v Secretary of State for Justice (2017): not bound by existing domestic authority – including *Pretty* and *Nicklinson*; blanket ban on assisted suicide in s 2 of the Suicide Act 1961 was compatible with Art 8.

Ross v Lord Advocate (2016): petitioner unsuccessfully sought a declarator that the Lord Advocate's failure to publish a policy that identified the facts and circumstances that would be taken into account in deciding whether to prosecute a person who had assisted someone to commit suicide, did not constitute an interference with Art 8. It is not a crime *per se* in Scotland to assist a suicide, but criminality will depend on a combination of *mens rea* and causation.

HM Advocate v Brady (1996): a man fed tranquilisers and alcohol to his brother suffering from end-stage Huntington's disease. Although, technically, a murder charge was possible, he was found guilty of culpable homicide and admonished.

R v Cox (1992): where there is no therapeutic purpose to the treatment that hastens the patient's death, the doctrine of double effect is inapplicable, and a prosecution of murder will follow.

Re AK (Medical treatment: consent) (2000): 'do not resuscitate' orders were recognised as valid.

GLOSSARY

A

actio iniuriarum: Roman law action for injury to a personality interest

actus reus: physical element of a crime

admixed [embryo]: artificial creation that behaves like an embryo and contains both human and animal material

advance statement: formal directive indicating one's treatment preferences in the event of future incapacity

Aquilian liability: action for patrimonial (monetary) loss

affront: injury to feelings, see 'nervous shock'

ante-natal: before birth

assisted suicide: assistance given to a person to end their own life

B

bailment: transfer of physical possession of property from one person to another

biopsy: procedure to remove tissue for examination

C

chromosome: DNA molecule containing genetic material of a cell

civilian law: legal system originating in continental Europe, in contrast to the common law

clone: production of individual organisms with identical genomes

corpus juris civilis: body of civilian law

Court of Session: supreme civil court of Scotland

contumelia: legal insult

culpa: legal wrong

curator *ad litem*: court-appointed legal representative

D

damages: categories of payment resulting from a judgment

damnum: harm

damnum injuria datum: harm to a natural person caused by unreasonable conduct

dominus: master or owner

E

EEA: European Economic Area

embryo: multicellular organism in its earliest stage of development

euthanasia: intentionally ending a life in order to relieve pain and suffering

ex lege: [arising] out of or from law

ex turpi causa non oritur actio: no action arises from immorality

F

fraud: deception with intention of making a gain and depriving a victim

futility: medical condition in which treatments on behalf of the patient will not serve the desired medical ends

G

gamete: cell of a sexually reproducing organism that will fuse during fertilisation (sperm or egg)

gender affirming: treatment or therapy to align or affirm a person's chosen gender that may not align with the gender assigned at their birth

germ line therapy: treatment to correct a condition in a person's genetic make-up

guardian: person appointed to act for an adult during their incapacity

H

High Court: senior court in England and Wales, or criminal court in Scotland (High Court of Justiciary)

House of Lords: United Kingdom upper legislative House, or until 2009 (origin of the Supreme Court), the highest court.

hypoxia: lack of oxygen

I

indemnity: insurance

institutions [Roman law]: the *Institutes of Justinian and Gaius*, a sixth-century BCE codification of the *corpus juris civilis*, or 'body of civilian law', received into Scots law

inter alia: additionally, as well as

interdict: authoritative prohibition (injunction in England)

in vitro fertilisation/IVF: assisted reproductive technology that takes place in a laboratory

intra-uterine device (IUD or 'coil'): form of mechanical birth control placed in the uterus

imperitia culpae adnumeratur: want of skill is regarded as a fault

implantation [of embryos]: adhesion of an embryo to the endometrium of the uterus, resulting in pregnancy

L

Lord Advocate: chief legal officer of the Scottish Government

M

mens rea: mental element of a crime

minimally conscious state: reduced consciousness following brain injury that falls short of a permanent vegetative state

miscarriage: natural death of an embryo or foetus

morbidity: illness or medical complications

morning after pill: medication that prevents implantation of a fertilised human egg in a woman's uterus

N

negotiorum gestio: voluntary management by one person (the *negotiorum gestor*) of the affairs of another (the *dominus negotii*) without the consent or even the knowledge of that other person

nervous shock: psychiatric harm suffered as a result of negligence

novus actus interveniens: a new act intervening to break the chain of causation between a negligent act or omission and the harm it caused

O

obiter: judicial statement that does not form part of the reasoning of a case and has little value in precedent

occupatio: occupation or possession

organ: body part, including blood

P

patrimonial: monetary

parens patriae: [jurisdiction] of the court to act on behalf of a minor

pars viscerum matris: the foetus being an integral part of the expectant mother

post-mortem: after death

permanent vegetative state (PVS): permanent disorder of consciousness following severe brain damage

primitive streak: a period of up to 14 days from the day on which the process of creating an embryo began

principal: main party (to a contract)

Procurator Fiscal: public prosecutor in Scotland

pro rata: divided proportionately

proxy: on behalf of

puberty blocker: treatment to delay the onset of puberty

S

Sheriff Court: principal local civil and criminal court in Scotland

sine qua non: 'but for' test for causation: there will be liability if the loss would not have occurred but for the negligence

solatium: delictual (Aquilian) pain and suffering caused by a legal wrong

somatic gene therapy: treatment that aims to correct a condition in the person treated

statutory: to do with legislation

spondet peritiam artis, et imperitia culpae adnumeratur: he is responsible for skill in his profession, and the want of such skill is regarded as a fault

sterilisation: procedure to render a person unable to produce offspring

surrogate (mother): person who carries a baby on behalf of another

Supreme Court (UK): highest court in the United Kingdom (since 2009)

T

tissue typing: the assessment of tissue from separate sources for immunological compatibility

tubal ligation: permanent blocking, clipping or removal of fallopian tubes to render a woman sterile

tutor dative: court-appointed person who exercises the functions of the court's *parens patriae* jurisdiction on behalf of those incapable of acting on their own behalf

V

vasectomy: surgical procedure to cut or tie the vas deferens and render a man sterile

viable [foetus]: foetus capable of sustaining life outside of the uterus

vicarious liability: an employer is held liable for the wrongs of their employee

volenti non fit iniuria: voluntary assumption of risk

W

ward: minor or incapable adult placed under guardianship

wrongful birth: parental claim for the negligent failure to terminate a pregnancy

wrongful conception or wrongful pregnancy: parental claim in negligence for failure to prevent a pregnancy

wrongful life: claim by a child for negligent failure to prevent, or later to terminate, the pregnancy that led to his birth

welfare attorney: person granted powers relating to the welfare of a person lacking capacity

X

xenotransplantation: cross-species organ grafting

INDEX

voluntary, involuntary or non-voluntary,
216
**exceptions to confidentiality and
privacy**
see also **confidentiality and privacy**
anonymised data, 158
clinical audit and express consent,
153–154
deceased patient, 157
disclosure, 156
legislation, 154–155
litigation, 155
medical information, parents of
adopted children, 157–158
duty to breach confidence, 158–159
genetic information, 157
health care team, 153
incapax
incapable adults, 156
minors under the age of 16, 155–156
victims of neglect or abuse, 157
express consent, 154

family, right to found a, 45
fertility, control of
abortion, 65–67
ante-natal injury, 67–68
contraception, 64
foetus, 64–65
methods, 63
non-consensual sterilisation, 71–72
wrongful life and birth, 68–71
fitness to practise
chiropractors, of, 37
dental care professionals, 26
dental practitioners, of, 19–22
health and care professions, 37–39
health visitors, of, 27–28
medical practitioners, of, 13–16
midwives, of, 27–28
nurses, of, 27–28
opticians, of, 33–34
osteopaths, of, 35–36
pharmaceutical chemists, of, 31–32
foetus, 64–65
freedom of information, 165
futility, medical
adults with incapacity, 207
advance statement, 208–210
generally, 196
incapacity and *see* **adults with
incapacity medical treatment of**
language of 'futility', 196

life-sustaining treatment, 197
selective non-treatment of children,
196–201
withdrawing/withholding treatment from
adults, 201–207

GDC *see* **General Dental Council**
gene therapy, 72
General Chiropractic Council, 6, 36–37
**General Data Protection Regulation
(GDPR)**
access rights, 163–164
exemptions, 163–164
legal framework, 162
remedies, 165
six data protection principles, 162–163
third party rights, 164
General Dental Council (GDC)
changes to register, 21–22
committees of, 17, 19–20
composition of, 16
functions of, 16–17
Health Committee, 19, 20
Interim Orders Committee, 20, 26
Investigating Committee of, 20–21, 26
objective of, 16
Practice Committee of, 20–21, 26
Professional Conduct Committee, 19–22,
25
Professional Performance Committee, 20
Registration Appeals Committee, 20
registration function of, 16–18
sanctions of, 22–23
General Medical Council (GMC)
committees of, 12
composition of, 8
creation of, 8
Education Committee, 9, 11
Fitness to Practise Panel, 13
licence to practise, 10
practitioners disqualification, 10
proceedings of, 12
publishes guidelines, 14, 16
qualification, 9, 11
registration function of, 9, 10
responsible officers, 10, 13
training, 10
General Optical Council, 33–34
General Osteopathic Council, 6, 34
General Pharmaceutical Council, 8
continuous professional development, 29
false representation, 30
functions, 28